The Defeat of the Luftwaffe Fighter Force Over the Western Front

1944/1945

Werner Girbig • SIX MONTHS TO OBLIVION

Werner Girbig

SIX MONTHS TO OBLIVION

Schiffer Military History
West Chester, PA

Cover artwork by Steve Ferguson, Colorado Springs, CO

FIGHT OF THE LONG NOSES
The painting shows an encounter between the Spitfire Mk. 14's of 130 Sqn. and the Focke-Wulf Fw 190 D's of JG 54 in late December 1944. The Fw 190 "Dora's" of III Gruppe, who introduced the type to combat in September, were led by *Hptm.* Robert "Bazi" Weiss, an Experten of more than 100 victories. *Kommandeur* Weiss and his Dora pilots were continually engaged with the 2nd Allied Air Force mad up of RAF and USAAF units based in northern France and the Lowlands. On December 29, the odds against Weiss and III/JG54 took a devastating toll; the *Kommandeur* and five wingmen failed to return after a sprawling dogfight against a larger Spitfire wing. December also encompassed the additional losses of more than 100 Jagdfliegers. After the debacle of the New Year's Day "Bodenplatte", *General* Galland had lost most of his veteran fighter pilots – the Jagdfliegers never recovered.

The title of the painting refers to the later models of the Fw 190 and Spitfire that were powered by larger engines which elongated the aircrafts' fuselages. Both Luftwaffe and RAF fighters carry dark grey and green camouflage, typical of late autumn schemes for both air forces. Weiss' Dora is marked with a fuselage band of dark blue, a "Reichverteidgung" defense designation for JG 54, although it was not always used.

Acknowledgements:
A chronicle of this scope could not have been compiled without the help of former Luftwaffe fighter pilots and/or their relatives, members of ground crews and administrative personnel, and last but not least the wide circle of individuals who have knowledge of the events at second hand. The details they furnished here often provided the clues with which to unravel the documentation available. I should like to thank the following in particular for the help, support, suggestions and information which they have provided: *Major* Helmut Ballewski (Porz-Lind), *Brigadegeneral* Dieter Bernhard (Munich), Emil Bischof (Garbsen), *Oberst* Georg Füreder (Wiesbaden), *Oberstleutnant* Hans Harms (Munich), Günter Izquierdo (Hamburg), Armin Köhler (Giessen), Gerhard Kott (Neu-Isenburg), Dieter Krägeloh (Soberheim), Kurt Loll (Berlin), Siegfried Luckenbach (Karlsruhe), Eugen Lux (Offenbach/Main), Arno Paffrath (Bergisch Gladbach), Heinz Polak (Kelkheim/Ts.), Hans Ring (Munich), Friedrich Scheer (Neukirchen), Karl Schubert (Lohr/Main), Friedrich Trenz (Vienna), Heinz Wischhöfer (Regensburg), Gerrie J. Zwanenburg (Baarn/Holland).

Photographs:
Bischof 2, Broeckelschen 1, DRK-Suchdienst; Eder 2, Hawker 2, Herwig 1, Col. Holt 1, Imperial War Museum 5, Col. Moon 2, Nauroth 2, North American 1, Polak 1, Republic 1, Robinson 2, Royal Air Force 2, Süddeutscher Verlag 1, United States Air Force 14, Waal 3, author's files 14, and 16 the origin of which cannot be traced.

Maps by the author.

Translated from the German by David Johnston & Richard Simpkin.

Library of Congress Catalog Number: 91-67054

Printed in the United States of America.
ISBN: 0-88740-348-4

This unabridged English edition was originally published under the title,
Start im Morgengrauen,
© 1989, by Motorbuch Verlag, Stuttgart.

We are interested in hearing from authors with book ideas on related topics.

Published by Schiffer Publishing Ltd.
1469 Morstein Rd.
West Chester, PA 19380
Please write for a free catalog.
This book may be purchased from the publisher.
Please include $2.00 postage.
Try your bookstore first.

Contents

Maps

To all unknown fighter pilots,

To those who fought alone,
To the unnamed wingmen,
And to the commanders,

To the host of young pilots,
Never named and never credited with a victory,
Whose courage and readiness to give their lives
Was nonetheless equal to every demand made of them
In pitting themselves against the enemy's strength,

To the "men in black" of the ground staff,
Without whose unflagging support
These fighter pilots would never have taken the air,

And to former enemies -
The pilots of the Mustangs, Thunderbolts and Spitfires.

Introduction

Many historians take the view that the decline of the German fighter force became evident as early as 1940 and 1941, as the Battle of Britain ran its course. There is of course some truth in this, for the drain on its manpower that the Luftwaffe suffered at that time must indeed have influenced the subsequent course of the war. Yet at that stage British Fighter Command was so severely battered that, had the Germans stuck to their plan of attack and concentrated exclusively on putting the enemy fighter force out of action, it too could scarcely have survived. In truth it was not until the autumn of 1944 that the German fighter force set foot down the sacrificial path; and it was the controversial Operation "Bodenplatte" of January 1, 1945 that dealt this force a mortal blow and sealed its fate. What happened from then on was no more than a dying flicker.

It is this operation, which took such an appalling toll, that provides the focal point of this account. But no report on Operation "Bodenplatte"would be complete if it did not also cover the final obliteration of the German *Jagdwaffe* (fighter arm).

A study of many existing publications dealing with the Luftwaffe's battle against the Allies and the heavy fighter pilot casualties in the Western Theatre and over Germany itself inevitably leads to the question: "Did the fighter pilots let the side down?"

Today we can only record how they took off time and again in face of overwhelming odds and well knowing what a slender chance they stood of getting home again. Day after day they found themselves facing the packs of the Allied fighter escorts, which so outnumbered them, and took up the unequal challenge anew. To begin with Göring, not realizing the true situation, may have boastfully asserted that, "his Air Force would soon fix that"; but when the setbacks came he lost little time in trampling the fighter pilots underfoot with accusations of incompetence and cowardice. But was it really their fault that one city after another succumbed to the hail of bombs and that they had little to set against the enemy's material superiority except their fighting spirit, bred of a cross between courage and desperation?

The purpose of this chronicle is not to resolve the question of who should bear the blame, but simply to abide by such hard facts as have emerged from the folly of that last world conflagration. In any event no distinction can be drawn between the Allied bomber crews who rained down bombs on Germany's cities in full conviction of the justice of their mission, and the fighter pilots who, with a like belief in the rightness of their actions, did battle against those detestable bombers. Men of both sides alike, on the one the simple sergeant with his eye to the reflector gunsight of a 1,400 HP Messerschmitt and on the other his opposite number behind the Browning machine-gun in the rear turret of a Flying Fortress, went into battle under the same orders – to ward off and destroy the enemy.

But scapegoats always have to be found when the plans of the high and mighty begin to go awry; and so it was that from summer 1943 onward, German fighter pilots were time and again to become the butt of harsh reproaches, to be accused of having lost mastery of the air through their own fault and of failing through personal shortcomings to exploit the superiority of their equipment. Pleas and factual reports alike from commanders right up to the level of *General der Jagdflieger* himself simply glanced off the obstinacy and imperception of the High Command, and were frequently even dismissed as unworthy of credence. But the heavy casualties which the fighter force suffered tell rather a different story, and the real reasons for the inadequacy of our home air defense must be sought in quite different quarters.

Right from its inception the whole Luftwaffe was tailored to suit an offensive strategy, and in the light of early campaigns this decision may have looked sound enough. Unfortunately, however, no one at that time devoted any thought to the course the war might subsequently take. The lessons that the bitter experiences of the Battle of Britain taught were not learned, with the result that offensive thinking remained in the ascendant. Meanwhile the enemy, having formed a correct appreciation of the likely turn of events, was able to build up a powerful strategic air capability.

By the time the High Command of the Luftwaffe realized the danger, it was almost too late. The fighter force, suddenly thrown onto the defensive, had no choice but to spread itself out geographically in penny-packets and found itself short of manpower and equipment, while the Allies with virtually unlimited logistic resources at their disposal had no need to disperse their forces. The German side also suffered from a lack of advanced aircraft; right to the end of the war the fighter force was flying the same old types, the Bf 109 and the Fw 190, much modified and thus increasingly prone to problems.

Insufficient attention was paid to aircraft production, and faulty appreciations led to new developments either being shelved in favor of other, seemingly more attractive projects while still in the experimental stage, or only reaching quantity production in face of the gravest of difficulties. Moreover on the one occasion when the opportunity existed to put into production a fighter with a performance that represented a revolutionary step forward, the machine had to be switched to a role wholly foreign to its concept.

Continued underestimation of the worth of the enemy's long-range fighters proved to be a grievous mistake which was to have disastrous consequences. Again, there was no proper coordination of the formations assigned to home air defense. Last but not least the failure to build up a realistically planned, adequate and coherent fighter command in Germany itself clearly demonstrates a gross lack of foresight in the highest quarters. All this enabled the enemy to pin down the German units stationed in the West and thus overfly Germany at greatly reduced risk.

When the war in the air took on menacing proportions, it was all too easy to lay the blame for failure at the door of the fighter pilots, who in reality were achieving extraordinary feats. But their dash, courage and fighting spirit could not of their own suffice to offset the omissions and mistakes of the Luftwaffe High Command.

In the very few instances where statements supporting the fighting men's pleas made themselves heard in high places, these were in blatant contradiction to earlier rejections of the same pleas – yet another indication of perplexity in the highest places and of their inability to coordinate the employment of the Air Force and to take logical decisions. In response to accusations that the fighter pilots lacked the will to win, Hitler had this to say at a review of the situation on November 6, 1944:

> "This proves once and for all that either the pilots or their

> machines are no good. We can't argue that it's the pilots, because it's they who get shot down.
>
> So it must be the machines. But I have quite the opposite view of the Luftwaffe – their aircraft are good. The whole thing's ridiculous."

Hitler then went on to say that under the circumstances there seemed no point in making any more fighter aircraft at all.[1]

And the Supreme Commander of the Luftwaffe? During a tour of inspection in Berlin after a heavy raid on that city in November 1943, Göring turned to his aides with the words: "Air raid precautions? What we need is fighters. Fighters!" In September 1944 fighter production in fact reached its peak for the whole War – 2,876 Bf 109s and Fw 190s. But by this time, thanks to the grave consequences of the turn for the worse the war in the air had meanwhile taken, to our losses brought about by the enemy's superiority and inadequate training of our own pilots, and to mistakes in the deployment of air defense resources. Göring had become convinced that the fault must lie with his pilots.

In the light of our knowledge today, one more factor must be adduced to round off this expose of the collapse of the German fighter force in the final phase of the war. This is done not for the sake of flinging mud at a system without a conscience, rather to take an opportunity to erect a Bauta Stonet[2] to those who were just unknown pilots. To make the point, the key events in the air defense of Germany between the beginning of 1943 and October 1944 must be reviewed.

1943

At the turn of 1942/43 the Luftwaffe in the East had taken its hardest knock so far at Stalingrad; and in the West too, as 1943 began, the fighter force, although still claimed to be superior, was encountering an enemy whose strength was mounting steadily, and was having to face a superiority in equipment that was patently on the increase.

Then something happened which a few months earlier would have been thought impossible or at least incredible – the Americans joined in the bombing offensive against Germany. As early as January 27, with a raid on

Wilhelmshaven, the US Eighth Air Force made its first daylight attack on a city in German territory. The Luftwaffe High Command attempted to reinforce the inadequate defenses by using a number of night-fighter units by day. But the night-fighter crews, accustomed as they were to completely different conditions, found it difficult to adjust to the daylight role; crews with a good record of success by night were not up to their new task and took damaging losses.

On May 4, the German fighters in the West made the acquaintance of the American Thunderbolt on its first operation as escort to the heavy bombers. The target was the port of Antwerp. And from this day on the sturdy P-47s provided a constant escort for the Flying Fortresses and Liberators of US Eighth Air Force. The fact that American fighters too were now operating over the Low Countries was of course realized on the German side, but its significance was not. Despite the technical data available on them, no one wanted to believe that the depth to which these American fighters could penetrate would very soon increase. Göring exploded with rage when Galland put forward the view that the Ruhr would soon come within reach of enemy fighter escort operations.

Then came the moment when the American escort fighters suddenly began to escort the bombers even further. The Thunderbolts were carrying supplementary fuel tanks which gave them a considerably increased radius of action. Göring, however, continued to ignore this threat. In the middle of the year the US Ninth Air Force, joined later by the Fifteenth, started to launch raids on Austria and South Germany from Italy; this opened up a new front on which appropriate defenses had hurriedly to be set up. And the German heartland remained as it had always been – a fortress without a roof. The fighter production programme initiated by the Head of Luftwaffe Procurement, *Generalfeldmarschall* Milch, unfortunately failed to come up to expectations; for no account had been taken of enemy destruction of production facilities, of the loss of fuel stocks in previously occupied territories or of a difficult pilot reinforcement situation. The only hope of success lay in the concentration of fighter units in German territory proper.

To quote Galland on the escort fighter problem: "Outside fighter escort range our pursuit and night fighter operations are successful. If we gave up any serious attempt to engage on the peripheries and pulled our fighters right back, we should, in logic, at the same time be able to use them in high concentration at key points." But Göring would have none of this, for he at once underestimated the enemy and had an exaggerated view of our own capabilities. So the existing concept continued unchanged. This may have been simply because the considerable numbers of enemy aircraft shot down by German day and night fighters gave cause for confidence, while against this broad background the losses so far suffered were not particularly striking and could readily be regarded as acceptable.

It is true that in late summer 1943 the Allies were still a long way from dominating German airspace; but the mounting intensity of attacks on fighter production plants presaged a major weakening of the fighter force, which would sooner or later be bound to bring about a shift in the relative strengths in German skies – in other words, the loss of German air superiority. The Luftwaffe High Command, on the other hand, shut its ears to pleas and facts alike and allowed itself to be deluded by the major local defensive successes the fighter pilots had achieved.

US 8th AF, based in England, was clearly deeply concerned at the bomber losses it was sustaining, particularly those suffered in the daylight raids on Schweinfurt and Regensburg on August 17 and October 14, to the point indeed where mass attacks on Germany were temporarily suspended. The Allies still lacked fighters which could accompany and screen their bombers deep into the German heartland; limited radius of action meant that escorts could be provided only over short distances within the German frontiers. From that point on the bombers had to make their flight to the target and back on their own and were at full risk.

Nor did British Bomber Command escape unscathed. Night-fighter kills reached their peak in 1943, even before the battle of Berlin. On the night of August 23 over 50 four-engine bombers were shot down, and this success was repeated on the night of September 1 when 47 British machines failed to return to base.

Dispersal of the units assigned to home air defense over numerous airfields, creating less than ideal conditions for successful operation; disregard of the fighter escort problem; and last but not least the bad weather of autumn 1943 – all these factors combined to produce a striking increase in fighter casualties. In fact the bad weather itself led to substantial losses of pilots and machines, for both the requisite pilot training and even the simplest of navigation equipment were lacking.

For the first time the shortage of commanders began to make itself felt. "It is true," Galland observed, "that the Luftwaffe as a whole has 60-70 thousand officers; but this same air force has never got beyond the figure of 7,000 aircrew officers."

Now for the first time the thoughtlessness and irresponsibility of disregarding the clearly recognizable trends the war in the air was to follow were exposed. At a time when German forces were being forced back on all fronts, giving up more and more ground and with it precious sources of raw material and at the same time having to accept bitter defeats, the Supreme Command failed to build up sufficient strength to protect Germany itself. But every time the subject of air defense was raised, Göring took care to change the subject a few minutes later.

In these circumstances the omens for the defense of Germany in 1944 were gloomy enough. It seemed as though the stockpiling of equipment, the build-up and the reorganization that were going on in British bases, in fact the whole development of Allied air strength remained hidden from the High Command of the Luftwaffe.

1944

The operational command, Jagdkorps I, took a far more realistic view of the situation; in the light of the enemy's mounting strength, an intensification of his offensive operations was only to be expected for the spring.

At the beginning of the year the new escort fighter, the P-51 Mustang, arrived in England, and as early as January and February long drawn-out, wide-ranging air battles developed over North Germany. Although they were inferior to the Americans in numbers, the fighting capability of the German units sometimes sufficed to deal a painful blow, as the events of January 11 show. In a daylight raid on the Brunswick and Oschersleben aircraft plants US 8th AF lost about sixty four-engine bombers, even though this cost some forty German fighters – losses which made it impossible for the fighter force to sustain this type of defensive operation, for so far that year, home air defense had received scarcely a single replacement aircraft.

During the week of February 20-25 ("Big Week") a large scale operation was directed mainly at the German aircraft industry. Enemy losses in this week were appreciable, but the fighter force was unable to prevent a single one of the mass raids. The fact could no longer be overlooked that the ratio of kills to losses was so unfavorable as to leave no doubt that defensive operations would shortly become in some degree uneconomic.

For the night-fighters the situation looked rather better. Here the intensity of operations was stepped up considerably, to reach its peak with the shooting down of 96 British bombers in the RAF raid on Nuremberg on the night of March 31, 1944. Despite this success the German night fighters remained virtually helpless against enemy electronic countermeasures. Inadequate situation reporting, a command weakness rather than a technical problem, was another sore spot – and one of the reasons for single-engine night fighter units being disbanded during March.

Finally in April the Americans succeeded in gaining effective air superiority over German airspace. Time and again they struck hard against the aircraft industry and Luftwaffe stations. Unremitting losses imposed on the German fighter pilots a heavy physical and moral burden which inevitably affected their fighting potential.

Then in May air defense units once again had a wave of abuse flung at them; the fighter pilots were accused of cowardice. But it was in that same month of May 1944 that the fighter force was engaged in bitter fighting and achieving particularly notable results. According to the Military Statistical Bureau of the time and to I Jagdkorp's War Diary, they shot down 530 American machines for a loss of 384 aircraft, representing 10.7% of the sorties flown.

In June things were comparatively quiet over Germany, all enemy resources being focussed on the landings in Normandy. But the German fighters committed to the Western theatre had to pay a heavy price; the superiority of Allied strength was simply too great. This breathing-space did not however last long, for once the enemy troops had gained a firm footing and begun to advance, the air war over Germany flared up again.

On June 20, US 8th Air Force launched a major air offensive, this time with the fuel industry on the target list. The raids were so heavy that for the first time the damage caused in the various installations led to a sustained shortfall in production. These raids continued until, towards the end of the year, a fuel shortage had set in. This was to have a decisive effect on the whole course of the war; the time had arrived when fighters stood ready on the airfields but could not take off for lack of fuel.

There can be no doubt that the appearance of good long-range fighters on the Allied side constituted a turning-point. During the year the American High Command decided to give its fighter units greater freedom of action; this represented a new tactic in the development of the war in the air, to which German day fighters had to adjust. For now the enemy fighter escorts no longer had to stick close to the bomber formations but could seize the initiative in seeking out and hunting down their attackers. "Germany is not within range of American fighters. The bomber is our main enemy." So the *Reichsmarschall* was saying as late as Autumn 1943. Thus the training of pilot reinforcements remained confined to the engagement of bombers. Once the Mustang formations dominated the airspace and adopted true offensive tactics, it was inevitable that German fighter losses should rise rapidly.

The German fighter pilots found it more and more difficult to get at the bombers. An effort was made to offset the disadvantage in strength by forming so-called "*Sturmstaffeln*," equipped with heavily armed and armored machines. Under this concept, the *Sturmjäger*, or "assault fighters," would ignore the escort and close with the bombers, penetrating the screen in close formation, while "high-altitude Staffeln" intercepted and pinned down the enemy fighters. Good initial results seemed to prove the proponents of this offensive tactic right and led to the establishment of further assault Staffeln. But in the last resort these too were unable to achieve any really decisive effect. It is true that the assault fighters were sometimes able to inflict serious losses on the enemy; but to achieve the same kill-rate, the other fighter units had to commit at least four times as many aircraft using normal tactics. The net result was that despite local successes, losses continued to rise. On top of this US 15th Air Force based in Italy, now began to step up the frequency of its raids on Southern Germany and Austria, forcing the Luftwaffe to deploy additional fighter units in defense.

By autumn the number of kills had ceased to bear any relation to the losses. Air battles on a scale so far unimagined raged over Germany, and the enemy superiority steadily became more obvious. While the total monthly losses on the enemy side remained with few exceptions under 1% of sorties flown, equivalent figures for the German fighter force were lying between 10% and 20%. It was not difficult to calculate the point in time at which the unprofitability and futility of our operations would culminate in a fiasco.

In the middle of September, on a massive scale comparable with that of February's "Big Week", the American and British air forces struck at the armaments industry and at communications targets of all kinds. Complementary attacks on almost every airfield in Germany were probably to be seen as preparation for the major Allied airborne operation at Arnhem which began on September 17.

In the same period a large concentration of German fighter units in Central Germany took place. On September 12, over 400 machines stood ready for a defensive operation, but the order for take-off was cancelled because of bad weather. Göring however did not agree with this decision and personally intervened to order the fighters into the air. This nonsensical order is said to have cost the fighter force some 10% of the machines that took part, which made the September balance-sheet look less encouraging. The fighter units engaged in home air defense shot down 307 aircraft for the loss of 371. Since however the number of Allied aircraft entering the area was 18 times greater than the number of sorties by defending fighters, the respective loss ratios were 0.7% as against 14.5%. And that looked worse than unprofitable.

At the beginning of October the aircraft strength of first-line day-fighter units in home air defense amounted to 347 serviceable machines, excluding units on conversion or refresher training. After the costly and bitter fighting in the West following the Allied landings and then during August and September over Germany, Galland, in his capacity as *General der Jagdflieger*, succeeded in gaining for his units the breathing-space that had become indispensable and was mainly devoted to bringing the day-fighter wings up to strength. By the end of October the number of serviceable aircraft had almost been doubled.

Meanwhile, the intensity of Allied air activity continued to increase, with hydrogenation plants as the priority targets, and this bombing of fuel resources still further impaired their capacity. But the major communications nodes in West Germany also stood high on the list, and the armaments industry within Germany was a third focal point for sustained attack.

In the I Jagdkorp's area operations were almost at a standstill from units being grounded; but this gave opportunity for the squadrons to be re-equipped with new aircraft and brought up to strength with pilots. A further trend was to abandon individual attacks, which had proved useless, in favor of working in large formations; only a force equalling the enemy in numbers could hope to achieve a worthwhile measure of success. Out of this the "Big Blow" plan was born; its aim was to establish a defensive strength of 2,000 fighters and regain air superiority. Both those goals proved unattainable.

It was thanks to Galland's unremitting efforts that, in October, after protracted hesitation, the *Reichsmarschall* finally arranged that, of the Me 262 jet fighters coming off production, all of which had so far been allotted to the hit-and-run bomber role on Hitler's orders, every twentieth machine should be handed over to fighter units. This finally made it possible to set up at Rheine, under *Major* Walter Nowotny, a fighter detachment equipped with the Me 262. On November 1, 1944 *Kommando Nowotny* had all of nine Me 262s serviceable.

Notes

[1] The subject of this review was the heavy fighter losses sustained over Central Germany on November 2, 1944.

[2] A prominent uncarved tombstone or memorial used to honor heroes of the Viking era.

I

AIR BATTLES OVER GERMANY

Operational Bases of the Tagjagd and Nachtjagd
November 1, 1944
695 Day Fighters
633 Night Fighters

November 1944 - The Losses Mount

Thursday, November 2, 1944

Late on the morning of Thursday November 2, 1944, two bomber formations from US 8th AF crossed the Dutch coast heading east. One, 325 heavy bombers strong, was directed onto the fuel installations at Gelsenkirchen and Castrop-Rauxel, while the other, of 650[1] machines, flew on towards Central Germany, its target being the Leuna hydrogenation plant about 22 miles southeast of Merseburg, a plant which had previously been subjected to a series of heavy raids over the preceding five months.

By this stage in the war it was no longer unusual for Allied bombers to penetrate to Central Germany, but on this occasion it was noticed that the bomber formations were surrounded by a particularly strong escort, consisting of about 600 Mustangs from 8th AF and a small number of Lightnings from 9th AF. Even before the attack proper had begun several Mustang flights appear to have spotted through a gap in the clouds an airfield occupied by German fighters. Without further ado they dove and brought fire to bear on the parked machines. It was Borkheide, where I Gruppe, Jagdgeschwader 300 was stationed; the low-level attack took place just as the Messerschmitts were standing on the runway ready to take off. In a few minutes the Gruppe had lost an appreciable number of machines; according to a private source, 25 Messerschmitts were totally destroyed and a further nineteen damaged in this attack, but these figures appear to be on the high side. They would have meant that almost the entire Gruppe had been put out of action, and this is contradicted by the activities of Jagdgeschwader 300 in the following days and weeks. Further the Geschwader reported not a single personnel casualty on November 2. If 25 machines waiting to take off had been so severely shot-up as to become a total loss, at least one of the pilots must have suffered some kind of wound.

Meanwhile however nearly 500 home air defense fighters were scrambling, briefed to take on Allied units flying in over Central Germany. Apart from a few largish gaps there was 90% cloud cover down to 1,500 to 3,000 feet over Germany, with 1.5 to 2.5 miles visibility[2] – not exactly ideal weather for an operation of this kind. Since however there was a strong stationary front over the Rhine-Main area where Jagdgeschwader 2 was stationed, the Geschwader could not get through to the Americans, so that of the machines which took off in defense only some 300 made contact. But the German fighter force was flying into its heaviest defeat so far.

Shortly before noon the 3rd Air Division, which was controlling the whole bomber force on that day, reached the target area. It was probably the 55th Fighter Group under Major Ryan which first joined battle with the German attackers. Ryan's Fighter Group reported nineteen Allied aircraft shot down and one Mustang lost. Next came US 1st Air Division, with Major Preddy's 352nd Fighter Group at its head. 352nd Group first made contact at 12.21 hours and in this engagement Capt Bryan claimed five kills on his own account. At its debriefing 352nd Group claimed 38 German fighters shot down, while 20th Fighter Group claimed 28 kills, of which Lt.Col. Montgomery himself accounted for three.

The Americans reported a total of 134 German machines destroyed, three unconfirmed and a further 25 damaged. 8th AF Fighter Command gave its losses as only eight P-51s.

On the German side the greatest success went to the two assault Gruppen, IV Gruppe, Jagdgeschwader 3 and II Gruppe, Jagdgeschwader 4. With a total of 61 armored Fw 190 A-8/R2s and A-8/R6s they succeeded in shooting down thirty four-engine bombers around midday, albeit at the cost of some thirty of their own machines. Over Bitterfeld *Oberleutnant* Werner Gerth, *Kapitän* of 14 (Sturm) Staffel, Jagdgeschwader 3, rammed a B-17. He managed to bale out of his Focke-Wulf, but his parachute failed to open. *Oberleutnant* Gerth, wearer of the Knight's Cross, died with thirty kills to his credit. Shortly after this two of his wingmen were fatally hit over Eisleben and crashed, while *Unteroffizier* Küttner was wounded for the second time and had to bale out (the first time had been in August over the Lechtal Alps when he was caught in the fire of a B-24 Liberator he was engaging).

As IV (Assault) Gruppe, Jagdgeschwader 3, under *Hauptmann* Mortiz landed in dribs and drabs back at Schafstädt, fifteen pilots were missing. Four had been wounded and had landed by parachute; the other eleven were killed.

Stab and II (Sturm) Gruppe of Jagdgeschwader 4 took off from Welzow. They climbed through the towering cumulus, reached the specified grid squares KE-KD in barely twenty minutes and came upon the enemy over Köthen. It is difficult to imagine how cooly the pilots tried to break through the American screen and get at the bombers. And they succeeded. While III and IV Gruppe of Jagdgeschwader 4 from Alteno and Finsterwalde with their Bf 109 G-14s took on the Mustangs, the "*Rammböcke*" ("battering rams")[3] closed with the bombers. The first B-17 showed signs of being hit and a few seconds later plunged steeply earthward with two engines on fire – a score for *Oberleutnant* Markhoff. *Unteroffizier* Scherer also had success, his Fortress diving away just as it had scored a hit on *Hauptmann* Jugel. The *Kapitän* of 5 Staffel leader and his Fw 190 crashed near Klein-Badegast.

While elements of the leading bomber units had already bombed the Leuna hydrogenation plant and the head of US 3rd Air Division was already on its way back, the follow-up bombers were just opening their bomb-doors. The Americans may have been able to ward off most of the German fighter attacks so far, but when the four-engine machines got over the target it was quite another story. Here they came under fire from Flak positions concentrated round Merseburg. 14th Flak Division succeeded in shooting down 32 more Flying Fortresses and damaging others. Despite his wounds, Lieut. Femoyer, navigator of a B-17G of the 447th Bomb Group, managed to limp his aircraft, half shot to pieces and almost uncontrollable, back to England, only to die of his wounds shortly after landing. He was posthumously awarded the Congressional Medal of Honor.

Still the battle raged on. The Mustangs were dominating Central German airspace, and one German machine after another went down or blew up in the air. Near Lebendorf *Feldwebel* Bilek of 3./JG 3 was injured in an attempt to belly-land his damaged aircraft. The *Kapitän* of 1 Staffel, *Oberleutnant* Zwittning, crash-landed his Bf 109 G-14 near Halle, while *Unteroffizier* Machalosowitz was shot down and parachuted to safety. Two other members of 6 Staffel, *Leutnant* Becker and *Unteroffizier* Müller, were shot down and killed. The *Kommandeur* of II./JG 3, *Hauptmann* Kutscha, was forced to write casualty reports for 13 men of his Gruppe.

12 Staffel, Jagdgeschwader 4, also had three killed, among them *Unteroffizier* Brüggemeier, who was shot down by a Mustang while leading

at Halle-Nietleben. *Unteroffizier* Jessen, of 10./JG 4, also had to bale out, but he was one of the few German pilots who lost their machines in the operations of November 2 and escaped unwounded.

As if battle casualties on this November day were not enough, bad weather and technical limitations caused further losses. As the Bf 109s of 2./ JG 4 were forming up over Lübbenau, the "Black 12" of *Unteroffizier* Gaismann rammed the Messerschmitt being flown by *Oberfähnrich* Schulz. Fortunately both men were able to bail out of their crippled fighters. As II (Sturm)/JG 4 was taking off from Welzow, the Focke-Wulf of *Fahnenjunkerfeldwebel* Frank collided with another machine, Frank being killed.

I Gruppe, Jagdgeschwader 400, equipped with the rocket-propelled Me 163B fighter, had been stationed since summer 1944 at Brandis, east of Leipzig. This Gruppe, under *Hauptmann* Olejnik, had the special task of close protection of the Leuna plant and November 2 found it in action. But things went wrong from the start. *Oberfeldwebel* Rolly in BQ+UJ crashed on take-off, and *Oberfeldwebel* Bollenrath and *Oberfeldwebel* Straznicky were shot down; all three were killed.

Jagdgeschwader 27 under *Oberst* Rödel had been split up over various fronts and now after a long gap was together again, assigned to the defense of Central Germany. From October onwards its four Gruppen had been stationed in Saxony, and November 2 was at once their first major operation as a group and the darkest day in the Geschwader's history. They met the Americans over the Leipzig area, but the Messerschmitts could not get through to the bombers. I Gruppe under *Hauptmann* von Eichel-Streiber, having taken off from Leutewitz in its Bf 109 G-14s, was suddenly attacked near Köthen by enemy fighters in great strength and immediately became involved in bitter fighting. III and IV Gruppen had a similar tale to tell. II Gruppe under *Hauptmann* Keller suffered the lightest casualties, with only one killed and two wounded.

Widespread air combats took place over Merseburg, Leipzig, Zerbst and Naumburg. German and American fighters chased each other through the skies above Saxony and Thuringia. Finally the situation reached dramatic proportions. The Germans fought desperately but the odds were too great. A continuous stream of reports of crashes, parachute descents and forced landings flowed in. Pilots were not always in a position to see the final dive of their shot-down comrades; and even when they were eyewitnesses of a crash they often looked in vain for the white silk mushroom of a parachute bringing the pilot safely to earth.

With 11 killed, I Gruppe, Jagdgeschwader 27, probably took the heaviest punishment, *Oberleutnant* Winkler's 1 Staffel alone lost five killed over Köthen and Zerbst, while 3 Staffel lost two pilots whose parachutes failed to open – another of the cards stacked against the airman.

By the end of the day, Jagdgeschwader 27 had lost 25 pilots killed and one missing; and of the twelve pilots wounded in dogfights one died of his wounds the following day – losses amounting to 38 pilots in all for the destruction of only seven Mustangs.

A comparison of the figures reported by both sides, in so far as these are available or accessible for evaluation, shows widely differing results. This is true not only of November 2, 1944, and it must be said that the respective figures are very rarely an approximate match or even lie in any demonstrable relationship to one another. Thus differences between one side's victory claims and the other's losses are nothing unusual, enemy losses usually being overstated. Sometimes a kill report may lead to disappointment because the enemy's reaction, a power-dive with emergency boost for instance, is misinterpreted; and some kill reports have to be revised the next day or even weeks later. In the same way a side's own losses are frequently under quoted, especially in official announcements or communiques.

According to German casualty reports the fighter force lost at least 98 aircraft on November 2, 24 of these in the assault units. I Jagdkorps documentation puts the figure at 120, with thirty in the assault squadrons; and the Americans, as already mentioned, reported 134 confirmed fighter kills.

The official US 8th Air Force figures gave a loss of forty four-engine bombers in all, 26 of them shot down by German fighters. The Americans placed particular emphasis on the use of the assault Gruppen, attributing a quarter of the losses to Jagdgeschwader 4. The report goes on to state that the 457th Bomb Group lost nine Flying Fortresses and the 91st Bomb Group as many as twelve from the attack of a single assault flight. If this refers to IV Gruppe, Jagdgeschwader 3, it amounts to a further 21 B-17s. This gives a total of 27 four-engine machines, and in their own reports the two assault Gruppen, IV./JG 3, and II./JG 4, claim thirty bombers shot down against thirty of their own aircraft lost.

Since other fighter units also achieved a significant success, the number of bombers destroyed in air-to-air engagements amounts to around fifty. There can be no doubt that the US 8th Air Force losses were higher than the forty quoted in their Official History, for with flak claiming 32 aircraft shot down, the total losses of bombers would come to about eighty.

One thing is quite clear, German fighter losses on November 2, 1944 were astonishingly high. In case the bare figures do not bring their severity home to the reader, it is worth mentioning by way of illustration that the fighter units deployed over central Germany that day had higher losses than for instance Jagdgeschwader 27 suffered in its whole twenty months in the North Africa campaign.

For the first time the very existence of the fighter force was threatened.

Fighter Losses on November 2, 1944

Units Involved	Killed/ Missing	Wounded	Total Casualties	Aircraft	Locale
I/JG3	4	5	9	Bf 109 G-14	Aschersleben
II/JG3	11	2	13	Bf 109 G-14	Dessau, Halle
			22		
I/JG4		2	2	Bf 109 G-14	Dessau
III/JG4	3		3	Bf 109 G-10/G-14	Kothen
IV/JG4	5	1	6	Bf 109 G-14	Zerbst
			11		
I/JG27	11		11	Bf 109 G-14	Dessau
II/JG27	1	2	3	Bf 109 G-14	Kothen, Leipzig
III/JG27	5	4	9	Bf 109 K-4	Leune
IV/JG27	10	5	15	Bf 109 G-14/K-4	Merseburg, Zerbst
			38		
I/JG400	3		3	Me 163B	Brandis, Leipzig
Assault Gruppen					
IV/JG3	11	4	15	Fw 190 A-8	Bitterfeld, Eisleben, Halle
II/JG4	6	3	9	Fw 190 A-8	Kothen, Zerbst
			24		
Total Losses (Germany)	70	28	98 (including 3 Staffel leaders killed and 3 wounded)		

Hitler's Reaction

Monday, November 6, 1944
Tuesday, November 7, 1944
Wednesday, November 8, 1944

During the situation briefing at Hitler's headquarters on November 6, 1944 the events of the major air battle of four days before were discussed in some detail, albeit without getting any nearer to the real underlying reasons for the setback. But some very revealing remarks were passed, and an extract from the discussion is given below:

Hitler: I've had another look at this business – I don't know whether *Reichsmarschall* Göring is fully in the picture. I've taken another fresh look at the whole thing and my conclusion is that eighty machines have recently been shot down.

Büchs:[4] 82.

Hitler: Of those eighty, fifty were shot down by fighters and thirty by AA. We'll discount the thirty for the moment. The Luftwaffe had 490 machines.

Büchs: 305!

Hitler: Right, 305 made contact. But you just said 490.

Büchs: No, 305. The whole fighter wing at Frankfurt failed to make contact, and of Jagdgeschwader 4 . . .

Hitler: All right then, 305 – it comes to the same thing. And among those, he said, an assault Staffel with 42 machines was committed. This assault Staffel shot down thirty machines on its own.

Büchs: Both assault Gruppen. There were two assault Gruppen.

Hitler: With altogether. . . ?

Büchs: With altogether 63 aircraft. 61 of those made contact.

Hitler: Right, 61.

Büchs: They shot down thirty heavy bombers.

Hitler: That leaves twenty. If you take away these sixty machines from 305, that leaves 240. So 240 machines made twenty kills in all, and themselves lost . . . thirty in the assault Staffel?

Büchs: Yes, thirty in the assault Staffel.

Hitler: And the rest lost ninety. Then we have 240 sorties with ninety lost and twenty kills altogether.

Christian:[5] One other thing. The assault Gruppe has another Gruppe with it which covers it.
Hitler: I don't give a damn about that. The covering squadron must shoot too. It wasn't just bombers that were shot down – some fighters were too.
Büchs: Yes, that's clear.
Hitler: Then the result is thoroughly unsatisfactory.
Christian: The key point is still that the thirty kills by the assault Gruppen . . .
Hitler: Do you have someone with you to make a planned analysis of all these things? Anyway, the Reichsmarschall isn't in the picture. When he was here just now, he had no idea that our losses were so high – these damned "failed to return" reports confuse the whole issue.
Christian: This comes up every day.
Hitler: I want to see the whole thing properly worked out. This proves once and for all that either the pilots or their machines are no good. We can't argue that it's the pilots, because it's they who get shot down. So it must be the machines. But I have quite the opposite view of the Luftwaffe – their aircraft are good. The whole thing is ridiculous. If I try and work it out, I can't make the answer add up.
Büchs: 65 machines were originally reported missing after this operation. Up to today, 38 of these in all have been traced, and 27 are still missing. All 38 aircraft were complete write-offs; 32 people were killed and six have come back wounded or unhurt.
Hitler: It takes a bit of time to sort all this out. The other day I was given the figures for one month. But someone should have said how many sorties were flown. For a month it looks crazy. But the number of sorties is what really . . .
Büchs: I put in the number of sorties, but the figures aren't available for the whole month.
Hitler: That's the whole point! It's minute.
Christian: But Führer, those are percentages.
Büchs: Führer, I'm now tracing through all these operations from the 1st onwards and looking specially at aircraft reported missing.
Hitler: There must be someone to go through all these things properly and set out the deductions and conclusions. It must somehow be possible to draw proper conclusions. We can't just

say 'Well, that's the way it is.'
Christian: Führer, we're drawing up planning figures and forecasts all the time – *Generaloberst* Stumpff as Commander Air Forces Germany is responsible for this. Galland as Inspector can talk to the units. The Reichsmarschall always has at his side . . .
Hitler: Well, all I can say is no one has ever shown me any figures of this kind.
Christian: Führer, I've got these tables all drawn up.
Hitler: But I've never really taken them apart. One's got to do that kind of thing for oneself.
Christian: These figures are just preliminary ones. The assault Gruppe shot down thirty heavy bombers.
Hitler: Thirty. And the AA shot down thirty. That leaves twenty. And these come from 260 engagements. That's a rotten result. I put in 260 fighters and get twenty kills. So if I put in 2,000, I'd get 200 kills. This means I just can't count on those machines producing any . . . and they're pouring out of the factories at the devil's own pace. They're just eating up labor and materials.
Christian: The real reason, Führer, is that the boys hadn't flown for ten days.
Hitler: Reasons, reasons! We're always hearing about 'reasons.'
Christian: Well, that's the way things are. By contrast the Jagdgeschwader that took off in bad weather in the West landed back without loss, because it's flying every day, even in bad weather. You just can't get away from it.
Hitler: I don't want to say anything against the pilots. Let's stick to the kill figures for the moment; nothing can change those. It means that with 2,600 aircraft I can expect 200 kills. In other words any hope of achieving decimation by mass tactics is right out of court. So it's nonsensical to keep on making machines just for the Luftwaffe to play numbers-games with.

November 1944 was to be the month of the "Big Blow", the simultaneous commitment of all the fighter units concentrated in Germany. But the air battle of November 2 put paid to this; a large proportion of the units which had been grounded for some three weeks were committed and wiped out. Analysis of the results of the day's fighting left no doubt that the planned mass operation was, for the time being at least, quite out of the question. And since the success of an operation of this kind would in any case be dependent on the weather, Hitler, who was by now convinced that his own fighter aircraft were inferior to the Allies on every count, decided to engage with small forces too if the enemy should come in with similar numbers.

Meanwhile on November 7, Göring had issued the following edict to "his fighter pilots":

> "For months now the Army has been heavily engaged in decisive battles whose outcome spells victory or defeat. The Luftwaffe has failed to meet the demands made on it.
>
> Comrades, our time is up! Now we must go to it and show the world that we can forge the German fighter force anew – stronger and fuller of fighting spirit and resolve than ever. Now we must prove that the hopes of the German people have not been unfounded, and that the German workman has not toiled in vain.
>
> Fighter pilots, it's up to you! The major fighter operation that lies before us must be the hour when a new Luftwaffe, stronger and full of victories, is born."

If the words of this exhortation are anything to go by, the Supreme Commander of the Luftwaffe simply does not seem to have taken in the events of November 2.

In the meantime *Versuchskommando Nowotny*[6] had been formed at Achmer and early in the month flew its first operational missions. It was hardly in a position however to forge the Messerschmitt 262 jet fighter into a decisive weapon, first because low production figures meant that the Me 262 was only trickling through to first-line units and second because the bulk of them were still being allocated to bomber wings.

On November 8, *Major* Walter Nowotny and his unit scrambled against an incursion by heavy bombers. They made an immediate interception and fought the whole of their action above the clouds. *Leutnant* Schall, holder of the Knight's Cross, brought down three Mustang escort fighters, and Nowotny himself had just reported his third kill. But then suddenly the men down in ground control heard his desperate calls. Something was wrong with one of the jet engines. Seconds later, the Me 262 plunged out of the clouds to explode in a meadow outside the hamlet of Epe, near Bramsche. Nowotny, holder of the Knights Cross with Diamonds and with 258 kills to his credit, was dead. The actual cause of the crash was never established.

This was also to be the last operation from Achmer, for the trials detachment with its Me 262s moved to Lechfeld, where it was later to form the nucleus of the new Jagdgeschwader 7.

Saturday, November 18, 1944

"18.11.44

Yesterday *Feldwebel* Damm (13) stalled over the airfield at Hüfingen, crashed and was killed. Meimberg's II./JG 53 engaged enemy aircraft in the Karlsruhe area, *Fähnrich* Schliwinski killed.

. . . the Americans were over Southwest Germany today with strong formations of P-47s and P-51s. II and III./JG 53 intercepted, resulting in the loss of eight pilots. *Leutnant* Kupfender (12) is missing. *Unteroffizier* Sommerhof (11) bailed out over Irrendorf.

Unteroffizier Pläschke was shot at and wounded in his parachute north of Bietingen. *Unteroffizier* Weitzel (5) and *Feldwebel* Fischer (8) bailed out over the Speyer area.

Within three weeks IV Gruppe has lost a *Kommandeur* and a *Staffelkapitän* , *(Hauptmann* Morr, *Oberleutnant* Kayl), bringing its losses to seven killed and two wounded."

Tuesday, November 21, 1944

On November 21, 8th Air Force bombers, escorted by some 650 Mustangs, again flew in over Central Germany, following the same path as they had on November 2. The weather was absolutely wretched. It was raining heavily in places, the whole sky was overcast and the lower and middle layers of this cloud were thick enough to provide about 80% cover. Only at ground level was visibility more than three miles.

At their various airfields some 400 machines of I Jagdkorps had been waiting for some time, some of them at cockpit readiness. But the order to scramble did not come, and only a few knew the real reason for this. It had been clear since winter 1943 that bad-weather operations were barely feasible; in the day fighter force the aircraft lacked the requisite radio installations and take-off and landing aids, and the pilots lacked the necessary training. In November 1944, a year later, only two Geschwader were capable of operating under these conditions. These were the all-weather JG 300 and JG 301, both formerly "*Wilde Sau*" single-engine night fighter units. The Gruppen of JG 300 were stationed in the Brandenburg area south of Berlin, and those of JG 301 in the area Salzwedel-Sachau-Stendal.

Furthermore, Headquarters, I Jagdkorps tended to be hesitant in com-

Fighter Losses on November 21, 1944

Units Involved	Killed/ Missing	Wounded	Total Casualties	Aircraft	Locale
I/JG1	15	5	20	Fw 190 A-8	Eisleben, Erfurt, Gardelegen, Weimar
III/JG2	1		1	Fw 190 A-8	Rhine-Main
III/JG4	1	3	4	Bf 109 G-14/K-4	Osterhausen, Querfurt
II/JG27	4	1	5	Bf 109 G-14/K-4	Cologne, Monchen-Gladbach, Neuss
IV/JG54	2	3	5	Fw 190 A-8	Krefeld, Munster-Handorf
I/JG300	2	1	3	Bf 109 G-14	Braunschweig
IV/JG300	3	1	4	Bf 109 G-10/G-14	Gifthorn, Hanover, Hildesheim
			7		
I/JG301	8	4	12	Fw 190 A-9/R11	Eisenach, Erfurt
II/JG301	4	3	7	Fw 190 A-9/R11	Gotha, Jena
III/JG301		1	1	Fw 190 A-8	Koenitz, Stendal, Zeitz
			20		
Total Losses (Germany)	40	22	62 (including 1 Gruppe commander killed, 2 Staffel leaders killed, 1 Staffel leader wounded)		

mitting its aircraft in bad weather as it was anxious to avoid wasting pilots in a type of operation for which they were still ill-prepared. This is what happened on November 21.

There was little doubt about the Americans' target for that day; the flight path pointed to another raid on Merseburg. With a severe storm front stationary over West Germany, the Germans reckoned on the likelihood of the bomber formations turning back. But the Americans pressed on and set about breaking through the storm front in the Hanover area. Only at this point did Luftflotte Germany pass the order to engage to the individual Jagddivisionen.

In any event they took off too late, and the American bombers had been over the target area for some time when the fighters got there. First contact took place in cloud, when the strong Allied escort took the bulk of German aircraft by surprise while they were still forming up. It appears to have been the three Gruppen of JG 301, with their Focke-Wulf Fw 190 A-9/R11s,[7] which first engaged the stream of bombers. The encounter with the Mustangs of the 352nd and 359th Fighter Groups had been so sudden that the Germans scarcely had time to jettison their drop-tanks. The unequal battle, fought in cloud and rain, was soon over.

JG 301 reported ten pilots killed and two missing. A further eight were wounded, three of them having baled out. *Feldwebel* Böwer of 1 Staffel, one of the eight wounded, was chased by Mustangs, but nevertheless managed to put his grey-painted Focke-Wulf down at III./JG 301's base at Stendal. *Oberleutnant* Kretschmer, the *Kapitän* of 7 Staffel, had no such luck. Whether it was the bad weather or his dwindling fuel state which led him to attempt a landing at Wenigenlupnitz, east of Eisenach, is unknown. In any case he was pursued by several Mustangs and shot down as he approached to land. Also lost was *Gruppenkommandeur Hauptmann* Burggraf, who was shot down over Jena.

Once again large numbers of white parachutes bloomed in the skies, plainly visible in those areas where the cloud cover was not so dense. Far higher, however, was the number of pilots who failed to escape from their fighters as they plunged earthward.

Meanwhile I and IV Gruppen of JG 300 had scrambled from Borkheide and Reinsdorf. They met the Mustangs in the Hanover-Brunswick area. I Gruppe suffered two losses in this operation which were not attributable to enemy action. Over Hildesheim a Focke-Wulf, probably from 2./JG 1, rammed *Unteroffizier* Horstkötter's Bf 109. A second Messerschmitt, *Unteroffizier* Hennersdorf's "White 8", was unfortunately shot down by German anti-aircraft fire.

I Gruppe, Jagdgeschwader 1 took off from Greifswald, where it had been in refresher training since the beginning of October, and headed south, guided by ground radio, to meet the bomber force over Thuringia. But the Geschwader must have taken the heaviest losses of any German formation that day, for the one Gruppe which took part in the operation was virtually wiped out. At least twenty aircraft went down, eight of them over Erfurt alone. That was two thirds of the Gruppe's strength. For these pilots November 21 was their first operational mission for some time – and for many it was also to be the last. We will never know if *Gefreiter* Simmel of 3 Staffel gave the possibility any thought as he climbed into his "Yellow 14," because he met his end over Sangerhausen. Simmel and three other young pilots of the Staffel were shot down and killed by a swarm of Mustangs. The only pilot to survive the encounter was *Oberfähnrich* Seume, who bailed out of his Fw 190 A-8 over Alsdorf. The German pilots had fought desperately to hold off the Mustangs, but were unable to prevent the loss of five Focke-Wulfs. 4 Staffel lost six aircraft, their pilots being listed as killed or missing. Only one, *Unteroffizier* Fendler, managed to bail out over Erfurt.

The American bombers had long since reached the Leuna plant and almost without hindrance dropped their 475 tons of bombs on the fuel installations. Here it was only Jagdgeschwader 4 which tried to get its III Gruppe through to the bombers; but it was no more successful than 1 Geschwader had been in splitting open the Mustang screen. Its losses were less devastating, however, with one killed and three wounded.

When the order to scramble reached II Gruppe, Jagdgeschwader 27 and IV Gruppe, Jagdgeschwader 54 (which was attached to JG 27) at Hopsten, the Americans were already well on their way home. The German fighter formations made contact with the returning bombers over the Ruhr, only to get a prompt hot reception from the fighter escorts, this time Thunderbolts of the 366th Fighter Group, US 9th Air Force. In engagements over the Cologne-Düsseldorf area the Thunderbolt pilots claimed ten machines shot down and three unconfirmed. By contrast the II Gruppe, Jagdgeschwader 27 diary gives only five losses. However IV Gruppe, Geschwader 54 lost five Focke-Wulfs, among them the two Fw 190s which crashed after colliding over Münster-Handorf.

There is no question but that the day's entire defensive operation must be seen as a total failure. Attacks were broken up or frustrated before they had begun. The Allied fighter escorts succeeded in involving the German fighter force in dogfights to the point of inhibiting the real business of the day, a breakthrough to the bombers. On November 21, the German fighter force lost at least 61 aircraft against 25 Flying Fortresses and 15 Mustangs shot down, according to US documents – a heavy toll in blood for the fighter pilots to pay. But so many of these pilots lacked adequate operational experience that their actions had ceased to bear comparison with the proud fighter tradition that had seen the war in. The situation as a whole had long since prevented more comprehensive training, and young students from the flying and fighter schools were being posted to first-line units almost before they had mastered circuits and bumps with the Bf 109, to find themselves, sometimes on their very first operation, swept up in the maelstrom of a dogfight from which there was no escape. The fighter pilots were now having to pay a ridiculous price for the failure to make timely and continuous preparations for a defensive strategy.

Sunday, November 25, 1944

The American offensive astride the Vosges had begun on November 14. After bitter fighting 3rd US Army under General George S. Patton took the ancient fortress of Metz on November 20, and three days later occupied Strasbourg. The opponents of the German fighter units which were flung into the Lorraine battle were the strong fighter elements of 9th US TAF,[8] which was supporting the ground forces. Whenever the weather allowed, the American P-47 Thunderbolts were constantly over the front, with the result that dogfights constantly developed, for the most part over Hagenau Forest.

At the end of October 1944 a new unit, IV Gruppe, Jagdgeschwader 4, was formed from elements of II and III Gruppen, Jagdgeschwader 5. This Gruppe, which had taken its first losses in the fighting on November 2, now prepared to move from Fürstenwalde to Rhine-Main.

> "25.11.44. First operation from Rhine-Main and five pilots lost. Attacked by P-47s in strength while flying cover for our own troops in the Strasbourg area and South of Hagenau Forest.
>
> Jupp Kunz's 13 Staffel lost *Uffz.* Mehrens wounded and *Fw.* Lautenschläger killed near Iffezheim. 14 Staffel also lost one wounded and one killed – *Uffz.* Blumenberg landed by parachute near Neuweiler and *Uffz.* Müller was shot down by P-47s near Rastatt. From 16 Staffel *Uffz.* Bintriem was wounded and baled out near Strasbourg."

The *Kommodore* of Jagdgeschwader 4, *Major* Michalski, was awarded the Oak Leaves.[9]

Sunday, November 26, 1944

As the crews of the 491st Bomb Group left the briefing hut next day no one among them had any idea that this flight over Germany was to cost their Group extremely dear. 491 Group's B-24 Liberators took off from North Pickenham at midday. The US 8th Air Force formations assembled over southeast England, forming up into several waves, and headed off across the Channel for the Continent – an armada of about 1,000 aircraft. Their target was the Misburg hydrogenation plant near Hanover.

Fighter Losses on November 26, 1944

Units Involved	Killed/ Missing	Wounded	Total Casualties	Aircraft	Locale
I/JG1	2		2	Fw 190 A-8/A-9	Helmstedt, Perleherg, Salzwedel
II/JG1	9	3	12	Fw 190 A-8/A-9	Uelzen
			14		
III/JG6	6	6	12	Bf 109 G-14	Salzwedel, Wittstock
III/JG26	1	1	2	Bf 109 G-14	Oldenburg
I/JG27	2		2	Bf 109 G-14	Bersenbruck
II/JG27	2	4	6	Bf 109 G-10/G-14	
III./JG27	4	2	6	Bf 109 K-4	Osnabrück
IV./JG27	3	1	4	Bf 109 G-10/K-4	
			18		
IV/JG54	2		2	Fw 190 A-8	Vechta, Vorden
I/JG301	13	3	16	Fw 190 A-9/R11	Brunswick
II/JG301	9	6	15	Fw 190 A-9/R11	Eimbeckhausen
III/JG301	4	4	8	Fw 190 A-8	Hamlin, Hildesheim, Wunstorf
			39		
Total Losses (Germany)	57	30	87 (including 5 Staffel leaders killed, 1 Staffel leader wounded)		

The storm front which had been stationary over West Germany a week earlier had long since moved on, and this time the Americans found the skies over Hanover almost cloudless. It was not only for the 491st Liberator Group that fate lay in wait, but for their immediate opponents too. For November 26th was to be Jagdgeschwader 301's blackest day.

The weather conditions were now more suitable for a counterattack, and the Germans on their side lost no time in preparing the bulk of their serviceable aircraft – some 550 fighters in all from I Jagdkorps and Luftwaffe Headquarters West. In the event about a quarter of these would fail to make contact with the enemy.

Meanwhile the bomber waves had passed Oldenburg in the north and were heading southeast towards the Elbe. The Gruppen of JG 1 and JG 6 scrambled from Mecklenburg, and JG 301 was brought to readiness on its airfields between Stendal and Salzwedel.

Long-range visibility was relatively good. The Americans' vapor trails were soon to be seen and the air defense fighters were able to set up their attack in good time. Guidance from ground control was almost superfluous this time; no one could miss the Allies tight-packed "combat boxes." A force of some 50-80 machines from III./JG 1 went in against the bomber formations on a broad front between Uelzen and Perleberg; but the Mustang escort was on its guard and had already formed up to ward them off, with the result that II./JG 1 alone lost five fighters in as many minutes. As if that were not bad enough, the aircraft flown by *Fähnrich* Peters rammed the Fw 190 of *Fähnrich* Hinrichs during the fighting over Uelzen. Both aircraft crashed and their pilots were killed.

At this point the bomber formations, now over Wittenberge, changed heading and turned south. Then they flew west past Stendal to cross the high ground at Gardelegen and run in on the target from the east.

Meanwhile three pilots from Jagdgeschwader 6 had baled out near Salzwedel, all of them escaping with wounds. *Oberleutnant* Wernhard Mayer, *Staffelkapitän* of 7 Staffel was shot down by the Mustang escort near Poppau and killed; *Fähnrich* Obrakat, also of 7 Staffel, met a similar fate over Salzwedel. But it was 9 Staffel which suffered the heaviest losses, with four pilots lost.

It was only with the entry of Jagdgeschwader 301 that the real drama began, however. On November 26, all three Gruppen took off from the fields at Salzwedel, Sachau, Stendal and Solpke. At this moment the leading American squadrons were already approaching Hanover, but JG 301 moved in swiftly and it was just to the south of the line Brunswick-Hanover that the fateful encounter with the enemy escort fighters took place. But this time the Germans found a few gaps which allowed them to get through to the bombers, and they soon had the 491st Bomb Group's Liberators in their sights.

Suddenly the air was full of the rattle of machine-guns. Engines screamed. The first Fw 190s plunged downwards, two at Mellendorf and one near Bad Münder, killing *Gefreiter* Henning, *Gefreiter* Dossmann and *Feldwebel* Handel. Over Rethen *Oberleutnant* Vollert, *Kapitän* of 5 Staffel, closed in on a Liberator; but the two Mustangs chasing him were faster, and after a wild dogfight Vollert's A-9 went down.

Three parachutes came down near Sarstedt and Peine. The pilots all belonged to 7 Staffel: *Unteroffizier* Stargardt, *Oberfeldwebel* Menzel and *Feldwebel* Röglsperger. All three were wounded, but survived.

All the while JG 301 was pressing home its attacks against the four-engine bombers and at the same time trying to ward off the horde of Mustangs. The escort, whose screen had been penetrated in places, now for the first time really seemed to wake up and redouble its efforts to intercept the German fighter attacks. The combat in the skies over Hanover grew more and more intense.

Two aircraft detached themselves from the ongoing battle. A Focke-Wulf with a "Red 1" on its fuselage was being pursued by a Mustang. The German pilot appeared to be having difficulty controlling his aircraft; the initial burst from the Mustang must therefore have hit something vital. The pursuit continued north across the Aller Canal and the Boldecker Land. Finally, however, the Fw 190 went down; 6 Staffel had lost its *Kapitän*, *Oberleutnant* Rudolf Schick.

Feldwebel Helmut Thiemann died east of Eimbeckhausen. Thiemann was seen to bail out of his "Blue 2" before the Focke-Wulf went down in flames, but was listed as missing. Not until December 18 was he found in a clearing in Stölting Forest. Also shot down over Eimbeckhausen was *Feldwebel* Werner Meyer, at twenty-seven one of the "older" pilots. He failed to get out of the aircraft, which crashed into a furniture factory in the town. I Gruppe suffered the most pilots killed that day. Among the dead were *Leutnant* Brinkmann, *Fähnrich* Raykrotzki and *Unteroffizier* Geibler, all shot down by Mustangs over Bad Münder. The others were brought down over Minden, Bückeberg and Hameln. 4 Staffel was somewhat luckier, with one pilot killed and three wounded. *Unteroffizier* Schäper managed to bail out near Bredebeck and was picked up with minor wounds, as was his Staffel comrade *Unteroffizier* Hellrieger.

Among the units of III Gruppe, 10 Staffel suffered the heaviest losses, among them *Leutnant* Franzel and *Leutnant* Karioth, both of whom were wounded in combat in the Braunschweig area. *Fähnrich* Voigt was shot down and killed over Wunstorf in his "Red 15."

At the end of the day Jagdgeschwader 301 had 26 killed or missing and thirteen wounded. Fritz Yung, who had been shot down and severely wounded over Erding at the end of April 1944, rejoined 301 Geschwader on his recovery. His first duty was to lay his comrades killed on November 26 to rest in the Wunstorf War Cemetery. This was a sad task for Yung, and many pilots remain unidentified to this day.

But the battle was not yet over. Having dropped a total of 862 tons of bombs on Hanover and turned for home, the American bombers ran into JG 27 and IV./JG 54, by now airborne after scrambling from Rheine, Hopsten, Achmer and Hesepe, and Vörden respectively. These units, operating under the command of 3 Jagddivision were waiting for the enemy units over the Teutoburger Wald and the Ems; but JG 27 was once again to taste the fury of the Mustangs' counterattacks.

The first Messerschmitts smashed into the ground in the flatlands astride the Mittelland Canal; and to the North, almost above their own airfield, the parachutes began to plume. 5 Staffel lost two machines over the Hesepe area, one of them belonging to the *Staffelkapitän*, *Leutnant* Bittner. Bittner escaped by parachute and returned wounded to his Staffel. *Oberfähnrich* Paffrath likewise survived, albeit wounded.

More skirmishes developed in the skies around Osnabrück and spread out northwards as far as Vechta and Bersenbrück. *Fahnenjunkerunteroffizier* Otz, who had become involved in a dogfight with 7 Staffel, fell near Bramsche, while the badly-wounded *Leutnant* Siegfried Dellin managed to bail out of his burning Bf 109 over Osnabrück. Dellin entered the hospital, but succumbed to his injuries on February 21, 1945.

III and IV Gruppen, Jagdgeschwader 27 each lost three pilots killed, and *Unteroffizier* Gerd Schmidt was reported missing. IV./JG 54 suffered a particularly tragic loss when *Oberleutnant* Heinz Sterr, Knight's Cross, was shot down by a Mustang over Vörden airfield as he was approaching to land. Sterr had a tally of 130 kills, 127 of them in the east; he had joined 16./JG 54 as *Staffelkapitän* only in the autumn of 1944, and his death cost the unit one of its more distinguished pilots. IV./JG 54's second fatality was *Unteroffizier* Schische of 13 Staffel.

Hauptmann Haase, *Kommandeur* of I./JG 3 Udet, was killed in an unfortunate accident. The Geschwader had received no orders for this operation, but the *Gruppenschwarm* had been scrambled. Shortly after takeoff, *Hauptmann* Haase collided with his wingman's machine over Erkelenz and crashed to his death.

The operations of November 26 added up to yet another painful blow for the home air defense fighters. The Gruppen taking part lost at least ninety machines, a figure for once not far different from the Allied claims. The 339th US Fighter Group reported 29 kills, Lieut. Daniel alone accounting for five Fw 190s. The 361st Group (Capt. Duncan) claimed nineteen kills, and the 356th Mustang Group (Lt.Col. Baccus) 23. Together with a figure of 27 for the 355th Fighter Group this amounted in all to 98 German fighters destroyed.

I Jagdkorps announced 35 four-engine bombers shot down, but at 34 the US 8th Air Force figures were far lower – among these were B-24 Liberators from 491st Group, mentioned earlier, and five Liberators from 445th Bomb Group.

The losses suffered up to this point had already made a mockery of continued talk of "home air defense." However, the commanding officers, or at least most of them, might strive to use their alertness and their experience to produce at least some slight improvement in their men's slender chance of survival, the final decline of the German fighter force was under way. Perhaps the Luftwaffe High Command thought otherwise; at least they did all they could to conceal this tragedy from the public. Thus it was that the Armed Forces communique for the "Black 26th" contained only a brief paragraph:

> "Anglo-American terror bombers penetrated by day to Northwest and Central Germany with strong fighter escort, dropping their bombs mainly in urban residential areas and on rural communities. Damage was particularly extensive at Hanover, recently the target of repeated enemy air-raids, and in Hamm."

November 27, 1944

The fine weather of the day before had changed. It is true that no rain was forecast, and visibility remained excellent; but cloud was forming and was later to give 40-60% cover. It was also a good deal colder.

Once again the observation posts reported Allied bomber formations airborne and forming up over the British Isles. It would not be long before General Doolittle's 8th Air Force formation set course for Germany. Sure enough, at 1100 the leading bomber wave was over the Channel, and an hour later the Americans were spread out on a broad front over the Ruhr.

The Allies was bound for communications targets in the Rhine-Main area, and was to reach them unmolested by the German defense. For strong forces of Mustangs and Thunderbolts in their hordes put a ring round the attacking waves, now flying alongside the bombers, now thrusting out ahead to spring upon the German fighters in good time. Far to the north and the east the Allied fighters threw out a screen which proved quite impenetrable. While the Fortresses and Liberators were starting their bombing-runs, fierce air fighting was in progress over Münsterland and the Harz.

Stationed at Fürstenau airfield, some fifteen miles east of Lingen, was I./JG 26 (*Schlageter*). A mere six Focke-Wulfs were serviceable and standing ready on the wet runway, but only four took part. The Messerschmitts of III./ JG 26 were scrambled from Plantlünne, and III and IV Gruppen of JG 27

Fighter Losses on November 27, 1944

Units Involved	Killed/ Missing	Wounded	Total Casualties	Aircraft	Locale
I/JG26		1	1	Fw 190 A-8	Iburg, Osnabruck
III/JG26	2	2	4	Bf 109 G-14/K-4	Munster, Rheine
			5		
III/JG27	3		3	Bf 109 K-4	Bersenbruck
IV/JG27	2	2	4	Bf 109 G-10/G-14	Munster, Werther
			7		
IV/JG54	3	1	4	Fw 190 A-8/A-9	Diepholz, Ibbenburen, Vorden
I/JG300	3		3	Bf 109 G-14 AS	Altenau, Aschersleben, Hahnenklee
II/Sturm JG300	7	4	11	Fw 190 A-8	Halberstadt
III/JG300	7	1	8	Bf 109 G-14	Nordhausen, Quedlinberg
IV/JG300	1		1	Bf 109 G-14	
			23		
I/JG301	6	3	9	Fw 190 A-9/R11	Brunswick
II/JG301	3		3	Fw 190 A-9/R11	Gottingen
			12		
Total Losses (Germany)	37	14	51 (including 1 Staffel leader killed,1 Staffel leader wounded)		

were in the thick of it again. Their operational area was right on their doorstep, for the American fighter formations had already penetrated to the general area Rheine-Osnabrück-Gütersloh-Münster. The party was on.

By 1215 *Oberleutnant* Gottfried Schmidt was hanging in his parachute, after a Mustang had shot up his faithful "White 21." Soon after Schmidt, the *Kapitän* of 9./JG 26, came down near Iburg. Five minutes later *Feldwebel* Niedermeyer, also of 9 Staffel, was forced to abandon his aircraft near Rheine. The third member of JG 26 to take to his parachute was *Unteroffizier* Brühan of 1 Staffel. He had been set upon by a pair of Mustangs and was forced to bail out suffering from splinter wounds. Two pilots of III Gruppe went missing between Osnabrück and Münster.

Along with the pilots from JG 27, about a dozen machines of IV./JG 54 took off from Vörden and headed southwest. Seconds after they were airborne and still in sight of the field, pilots and groundstaff alike were horrified to see a Focke-Wulf, apparently with engine-failure, lose height and go straight in, killing its pilot.

Between Bramsche and Bersenbrück *Oberleutnant* Kohl of 11./JG 27 found himself hard pressed; the pilots had scarcely had time to bring their Messerschmitts to combat height after their takeoff from Hesepe before enemy fighters were upon them. An unending stream of Allied machines seemed to pour from the sky, and not one pilot managed to catch even a glimpse of a bomber's silhouette. They simply could not force their way through to the bombers.

As the wild hunt with its bitter infighting swept on to the north of Bramsche, individual machines could escape the deadly enemy fire only by going down to treetop height. It was just after midday. By this time III./JG 27 had already lost three pilots: *Oberleutnant* Karl Kohl, *Oberfeldwebel* Sperlich and *Feldwebel* Schopper. On the other hand IV Gruppe found itself in action between Münster and Bielefeld. Two of the unit's pilots, *Unteroffizier* Reckhenrich and *Oberfeldwebel* Harbrecht, were shot down and killed.

It was hardly surprising that, in the massed dogfights of those times, pilots were taking friend for foe and vice versa. Thus in the heat of battle two *Feldwebeln* of 13 Staffel, JG 27 took each other on and shot each other down. One Messerschmitt crashed in a wood near Ascheloh and the other came down not far from it in a field at Werther. Luckily both pilots, although wounded, succeeded in baling out. History does not relate what *Hauptmann* Dudeck had to say about this incident at the debriefing. The same thing happened with the Americans. A Mustang pilot from the 353rd Fighter Group took another machine in his own unit for a Messerschmitt and duly despatched it; and Major Juntilla, commanding the 353rd Fighter Group, narrowly escaped the same fate. Nevertheless Juntilla's unit reported 21 kills that day.

Meanwhile the American fighter screens were fanning out over the Harz and the Göttingen area. The Americans knew exactly where the individual fighter units of the German home air defense were stationed, and they were expecting another intervention from JG 300 and JG 301 based south and west of Berlin. To nip this plan in the bud, the US 8th Air Force fighters pressed way out ahead – a tactic which was once again to pay dividends.

II./JG 300, stationed at Löbnitz, under *Major* Peters, an assault unit set up on the proven model, was already airborne and had assembled with the Geschwader's other three Gruppen, based at Borkheide, Jüterbog and

Reinsdorf, to form a large tactical grouping, which two Gruppen from Jagdgeschwader 301 were also to join.

Jagdgeschwader 301, based in the Altmark, also was already airborne and was heading south over Brunswick to be guided on to the American formations.

Directed onto the same target, JG 300 was flying westward over the Brandenburg area and thence over Saxony. These fighters did not get far, for both Geschwader the Harz, or more precisely the area Salzgitter-Eschwege was the limit of their flight. There the Americans were already lying in wait for them, and the Mustangs, streaming in from all directions, went over to the attack.

It speaks well for the courage of the individual German pilots that they were able here and there, in dashing counter-actions, to press their numerically superior pursuers hard. Pushing their aircraft to the limits of maneuverability and beyond, they strove to get into favorable attack positions; but usually they failed and the pilot had to use all his skill to escape in one piece. The sky was full of well-trained enemy pilots, and on the German side there were too few fighter pilots with the experience called for by an all-out dogfight. At this stage many pilots quite simply lacked the training for this type of operation. In the heat of the moment they would often forget to push the safety-catch on the control column and press their thumbs sore until they became resigned to the fact that they could not get a single shot off and were thus defenseless. For the first time they were seeing the gruesome downward plunge of a friend who had managed to jump clear of his blazing "crate" only to find that his parachute would not open. For the first time they were confronted with death, with the reality of war. And then it happened. While the novice, fresh from flying school, was trying to grasp all these incomprehensible things and was staring wide-eyed at machines dropping out of the sky beside him and exploding as they hit the ground, he too, paralysed by what he had seen, fell prey to the Mustangs.

The bitterest fighting raged between the Harz and the Selling Hills. 1 Staffel lost two pilots at Alfeld on the Leine. With six killed and three wounded in I Gruppe, as well as three killed in II Gruppe, Jagdgeschwader 301 had been badly battered once again; like JG 27 it had been virtually decimated within a few minutes. The number of available serviceable aircraft had fallen drastically, and the pilot reinforcements needed to bring the Geschwader up to strength did not exist.

Over the Harz and to the east and south the whole of *Oberstleutnant*

Dahl's JG 300 became involved with enemy fighters. Once again the casualty reports piled up at Jagdkorps Operations Center in Treuenbrietzen. There was especially heavy fighting in quadrants "*Konrad-Anton*," "*Julius-Anton*" and "*Julius-Cäsar.*"

From 2 Staffel *Feldwebel* Hanauer was shot down in his "Red 1" near Quedlinburg and *Oberfähnrich* Krüger over the Nordhausen area. 3 Staffel, which was led by *Oberleutnant* Seeler, lost *Gefreiter* Schöffmann, likewise shot down near Nordhausen. *Hauptmann* Stamp's I Gruppe thus lost a total of three pilots killed. Schöffmann had earlier been wounded in air combat over Munich at the end of July. The *Kapitän* of 2 Staffel, *Oberleutnant* Manfred Dieterle, was also familiar with this area of operations. He had been shot down on September 28 and had bailed out of his "Red 17" over Halberstadt.

In the Herzberg-Duderstadt area *Hauptmann* Nölter's III Gruppe also suffered badly at the hands of enemy fighters. *Leutnant* Kamp and *Gefreiter* Müller, both of 12 Staffel, were killed. A wounded *Obergefreiter* Bernau managed to escape from his stricken machine by parachute not far from Goslar, and *Leutnant* Emil Kriegbaum failed to return and was listed missing in action. His Bf 109 G-14 was last seen somewhere in quadrant "*Konrad-Anton.*" A Messerschmitt of 11 Staffel crashed near Mühlhausen; the aircraft's pilot was unable to bail out.

However, it was the *Sturmgruppe* that took the highest casualties, with two killed and two wounded in 5 Staffel, two killed in 6 Staffel, two killed and two wounded in 7 Staffel and one killed in 8 Staffel. This Gruppe met enemy units over the eastern slopes of the Harz, in the triangle Halberstadt-Quedlinburg-Aschersleben. In a bitterly contested action they shot down several Mustangs, but at high cost. *Oberfähnrich* Schneider was found with the remains of his aircraft northeast of Halberstadt, and *Unteroffizier* Hinning as well as *Gefreiter* Hachmann near Blankenburg.

Most of JG 300's casualties had been younger, less-experienced pilots. In addition to those mentioned the Geschwader lost *Gefreiter* Sauttner, *Gefreiter* Vorpahl, *Obergefreiter* Bartsch and *Obergefreiter* Seelow. A preliminary examination of the incoming loss reports at the corps headquarters showed clearly who had borne the brunt of the fighting. With a total of eighteen dead and missing pilots, JG 300 had paid the highest toll in blood this day.

The outcome of the defensive operations of November 27 was catastrophic. I Jagdkorps took on the intrusion by US 8th Air Force with some

750 fighters, the strongest force it had yet fielded; but the American fighters succeeded in pinning down the German defense to the point where not a single bomber was destroyed. And against German losses of over fifty, only eleven Mustangs were shot down. The American fighter units – mainly the 353rd and 357th Fighter Groups, the latter led by Major Broadhead – claimed 98 German fighters. Although it had by this time become very difficult to establish exact figures for German losses in home air defense, this figure seems on the high side. It is however not known whether fighters destroyed on the ground or accounted for in other ways are included.

November 30, 1944

Early in the forenoon 1 Jagddivision at Döberitz received a report of strong American bomber forces headed towards Berlin. That meant bringing Jagdgeschwader 300 to readiness, for its four Gruppen had the special role of protecting the capital. But when the bad weather still had not cleared shortly before midday – visibility was down to less than 1 mile in places – the commanding officers considered any attempt at interception out of the question.

Nevertheless two Gruppen of Jagdgeschwader 300, I Gruppe at Borkheide and II at Löbnitz, were scrambled. Göring, who happened to be at Jüterbog airfield on an inspection that day, applied pressure for the *Geschwaderstab* and *Hauptmann* Nölter's III Gruppe to take off as well. An argument followed between the Commander-in-Chief of the Luftwaffe and *Oberstleutnant* Dahl, the *Geschwaderkommodore*, the latter flatly refusing to fly in such weather, since less than half of the thirty pilots briefed for the mission were qualified to fly on instruments. Thus a massed takeoff was out of the question and to take off individually would have been suicidal. In the middle of all this elements of JG 300's other two Gruppen made contact. But, predictably enough, the moment the pilots broke out of the cloud the American escort flights picked them off, hunted them down and sent them to the ground.

In any event the Americans were not in fact going for Berlin; their target was the fuel industry in Central Germany. More than 1,000 four-engine machines dropped a total of 1,920 tons of bombs, mainly blind, on the installations at Böhlen, Leuna, Lützkendorf and Zeitz.

Reports of German pilots bailing out poured into the operations rooms.

About midday the results of the operation became clear, it was ill-conceived and had therefore failed. Only a fraction of the machines that had taken off were still intact. Countless forced landings and parachute descents were recorded. Many had never caught so much as a glimpse of the Americans. The only good thing was that almost all the pilots were able to report back to their units fit for flying.

On the very next day *Oberst* Lützow, commander of the 4th Pilot Training Division at Altenburg, pronounced on this unsuccessful operation, and in particular on the delay in scrambling III./JG 300, and proposed that every pilot without exception must be instrument-trained. This requirement was by no means a new one, but no one seemed to have attached much importance to it. This despite the fact that JG 300 and JG 301 were designated as "all weather formations" – the only two of their kind in the whole of the home air defense!

Review of November 1944

Analysis of the Allied offensive air operations of November 1944 shows that, in addition to raids on communications targets, the level of attacks on synthetic fuel production was greatly stepped up. In October the Americans had dropped 12.5% of their total weight of bombs on fuel targets and the RAF 5.9%; but in November these figures rose to 33% and 25% respectively. On the other hand the intensity of strategic operations fell off somewhat from that of the preceding months, as the Americans' attention was focussed on the ground operations that were taking shape in Lorraine and across Belgium and Luxembourg.

On the German side, by contrast, thanks to conservation and accumulation of fighter resources in the previous weeks, we could put strong forces into the air. But the figures are deceptive. The "Big Blow" envisaged by *General der Jagdflieger* Galland never took place. For one thing the weather that November was not suitable for an operation of this kind; the bulk of the pilots lacked the requisite operational training; and in addition the results of operations were falling way below expectations. In the area of I Jagdkorps under *Generalleutnant* Schmid, 155 Allied aircraft were shot down for the loss of 404 German aircraft, while personnel casualties amounted to at least 300 on the four principal days alone. The November 1944 figure for day-fighter pilots killed or missing, excluding accidents, was 244.

Oberstleutnant Dahl, commander of Jagdgeschwader 300, put the situation of the past weeks in a nutshell when he said:

> "November 1944's flying was the toughest I had been through in the whole war. The odds were 20 to 1 and often as much as 30 to 1 against us. We were taking casualties every day. Our aircrew reinforcements were short on quality as they didn't receive enough training. And shortage of fuel was making itself more and more felt."

Shortage of fuel was indeed becoming more serious and was having its effect on the night fighters too; it was one of the handicaps from which the German defenses suffered that November, despite isolated successes. A new unit, II./NJG 11, was set up with the specific aim of countering the Mosquito; for these very maneuverable British harassing bombers with their high ceiling remained a problem to which the Luftwaffe could offer no real solution. The new squadron was at first equipped with Bf 109 G-14s, specially modified for night fighting and fitted with the Daimler-Benz 605 AS engine; but these were not man enough for the job. During November the RAF carried out thirteen mass night attacks, their main targets being Düsseldorf, Coblenz, Dortmund and various hydrogenation plants in the Ruhr. In the heaviest of these raids, on Düsseldorf, on the night of November 3, II./NJG 1 shot down ten enemy aircraft in the Höxter area for the loss of only one machine. The overall figures for November 1944 for home air defense night-fighters were 115 kills for 45 aircraft lost.

It is beyond dispute that the general level of activity in this month of November 1944 and the day-by-day response of German fighter pilots evidenced a fighting spirit that words cannot describe. They gave their all in face of an enemy many times stronger – and not altogether without success. Nonetheless it was now plain for all to see that the German fighter force had set its foot on the sacrificial path.

Notes

[1]683 according to US figures.

[2]In the English edition, flying distances, visibility etc are given in nautical miles, and ground-to-ground distances (eg between a town and a village) in (UK) statute miles.

[3]Nickname for the armored Focke-Wulf Fw 190 of the assault Gruppen.

[4]Military Assistant to the Chief of the Wehrmacht General Staff.

[5]*Generalleutnant* Eckhard Christian, Chief of Air Staff, 1944/45.
[6]Nowotny Test Detachment
[7]The R 11 equipment on the Fw 190 included the FuG 125 radio beacon receiver, which was mainly fitted on the machines of the all-weather units. This equipment also allowed the pilot to fly radio beam approaches in bad weather.
[8]Tactical Air Force
[9]Oak Leaves to the Knight's Cross of the Iron Cross.

II

THE WESTERN THEATRE

Drama Over the Ardennes and the Eifel

Saturday, December 2, 1944
Sunday, December 3, 1944

Even November's heavy losses did not altogether put an end the hope, given good weather, of achieving a major success with a mass fighter operation. But by this time Supreme Headquarters had quite a different idea, and preparations were already under way for large-scale operations by all fighter units in support of the planned December offensive in the West. In view of the scope of the ground support operations planned for the fighter force, the first half of the month was taken up by another breathing space to allow at least some units to be brought up to strength with reinforcement aircrew. New aircraft made their appearance too, but the best and most powerful of engines was little use when there was no fuel for it.

Nevertheless, according to *Generalmajor* Grabmann's figures, December 16, the day on which the Ardennes offensive opened, saw between 1,600 and 1,800 fighters at readiness. On December 1, the unit strength of aircraft in day fighter units in I Jagdkorps' area amounted to rather over 1,000.[1] But all these figures are misleading; strengths alone do not give a true indication of actual fighting capability. For the pilots of these aircraft, almost to a man, were new and green; their state of training was inadequate, and they were scarcely up to the extreme physical and psychological demands imposed by air combat.

Despite generally unfavorable weather conditions, the strategic air forces in England were very active at the beginning of the month. As early as December 2, they launched two major attacks on Cologne and Bingen, while the US 15th Air Force, based in Italy, bombed the hydrogenation plants and refineries at Blechhammer in Lower Silesia and Floridsdorf near Vienna. The following day the German squadrons were mainly engaged in tactical air support in the Aachen-Dren area and on the other side too the Allies committed mainly fighters over Germany. Then on December 4 the Americans put in a large-scale raid on the rail network Kassel-Bebra-Giessen-Mainz.

During this period air defense operations cost the Germans some 65 pilots, 47 of them killed or missing. On December 2, Jagdeschwader 3 *Udet* had 19 killed and 5 wounded. *Hauptmann* Wirges, commanding I Gruppe, JG 3, was killed over Damm, near Marburg. Just 24 hours later another squadron commander failed to return. *Hauptmann* Wienhusen, IV./JG 4, together with his 14 Staffel leader, *Oberleutnant* Scheufele, were shot down by AA fire on the Aachen sector. Scheufele was taken prisoner by the Americans, marking the point at which home air defense had to reckon with the loss of pilots shot down behind enemy lines and captured as well as of those killed, wounded and missing.

Tuesday, December 5, 1944

Raids carried out since the beginning of December by the Americans, and to some extent by the RAF, whose heavy bombers were now frequently operating over Germany by day as well as by night, once more made it clear that the Allies were by this time in a position to carry through his attacks regardless of weather conditions in the target area. On December 5, General James H. "Jimmy" Doolittle was ordered to bomb Berlin with his 8th Air Force. The skies above Berlin were completely overcast that day, with 90% cloud cover down to 500-1,000 feet in places. The forecast was heavy showers with the possibility of storms.

But heaped cumulus and indifferent visibility did not stop the Allies from flying in early that morning over the German capital from the Hanover-Brunswick area with 427 B-17 Flying Fortresses. And this date carries another significance too – December 5, 1944 was the black day of Jagdgeschwader 1.

Despite the November losses and the increasing disruption caused by fuel shortages, Jagdgeschwader 1 was able to put some 300 machines into the air, of which, thanks once again to bad weather, the majority failed to intercept. An unusually turbulent wind, gusting up to Force 6 and beyond, was sweeping across wide areas of Central and North Germany, creating an additional problem for pilots on both sides.

Luftflotte Reich had earmarked Jagdgeschwadern 1 and 301 for defense against the force attacking Berlin, and was then forced to commit the battered Jagdgeschwader 27 and the attached IV./JG 54 against an intrusion by British heavy bombers. The RAF's target was the railway yards at Soest, and this was one of eleven daylight raids made by the RAF during December 1944. With the exception of III Gruppe, of which *Oberleutnant* Clade was acting commander at the time, all JG 27's units took part in the operation. Taking off from the group of airfields Rheine-Achmer-Hopsten-Hesepe, they met Allied forces right over the Ruhr. But the British bombers too were well screened by escort fighters. Three Bf 109s were lost over Gladbeck, and *Unteroffizier* Hornberger of 5 Staffel and *Unteroffizier* Schiller of 15 Staffel were killed. *Unteroffizier* Liener parachuted wounded from his Bf 109 G-10. Hornberger was flying he *Gruppenkommandeur*'s machine that day, and the double chevrons on the fuselage may have proved fatal by giving the enemy to think that a particularly worthwhile target was being offered them. As to why Hornberger and *Major* Spies had swapped aircraft, only two explanations are likely. On the one hand a changeover of this kind was often made deliberately in some German fighter units to mislead the enemy; on the other this machine may have been fully serviceable while the other had tire or engine defects or such. Thus the NCO would switch to the officer's aircraft, because the latter, perhaps, was not flying in this operation or was himself flying some other aircraft, leaving his own available should it be needed.

Only 10-15 kilometers farther east, over Gelsenkirchen, *Unteroffizier* Gerlach of 6 Staffel was shot down. *Feldwebel* Prohaska was also shot down and parachuted from his aircraft. Battles with Spitfires were also under way in the Dorsten area and then over Dortmund. British fighters shot up the aircraft of *Unteroffizier* Käster, which went down in flames, killing the pilot. *Fähnrich* Schleimer's Bf 109 fell north of Dorsten; he too was killed. Against three victories JG 27 lost seven pilots: five killed and two who bailed out after being wounded.

Over the capital, it was about 1045 when the bomb bay doors opened and their lethal contents tumbled downwards through the unbroken cloud. Up to this moment the American crews had hardly so much as seen a German fighter. On this day too the Mustang escort proved so formidable as to make penetration to the bombers next to impossible. Elements of all three squadrons of Jagdgeschwader 301 had been flying on an eastern heading almost parallel to the stream of bombers, apparently without having so far been spotted by the Allied fighter escort.

The men in the Focke-Wulfs had a while to wait before the Jagddivision operations center at Döberitz gave the order to engage. This seemingly endless waiting put an enormous strain on the nerves and was affecting the many inexperienced pilots most of all – of the Allies nothing was to be seen. Every now and then fighter control passed the latest position of the bomber formation, at the same time correcting its own units' course.

Meanwhile the bombing of Berlin had gone unhindered, and the Americans had turned northeast, headed for Schorf Heath. The whole of Jagdgeschwader 1 *Oesau* was now scrambled from Greifwald, Tutow and Anklam to close on the stream of Fortresses and engage it on its way back to England. Then the long-awaited order to go in reached JG 301 too. Both Geschwadern made contact with the American fighter escort north of the capital somewhere between Oranienburg and Lake Werbellin. The Mustangs immediately went over to the attack in an effort to seal off the bombers completely. But this time they were not flying as far ahead of the bombers as usual, and now and then it was even possible to get a burst off at the real target, the bombers, while taking evasive action against the Allied fighter formations.

It was about midday, over the Uckermark and in particular over the Mecklenburg lakes, that December's first major air battle developed.

II./JG 301 attacked down the line of the Havel-Oder Canal. But the Mustangs were too much for them; elements of the Gruppe were forced right off into the Prenzlau-Angermünde area and almost wiped out. *Hauptmann* Rolf Jacobs, *Kommandeur* of II Gruppe, fell near Zirtow and 5 Staffel lost its *Kapitän*, *Oberleutnant* Poppenburg, over Angermünde. 7 Staffel had three and 8 Staffel two killed, including *Oberfeldwebel* Paul Becker, *Feldwebel* Pflüger and *Unteroffizier* Thorwirth. West of Eberswalde, near Finow and Finowfurt, 10 Staffel grappled with enemy units. *Oberfähnrich* Hörnig and *Unteroffizier* Marquardt were shot down and killed. I Gruppe had thrust farthest north. *Feldwebel* Leyer of 1 Staffel was shot down and killed over Fürstensee in his Fw 190 A-9/R11. *Feldwebel* Koch, also of 1 Staffel, was wounded near Neustrelitz. *Oberfähnrich* Ripper and *Leutnant* Max Kreil, both members of 4 Staffel, were shot down and killed in the same area. Thus Jagdgeschwader 301's total losses on December 5 amounted to 21 pilots – eighteen killed (including II Gruppe's commander) and three wounded.

The events of the previous month had already made clear how tragic it was that the German fighter force had to be brought up to strength mainly by green reinforcement pilots. This was proved yet again on December 5, especially in the case of Jagdgeschwader 1 which was still undergoing refresher training.

Over Schorf Heath the 8th Air Force bombers turned northwest, presumably on to their final homeward path between Neuruppin and Neustrelitz/Neubrandenburg. Their very strong fighter escort had concentrated on their northern flank; when Jagdgeschwader 301 had to break off the engagement, mainly from lack of fuel, the escort turned on Jagdgeschwader 1 and the curtain went up on one of the most unfortunate operations in that unit's history. I Gruppe was guided by ground control into quadrants "*Cäsar-Friederich*", "*Cäsar-Gustav*," "*Dora-Friederich*" and "*Dora-Gustav*." The Mustangs fanned out to intercept. *Unteroffizier* Stasch of 1 Staffel fell near the old Reichstrasse 96 near Dannenwalde. Not far away his Staffel comrade *Gefreiter* Hoppe came down by parachute, having been wounded during combat. Three further pilots of 1 Staffel bailed out of their aircraft, while *Oberfähnrich* Büttner suffered injuries when he belly-landed his damaged Fw 190 near Schönwalde. 3 Staffel also reported three pilots bailed out: *Feldwebel* Enderle, *Leutnant* Lecis and *Unteroffizier* Werner. Not far from Rheinsberg a P-51 Mustang pursued a machine of 4 Staffel at low altitude just above the trees. The German pilot had no chance and soon his "Red 8" was taking hits. After being hit several times *Oberfeldwebel* Essig went down with his aircraft.

On the western edge of Schorf Heath part of III Gruppe was trying to get to grips with the P-51s, while other elements from this Gruppe were involved in dogfights further to the north, near Neustrelitz. In the course of the battle *Oberleutnant* Müller, leader of 9 Staffel, was shot down and killed. *Unteroffizier* Prokay and *Unteroffizier* Dammeyer were listed as missing. *Oberfähnrich* Hans-Werner Kroll met his end near Zehdenick, when he was attacked by several Mustangs.

But II Gruppe, JG 1 was much harder hit, with no fewer than fifteen pilots killed or missing and two wounded. This tragic record made it seem all the more that fate had for once played a kindly trick when Leutnant Weissbrodt of 8 Staffel who had been seen to crash after a dogfight and whose name already stood on the casualty list reappeared safe and sound at Tutow. All of this Gruppe's Staffeln were in action in the Waren area and over Lake Müritz to the south. No one knows how many German fighter pilots were lost on December 5 in this lake which was over forty square miles in area. *Leutnant* Bock of 6 Staffel, *Oberleutnant* Rudolf Diesem, the leader of 7 Staffel, and *Unteroffizier* Fischer from 8 Staffel are known to have crashed into the lake. The *Gruppestab* also reported the loss of two pilots killed, *Unteroffizier* Rheinberg and *Oberleutnant* Rossmeisl, and one missing.

The entire drama was played out in quadrants "*Berta-Friedrich*" and "*Cäsar-Friedrich.*" The Fw 190 of *Unteroffizier* Wätzlich crashed near Bornkrug, and *Unteroffiziere* Hässler and Weichardt failed to return. Further combats took place to the northwest over two smaller lakes, the Kölpin See and the Fleesen See, in which *Unteroffizier* Bröckelmann and *Leutnant* Wilhelm Hasse were shot down and killed. 7 Staffel lost *Feldwebel* Teckel, while *Unteroffizier* Wiedenbeck was wounded by a burst of fire from a Mustang and abandoned his aircraft.

Gradually the pilots on both sides were forced to break off the engage-

Fighter Losses on December 5, 1944

Units Involved	Killed/ Missing	Wounded	Total Casualties	Aircraft	Locale
I/JG1	6	10	16	Fw 190 A-8	Furstenberg
II/JG1	15	2	17	Fw 190 A-8	Neuruppin
III/JG1	4	2	6	Bf 109 G-10/G-14	Neustrelitz
			39		
II/JG2		1	1	Fw 190 A-8	Bonn
I/JG3	2		2	Bf 109 G-10/G-14	Steinhuder Meer
IV/JG4	1	2	3	Bf 109 G-14	Darmstadt, Gosenheim
I/JG26	1		1	Fw 190 A-8	Furstenau
II/JG27	3	1	4	Bf 109 G-10/G-14	Dorsten
IV/JG27	2	1	3	Bf 109 G-10	Gelsenkirchen, Gladbeck
			7		
IV/JG54	1		1	Fw 190 A-8	Dortmund
I/JG301	4	1	5	Fw 190 A-8/R11	Angermunde, Finow
II/JG301	7		7	Fw 190 A-9/R11	Neustrelitz
III/JG301	7	2	9	Fw 190 A-8/R2	Prenzlau, Schorfheide
			21		
Total Losses (Germany)	53	22	75 (including 1 Gruppe commander and 2 Staffel leaders killed, 1 Staffel leader wounded)		

ment. The Americans still had a long flight home ahead of them, and on the German side the red fuel-warning lights were beginning to flicker. But the heavy bombers were still in German airspace and were now in II Jagdkorps' area. That morning I Gruppe of the *Schlageter* Geschwader (JG 26), based at Fürstenau, had been flying ground support missions over the American penetration in the Düren-Jülich-Linnich area, where they had already been involved with some Thunderbolts. As all 29 Focke-Wulfs came in to land the squadron commander, *Major* Borris, found the Inspector of Day Fighters waiting for him. A short extract from the I./JG 26 War Diary tells the rest of the story:

> "Landed in at 1041. *Major* Borris awarded Knight's Cross. *Oberst* Trautloft orders operations against bombers as they return. Five Fw 190s airborne at 1315. One Boeing shot down in flames by Borris at 1325; 5 men baled out. Landed at 1345. 1432-35 nine Fw 190s airborne. 1505-1515 engaged about fifty Thunderbolts without loss. Landed at 1601."

The Fortress shot down by Borris, which belonged to the 452nd Bomb Group, came down at Lohnerfeld, west of Lingen. A further B-17 which had been damaged by flak over the Ruhr crashed southeast of Lingen near Talge-Wilsten. Luckily the Gruppe itself lost only one pilot that day – *Oberfeldwebel* Buschegger, who crashed on landing at Fürstenau after an engagement with American escort fighters and was killed.

But even before the Allied bombers were back at their bases in England, it had become clear to the staffs at the Jagddivision operations centers that the German fighter force had suffered another defeat that day. Against a loss of 75 aircraft twelve American bombers and fifteen P-51s were shot down, according to US documents. 8th Air Force reported that ninety German fighters had been destroyed.

Tuesday, December 12, 1944

> "12.12.44. Two bomber formations 8th Air Force on Leuna fuel installations and rail targets in Rhine-Main area (Hanau and Darmstadt). Only isolated defensive operations, by JG 4 and JG 27. *Major* Walter Spies, commander II./JG 27, killed in action north of Greven. IV./JG 4 – three killed.

> I./JG 3 mission over the Ruhr against a British four-engine bomber force attacking Witten. Four pilots killed in action.
>
> Ground-support mission in 5th Jagddivision area. JG 53 reports two pilots killed and one wounded (*Uffz.* Betsch, parachute descent over Dammheim/Landau). Particularly tragic is the loss of *Fw.* Scholle, whose parachute failed when he attempted to bale out of his "White 5"; and of *Ofw.* Alexander Preinfalk. Preinfalk, holder of the Knight's Cross, only just 25 and with 78 kills to his credit, was shot by a P-47 while parachuting southeast of Graben (near Bruchsal)."

As already explained, the increasing difficulty of building up the operational picture and, no less important, the need for major fuel savings combined to produce an appreciable impairment of the success of night-fighter operations as well. The British had better means at their disposal for deceiving the German early warning system and causing confusion in the fighter control centers, to the point where coordinated large-scale defensive operations by night-fighters became impossible or at least bore little fruit – and this although German night fighter strength in December 1944 was greater than it had ever been.

The best example of this is the RAF raid on Essen in the evening of December 12. This once again demonstrated the helplessness of German defensive radar in the face of British interference. That night selected bombers carried, specifically for this purpose, whole batteries of Mandrel sets; when these were switched on a veritable veil was drawn across the German radar systems and identification of the actual bombers beams completely impossible. The Mandrel screen simulated a whole number of radar targets, depriving the German side of any clear idea of the actual course of the Allied operation.

British bomber formations flew in over the Dutch coast with 633 Lancasters and Halifaxes and was picked up by radar southwest of Aachen just before 1830, heading southeast. I Jagdkorps scrambled its night fighter units and directed them to Frankfurt/Main, while the British target was in fact Essen. Ten minutes later more night fighters took off from München-Gladbach. Then at 1906 radar spotted another enemy formation, and the observer posts had no idea that this was a small group of Mosquitos, which had separated from the main force to make a diversion raid on Osnabrück. A little later, when the target marker flares appeared over Osnabrück, it was assumed that a mass raid was about to take place there. And so at 1927, just three minutes before the actual mass raid on Essen, the night fighters were redirected to the Osnabrück area.

It is true that the main force of heavy bombers emerged clearly from the Mandrel screen just before the attack, but this was taken for a deception raid. At 1937 the night fighters were at last told that Essen was in fact the main target. But confusion became complete when only a short time later they were again given Osnabrück and then, after a few further minutes, told yet once more that Essen was the main target after all. By 1945 RAF Bomber Command's attack was over; the German night fighters were too late.

During December 1944, in the course of fifteen major raids, I Jagdkorps night fighters achieved forty kills for a loss of 66 of their own machines. On this basis the overall night-fighter figures for the month amounted to 66 kills and German losses to 114 machines.

Saturday, December 16, 1944

From the early hours of the morning the offensive in the West, the Wehrmacht's last great counterstroke, rolled forward. Between Monschau and Echternach, Army Group B under *Feldmarshall* von Rundstedt moved out from its assembly areas to pierce the American line and swept on westward. The Allies were completely taken by surprise. The offensive had been deliberately timed to coincide with a spell of bad weather; as a result it was only a full week later, on December 23, that the Allies were able to make extensive use of their air forces to bring relief to their hardpressed troops and, still more importantly, to halt the German advance.

By December 16 the redeployment of fighter units to the Western front was virtually complete. In effect only two units, Jagdgeschwadern 300 and 301 were left to protect Germany itself. And up to that date scarcely a single commanding officer had imagined that Supreme Headquarters would place this quite different interpretation on a "mass fighter operation." No longer was the destruction of the enemy in the air, and of his bombers in particular, the main task of home air defense; now they were to be dispersed in low-level strikes on ground targets, in the setting of an offensive which from the very beginning had been built on sand.

For the duration of the offensive all fighter units were placed under command of HQ Luftflotte West, which had its operations center at Limburg. In all there were twelve fighter Geschwadern with forty Gruppen, plus two Gruppen of JG 54 which were under command of other Geschwader.

JG 1	3 Gruppen	JG 26	3 Gruppen (+ III./JG 54)
JG 2	3 Gruppen	JG 27	4 Gruppen (+IV./JG 54)
JG 3	4 Gruppen	JG 53	3 Gruppen
JG 4	4 Gruppen	JG 77	3 Gruppen
JG 6	3 Gruppen	JG 300	4 Gruppen
JG 11	3 Gruppen	JG 301	3 Gruppen

With this change of role the Luftwaffe High Command had planned for Gene*ral* Peltz, the General in Charge of Bombers, to assume command of all fighter units – one more decision that gave rise to great bitterness among fighter commanders at all levels, who saw it not least as another blow for General Galland, the General in Charge of Fighters, whose position had become difficult almost to the point where he had been placed in cold storage. As the coming weeks were to show, it was also a decision which was to have grave consequences.

Over and above this, operational coordination was extremely difficult, for the fighter Geschwadern were based much too far from one another – over a breadth of some 250 miles between Oldenburg and the Rhine-Main area.

When the Wehrmacht went over to the offensive in the Eifel on December 16, things were at first very quiet on the German operational airfields. With few exceptions, bad weather kept the units on the ground.

Sunday, December 17, 1944

The second day of the offensive saw little change in the weather; the temperature was 45 degrees fahrenheit and it rained continuously. But despite the overcast sky, visibility was good enough to allow both sides' fighters to enter the battle. It was remarkable how, in concentrating mainly on logistic targets in the rear areas, the Americans were able to keep the German fighters away from the real scene of the fighting. The air battle in fact took place mainly over the Eifel.

December 17 was the Thunderbolts' and Lightnings' day. Germany, Britain and Russia alike all had good fighter-bombers and close-support aircraft; but perhaps no other type has ever seemed as well cut out for the fighter-bomber role as the Republic P-47 D Thunderbolt. It was its performance that made this aircraft outstanding. Although the heaviest single-engine aircraft used in the Second World War, the Thunderbolt had a top speed of some 375 knots at about 30,000 feet and excellent dive characteristics. By the same token, it was not just its climb-rate that made the name of the Lockheed P-38 Lightning, which, like the Thunderbolt, was used by the Americans in all theatres. It never ceased to impress German pilots h w this twin-fuselage machine, with its two powerful Allison engines, would be cruising along quietly and then suddenly, without any "run-up", rocket upwards at overwhelming speed – a maneuver which proved fatal for many an unsuspecting German fighter pilot.

It was still morning when things began to heat up to the west of the Rhine. The 404th Fighter Group of 9th US TAF was to attack Bonn-Hangelar airfield, where a tactical reconnaissance unit, NSG 20 and elements of Kampfgeschwader 55 were based. About 0930, 26 Fw 190s of Jagdgeschwader 26 were scrambled in bad weather; they could not find enemy aircraft and returned to Fürstenau without having made contact.

In the meantime however, over Euskirchen, II, III and IV Gruppe of Jagdgeschwader 27 intercepted the Thunderbolts which had taken off from St. Trond in Belgium. Germans and Americans alike jettisoned their drop tanks, and a dogfight rapidly developed. The Gruppen of JG 27 scored a number of kills but themselves had six pilots killed and four wounded. 8 Staffel alone lost four pilots, including the *Staffelkapitän*, *Hauptmann* Herbert Rehfeld, killed in action to the east of Aachen. *Gefreiter* Breiter and *Unteroffizier* Etzler were killed and *Obergefreiter* Lüders wounded. The *Gruppenkommandeur* was caught by Thunderbolts southwest of Zülpich over Vlatten. He too was wounded and escaped by parachute. III Gruppe lost two pilots killed: *Unteroffizier* Kummer and *Obergefreiter* Möllers. *Feldwebel* Völz abandoned his "Yellow 19" near Neuenahr. *Feldwebel* Fritz Hopf of 14 Staffel, initially listed as missing, was later found in the remains of his Bf 109 G-10 near Berg, in the Altenahr area.

Leutnant Budde's 14 Staffel of IV./JG 54 encountered enemy aircraft near Bonn and lost two pilots. *Unteroffizier* Winkler fell near Roggendorf, while the fate of *Oberfähnrich* Werner Timpes remains unknown. His aircraft, an Fw 190 A-9, was last seen in the Düren area. *Feldwebel* Schelnast of 13 Staffel was shot down and killed over the Ahr Mountains near Werthoven.

Thanks to this interception the Hangelar airfield itself remained untouched, so the Americans came back in the afternoon. This time Lt.Col. Moon sent all three squadrons of his 404th Fighter Group, and once again

Fighter Losses on December 17, 1944

Units Involved	Killed/ Missing	Wounded	Total Casualties	Aircraft	Locale
I/JG2	4	1	5	Fw 190 A-8	Bitburg, Giessen
II/JG2	4	2	6	Bf 109 G-6/G-14	Coblenz, St. Voth
			11		
III/JG3	1	2	3	Bf 109 G-14	Andernach, Bonn
IV/JG3	1	1	2	Fw 190 A-8	Nierendorf
			5		
I/JG4	3	1	4	Bf 109 G-14	Birresborn
II/JG4	3	1	4	Fw 190 A-8	Boppard, Cochem
III/JG4	3		3	Bf 109 G-14/K-4	Heidweiler
IV/JG4	1	1	2	Bf 109 G-10/G-14	Fronsfeld
			13		
II/JG6	1		1	Fw 190 A-8	Konigswinter
I/JG11	3	5	8	Bf 109 G-14	Munstereifel, Wittlich
I/JG27	4		4	Bf 109 G-14/K-4	Aachen, Beers
II/JG27	3	3	6	Bf 109 G-10/G-14	Duren, Eindhoven
III/JG27	2	1	3	Bf 109 K-4	Neuenahr
IV/JG27	1		1	Bf 109 G-10	
			14		
II/JG53		1	1	Bf 109 G-14	Kandel
IV/JG54	3		3	Fw 190 A-8/A-9	Bonn, Duren
II/JG300	7	3	10	Fw 190 A-8	Hochheim, Liegnitz
III/JG300	2		2	Bf 109 G-10	Meseritz, olomouc
IV/JG300	9	2	11	Bf 109 G-10/G-14	Prerov, Prossnitz
			23		
Total (Germany, Western Theatre and Sudetenland)	55	24	79 (including 1 Staffel leader killed, 1 Gruppe com mander and 2 Staffel leaders wounded)		

there was a sharp encounter between the Thunderbolts and the German fighters.

Rheine airfield was harboring the Me 262s of Kampfgeschwader 51 in addition to a variety of fighter units. Because of this the Allies kept it under constant surveillance, for with their superior performance the jets were at their most vulnerable when taking off and landing. On the morning of December 17, five Hawker Tempests of 56 Squadron, RAF, took off to "relieve the guard"; south of Nijmegen they met several Bf 109s of I./JG 27.

The dogfight which ensued was later joined by more British fighters and ended with the loss of 4 German pilots. The British by contrast landed back at Volkel without loss.

Col. Wasem's 474th Fighter Group was operating over the Moselle, in the Trier area. His Lightnings had already been in action that morning, scoring seven kills without loss; now they reported a further four Fw 190s shot down and four others damaged. In this second encounter 474th Group lost two machines, and a third P-38 belly-landed near Luxembourg. These may have been the three P-38 Lightnings shot down by Jagdgeschwader 26 on their second sorties of the day *Unteroffizier* Delor claimed two Lightning kills and *Leutnant* Günther a further one.

JG 26 survived the day without loss, but the *Richthofen* Geschwader (JG 2) reported a further four pilots missing, all from its I Gruppe. They were *Leutnant* Elser, *Gefreiter* Eube, *Fähnrich* Selpin and *Leutnant* Snobeck. *Oberfeldwebel* Nowack bailed out and *Gefreiter* Rebmann, who had initially been posted missing, returned later, albeit wounded. Both pilots reported a dogfight between 3 and 4 Staffeln and about fifteen Thunderbolts over the German-Belgian border. *Oberfähnrich* Kowalski of II./JG 2 was shot down and was taken prisoner near Krinkelt in Belgium, while *Feldwebel* Fester was hit by flak over the front and subsequently had to bail out near Adenau. *Gefreiter* Frischer was killed in combat with Thunderbolts near Oberstedem, not far from Bitburg.

Jagdgeschwader 3, 4 and 11 were also involved in the operations of December 17 and took heavy casualties. JG 4 was hardest hit, with ten killed, one missing and three wounded. *Kommodore* Michalski's Gruppen were on their way to the Western combat zone. At this time the fighting centered round St. Vith, which the Germans had retaken after bitter fighting. But very few machines reached the Belgian-German frontier, for behind the Hunsrück JG 4 pilots met a force of Thunderbolts. Below the Messerschmitts, although scarcely visible, lay the twists and turns of the Moselle, and at this early stage several machines plunged down through the clouds and were seen no more. One of the first to fall was *Leutnant* Heinz Krause, shot down over Cochem. The fate of Krause's Staffel comrade *Leutnant* Brindlinger was initially uncertain. It was later discovered that he had been shot down near Zemmern, north of Trier. 4 Staffel lost *Unteroffizier* Heyne between Zemmern and Zell on the Mosel. He too was killed in air combat.

In II./JG 4 it was 6 Staffel which suffered the heaviest pilot losses, with two killed and one wounded: *Leutnant* Lehmann, *Feldwebel* Lippold and

Unteroffizier Weichmann. The latter was wounded and came down near Pronsfeld by parachute. Southeast of the High Eifel elements of IV Gruppe suddenly found themselves facing about twenty Thunderbolts. *Unteroffizier* Henrichs was cornered by several enemy aircraft, but as the others had their hands full with the numerically superior enemy, none could follow the progress of the Messerschmitt. The young *Leutnant* crashed near Mürlenbach and was killed. III./JG 4 reported a total of three losses, with *Unteroffizier* Gras and *Unteroffizier* Walther killed and *Unteroffizier* Walter Ziegler posted as missing.

JG 3 *Udet* fought between the Bonner area and the Ahr Mountains. *Unteroffizier* Werner Thiel was wounded and forced to abandon his aircraft over Nierendorf. *Leutnant* Rolf Lahne went down in the Bonn area in his Fw 190 A-8 "Red 5" and was not seen again.

Also taking off with JG 4 was a Gruppe of JG 11, which was now based south of Frankfurt/Main. On December 17, 2 and 4 Staffeln were especially hard hit, each suffering four losses. 2 Staffel engaged large formations of Thunderbolts north of the Ahr Mountains in the Münstereifel area, which were soon joined by groups of P-38s. The result: four wounded. "Black 6" was shot down and its pilot, *Unteroffizier* Liebeck, bailed out. *Unteroffizier* Heyer shot down a P-38, but was unable to have the kill confirmed as there were no eyewitnesses. Soon after he was forced to abandon his A-8 with the "Black 1." As a result of his wounds Heyer's part in the Ardennes Offensive was over. The same applied to his comrades Sauseng and Wegener.

In the meantime 4 Staffel was struggling with the Americans between Wittlich and Gillenfeld. Although the Focke-Wulf pilots fought well the Thunderbolts emerged victorious, shooting down the aircraft of *Unteroffiziere* Dalecki, Grätzer and Schäfer. All three pilots were killed. *Unteroffizier* Alfred Winderlich was wounded.

The "winter battle in the West", as the Press called the offensive, caused the loss of 56 aircrew in German fighter units on December 17th. Jagdgeschwader 27, with nine killed, four wounded and one captured, had once again taken the hardest knock; but on this occasion the Geschwader had 16 kills to its credit. 9th US TAF claimed 68 German fighters destroyed and admitted the loss of sixteen aircraft – a figure that would tally exactly with JG 27 reports.

That same morning Jagdgeschwader 300, held back in Central Germany, also had to pay a heavy price – not indeed on the Western Front, but over Southeast Germany and the Sudetenland, where engagements between

German fighters and Liberator formations with a strong escort were spread over a wide area. The Allies clearly had two purposes in stepping up US 15th Air Force operations. The German counter-offensive increased the importance of destroying the synthetic fuel plants in East Germany, Austria and Poland. At the same time these raids tied down the German home air defense fighters, forcing their withdrawal from planned operations in the Western theatre or at least greatly reducing the strength available for these. These were the reasons for the intrusion of US 15th Air Force bombers into Poland to attack the hydrogenation plant at Auschwitz.

The Americans crossed the Gulf of Trieste in several waves, flying northeast over the eastern part of Austria, and penetrated into the area of Moravia. Action between the intruders and II./JG 300 Geschwader developed between Osomouc and Prerau and later over Upper Silesia. Il Gruppe, now in the assault role and equipped with Fw 190 A-7s and A-8s, lost seven killed and three wounded here. 5 Staffel reported two casualties and 6 Staffel four, with *Feldwebel* Funk, *Unteroffizier* Pöhner and *Oberfähnrich* Winter being shot down and killed. 7 Staffel also lost four pilots. *Oberfähnrich* Hohmann's "White 7" was hit and crashed near Prossnitz. The pilot was killed. *Unteroffizier* Martin and *Feldwebel* Paplowski were also shot down and killed by Mustangs.

Over East Sudetenland and the Klodzko Hills 13 and 14 Staffeln were trying to get their Messerschmitts through to the American bombers, only to take a knockout punch. This squadron had the heaviest casualties of the day – eleven pilots in all. Two pilots of 13 Staffel were killed: *Feldwebel* Baartz near Milawetz and *Leutnant* Stegmann over Bautsch. *Feldwebel* Grothendieck was posted missing. Where *Leutnant* Dieter Kaiser's "Yellow 6" went down is unknown. The Bf 109 G-14 of *Unteroffizier* Gresing also disappeared without a trace. 15 Staffel reported a total of two killed and three missing, as *Unteroffiziere* Knock and Riese were also shot down and killed, while *Feldwebel* Weinert escaped near Hochheim in the Sudeten with minor injuries.

Staffelkapitän Hauptmann Kowatsch was wounded near Grunwald. Like his missing sixteen Staffel comrade *Fähnrich* Weiss, he had been flying a Bf 109 G-10 with two additional 20mm cannon beneath the wings. *Hauptmann* Josef Puchinger of the *Gruppestab* was posted missing over Upper Silesia.

At the end of the day it was thus clear that, despite a readiness to take risks and press home dashing counter-attacks, the German fighter forces were not up to the task of hampering the execution of the American bombing programme. The Americans came away virtually unscathed, but Jagdgeschwader 300's defensive operations had cost it 23 machines and their pilots, bringing the total losses of German fighter pilots on December 17 to around eighty.

But the slaughter was only just beginning.

Monday, December 18, 1944

On the third day of the German offensive in the West the weather was again bad – but not bad enough to prevent US 8th Air Force flying in over Germany with some 950 bombers. Dropping their bombs blind through unbroken 10/10 cloud cover, the Americans took as their main targets communications nodes in the rail triangle Coblenz-Ehrang (Trier)-Cologne. That morning and on the days that followed it became evident that the Allies had now shifted the weight of their raids on to communications targets behind the combat zone to stop supplies getting through. Their next reaction to the German offensive was to be the ceaseless pounding of airfields on both sides of the Rhine.

Elements of Jagdgeschwader 1 were, it appears, sent up against the bomber incursion, for their 9 Staffel reported one man wounded following an engagement with four-engine bombers near Bonn. It was *Leutnant* Holz, who was able to escape by parachute. *Unteroffizier* Mietling of 4 Staffel was killed in the Malmédy area.

9th US TAF was active over Belgium and Luxembourg with twin-engine bomber formations, while its Thunderbolts probed deep behind the line of contact on the hunt for such targets as road convoys, locomotives or concentrations of armor. Jagdgeschwader 77, stationed around Dortmund, was committed for the first time. II Gruppe and Capt Köhler's III Gruppe were tasked to observe the movements of armored spearheads on the line of contact. But they never got that far, for south of Cologne their Messerschmitts were set upon by Allied fighter units. III Gruppe lost three machines, including the Bf 109 K-4s of *Leutnant* Rogall and *Unteroffizier* Schulze. Both pilots were shot down and wounded between Weilerswist and Lechenich. *Unteroffizier* Albin Micheliak was posted missing.

Between Aachen and Bonn, II and III Gruppen, Jagdgeschwader 2 engaged the Thunderbolts of the 365th and 368th Fighter Groups. Here

Fighter Losses on December 18, 1944

Units Involved	Killed/ Missing	Wounded	Total Casualties	Aircraft	Locale
I/JG1	1		1	Fw 190 A-8	Bonn, Malmedy
III/JG1		2	2	Bf 109 G-10/G-14	
			3		
II/JG2	2		2	Bf 109 K-4	Aachen, Bonn
III/JG2	1		1	Fw 190 A-8	
			3		
III/JG3	5	2	7	Bf 109 G-14/K-4	Bonn, Dortmund, Duren
III/JG6		1	1	Bf 109 G-6	Andernach
II/JG26		1	1	Fw 190 D-9	Almelo
III/JG26	1		1	Bf 109 K-4	Plantlunne
			2		
II/JG27		1	1	Bf 109 G-10/G-14	Cologne, Werl
III/JG27	5	2	7	Bf 109 K-4	Cologne, Werl
IV/JG27	1		1	Bf 109 G-14	Cologne, Werl
			9		
IV/JG54	2	1	3	Fw 190 A-8	Cologne, Vussem
I/JG77	2		2	Bf 109 G-14	Lechenich
III/JG77	1	2	3	Bf 109 K-4	Weilerswist, Scheuerheck
			5		
Total Losses (Germany and Western Theatre)	21	12	33 (including 1 Staffel leader killed)		

German losses were, fortunately, light. Only two pilots failed to return. *Feldwebel* Pfeiffer of 11 Staffel was killed and *Obergefreiter* Melda of 7 Staffel was listed as missing. His Bf 109 K-4 was last seen near Aachen in combat with fifteen Thunderbolts.

On December 18, the Spitfires of British 2nd TAF made their appearance alongside the American fighter hordes. 610 Squadron reported an engagement with some fifteen Focke-Wulfs. This was broken off without loss on either side owing to bad visibility; but a British flight leader failed to return for unknown reasons, and a further Spitfire was lost on the squadron's second mission of the day. 66 Squadron on the other hand was more successful. They were briefed to fly a twelve-strong armed-reconnaissance mission over Cologne and Coblenz. Over the combat zone they met four formations of Messerschmitts, engaged in some tactical mission, and a dogfight developed in the overcast sky. One Bf 109 went down in flames and four others were damaged; the British lost one Spitfire.

Meanwhile all hell broke loose in the skies around Cologne, where the Gruppen of JG 27 were involved with a large force of enemy aircraft. *Unteroffizier* Fink, the sole pilot of I Gruppe to be lost, was shot down by German anti-aircraft fire near Burgsteinfurt. III./JG 27 suffered heavier losses however. *Hauptmann* Richard Hasenclever went down near Rondorf in his Bf 109 K-4 "Chevron-Bar" and was initially listed as missing. Unteroffiziere Grote and Kauffeld, both of 11 Staffel, were wounded in combat. Following the mission *Gefreiter* Heinz Merkel failed to return; his Bf 109 K-4, "Black 4," was believed to have crashed into the Rhine. Merkel and another pilot who failed to return, *Unteroffizier* Fritzsche, were listed as missing in action. *Gefreiter* Merkel's fate was not discovered until four months later, on April 27, 1945, when his body was recovered from the Rhine. Two pilots were also initially reported missing from 10 Staffel, but *Obergefreiter* Herberg and *Unteroffizier* Wolf Scheiber both later returned to the unit unharmed after bailing out in the Cologne area. In contrast, the fate of *Unteroffizier* Wolf Korn of 12 Staffel remains a mystery to this day. At about 1045, IV./JG 54, which was attached to JG 27, also became engaged in air combat west of Cologne.

When the orders from Headquarters Luftflotte West to the units of II Jagdkorps reached Jagdgeschwader 3, all four Staffeln of III Gruppe took off from their bases below the eastern spurs of the Teutoburger Wald. *Hauptmann* Langer, the Gruppe's commanding officer and an experienced commander, was far from happy; it went against the grain to commit his men to an interception under such appalling weather conditions. He saw the many young faces among his pilots every day and, like other day-fighter COs, he knew only too well the price that this type of operation could and frequently did exact – as it always will. He had already had five of his squadron killed on December 2, including the leader of 11 Staffel, *Leutnant* Karl Willeke.

III Gruppe's machines flew towards the Ruhr before setting course for Cologne, where the messages from ground control told them the enemy bombers were to be found. Southwest of Bonn they suddenly came up against the American fighter escort, and when the battle was over they had lost eight pilots: two wounded, *Obergefreiter* Kaufmann of 10 Staffel and *Unteroffizier* Lehnen of 11 Staffel, as well as three killed and the same number missing, including *Feldwebel* Rinke and *Gefreiter* Riess of 9 and 12 Staffeln, respectively. Another member of 9 Staffel, *Unteroffizier* Horst Witzler, was fortunate and returned to his unit. Twenty-two days later he was not so lucky; *Unteroffizier* Witzler was killed near Münstereifel.

The Wehrmacht Communique of December 18 had this to say:

> ". . . German Air Force fighter and close support units covering our troop movements shot down 24 enemy aircraft. The fire of our long-range weapons on London, Antwerp and Liege continues at increased intensity . . ."

Saturday, December 23, 1944

From the early hours of the morning, intense activity reigned in the Allied air bases. The US 8th Air Force's heavy bomber units were taking off for Germany, and some 400 light and medium bombers from 9th US TAF were heading for the Ardennes combat zone and the Eifel. The RAF's heavy bombers were to attack Cologne. Strong Allied fighter forces streamed out far in front of the Fortress and Liberator formations to screen their northern flank, for experience had shown that it was from this quarter that the main German fighter threat was likely to come. And on the German side too the fighter units were at readiness; both small formations and large tactical groupings were dispatched to meet the massive Allied invasion.

Air activity on this day was on a scale that had not been seen for some time, for the weather had changed for the better almost overnight and the skies had begun to clear. The depression which had been stationary over the combat zone for a week since December 16, the day on which the German offensive was launched, was now filling. Here and there the sun even broke through. Fighter pilots on both sides, driven to desperation by the drizzle, snow showers, ground mist and low cloud, now felt more sure of themselves.

With a fighter escort over 400 strong, 417 8th Air Force bombers were directed on to rail junctions west of the Rhine to destroy the German lines of communication. For on the ground German pressure was mounting and the Allied armies were in an awkward position; St. Vith had fallen and Bastogne was surrounded.

The American bombers' primary targets were the communication systems in the areas of Trier-Ehrang, Jünkerath-Dahlem and Ahrweiler. At about 1015 a large German fighter formation, around ninety Messerschmitts and Focke-Wulfs from Jagdgeschwadern 4, 11, 27 and 54 had passed over Cologne and was now over the triangle Brühl-Bonn-Euskirchen. JG 4's three Gruppen flew on southward undisturbed, but the rest of the force suddenly found swarms of Thunderbolt's above their heads. These were the battle-proven pilots of Col. Schilling's 56th Fighter Group; in a flash they had dropped their jettison tanks and were diving on their enemy. The German pilots realized the danger, but the P-47s, coming from above, had the edge.

Just over Kottenforst a damaged Fw 190 broke away and tried to get clear of its pursuers, but near Röttgen the pilot, *Unteroffizier* Willi Bach of 16./JG 54, crashed to his death still in his machine. At about 1030, a second Fw 190 A-8 from the same wing appeared over the tree-tops and went down near the hamlet of Villip. This machine too had been hit earlier on, and *Unteroffizier* Klaus Gehring from Gerdauen in East Prussia had decided to bale out. But he failed to jump clear; his parachute fouled on the tail and he was killed when the aircraft hit the ground. Only a few hundred yards away, near the moated castle of Gudenau, a Messerschmitt struck with an incredibly violent impact and buried itself deep in the frozen ground. No parachute was seen, and it was to be 24 years, almost to the day, before more was known of this crash. It was the Bf 109 G-10 of *Oberfeldwebel* Heinrich Bartels, who had destroyed a Thunderbolt just before he was himself shot down. This was the 99th kill scored by this 26-year-old holder of the Knight's Cross from Linz on the Danube, who had been flying with IV./JG 27 since May 1943.

The three Gruppen from Jagdgeschwader 4, together with I Gruppe of *Oberstleutnant* Günther Specht's JG 11, tried to carry on with their mission and intercept the American bomber formations before the latter reached Trier. But this intention was largely frustrated by the Allied fighter escort and these units became involved in dogfights which spread out right across the Eifel.

Major Jeffrey of 479th Fighter Group personally accounted for three of the 12 Fw 190s shot down by his formation, this for the loss of one Mustang. 8./JG 4 was especially hard hit, and *Unteroffiziere* Haug, Nefzger and Walter were listed as missing. *Leutnant* Dietmar Bischoff and *Feldwebel* Höflich were captured. *Leutnant* Eduard Schmidt later reported back to his unit after bailing out of his Focke-Wulf "Blue 10." *Unteroffiziere* Jessen and Lemmer of 10 Staffel were wounded, while *Unteroffizier* Werner Dehr was posted missing. 11 Staffel lost *Fähnrich* Ernst Amman, and *Oberfähnrich* Rickling was wounded in combat with enemy fighters over Roth an der Sauer. IV Gruppe also suffered three losses. *Unteroffizier* Heinz Weber was killed over Ehrang, and *Oberfähnrich* Herdtle was listed as missing in the Trier area. Also shot down in the same area was the Bf 109 G-14 of *Unteroffizier* Karlheinz Witt.

But Jagdgeschwader 11 had suffered far worse losses. With twelve pilots killed and four missing it accounted for the bulk of the German casualties on December 23. Its three Gruppen were scattered over the whole area of operations, I./JG 11 together with IV./JG 4 engaged the heavy bombers over the Moselle. The other two Gruppen, operating under command of Jagdgeschwader 2 *Richthofen*, encountered fighter escorts from both 8th Air Force and 9th US TAF. *Fähnrich* Kaluza and *Oberleutnant* Georg Ulrici of 1./JG 11 were listed missing with their Fw 190 A-8s between Daun and Cochem. Ulrici was found dead near Kaisersesch in February 1945. *Unteroffizier* Ehrke and *Gefreiter* Eiden of 2 Staffel were killed in air combat near Gillenfeld. Three pilots of 4./JG 11 suffered wounds and *Oberfähnrich* Hansjoachim Wesener was shot down by American fighters south of Kaisersesch.

Using the fine weather to good effect, the US 9th TAF's fighter-bombers gave their ground troops all possible support. C-47 transport wings were at last able to drop food, ammunition and equipment to their troops surrounded at Bastogne, but German AA shot down eight of these aircraft. Before the morning was over 624 two-engine bombers, A-26 Invaders and B-26 Marauders, were on their way to take out the rail system immediately behind the line of contact. 9th Bomb Division suffered its heaviest losses so far; German AA and home air defense fighters shot down 36 bombers; a further six crashed or made forced landings later; and over 180 were damaged. Among 9th US TAF's first targets were the yards at Ahrweiler, which were bombed by some 60 Marauders from the 386th and 391st Bomb Groups. But suddenly about an equal number of grey fighters made their appearance – part of the tactical grouping made up from Jagdgeschwadern 2, 3 and 11. The Germans concentrated on the second wave of bombers as they flew on towards the Westerwald and accounted for sixteen Marauders from the 391st Group.

But the German losses were even higher. *Unteroffizier* Kleybrink and *Feldwebel* Land, as well as *Obergefreiter* Maas and *Unteroffizier* Pfeifer, members of I. and II./JG 2, respectively, were shot down by American escort fighters west of the Rhine. The Messerschmitt flown by *Oberfähnrich* Nidda crashed on takeoff, killing its pilot. *Oberfähnrich* Aickelin attempted to crash-land his damaged Bf 109 G-14 at the nearby Cologne-Wahn airfield, but the aircraft turned over on landing. Aickelin sustained injuries and was taken to hospital.

III Gruppe of JG 2 lost five pilots. *Feldwebel* Heinz Scheider was never found, but in January 1968 the body of *Unteroffizier* Burger of 12 Staffel was found near Meckenheim on Swistbach in his Fw 190 D-9, one of the first of this "long-nose" version to be lost in the West.

Jagdgeschwader 3 reported four parachute descents. One of these was *Fähnrich* Adolf Tham, who was injured when he rammed a Marauder with his Bf 109 K-4. The American aircraft may have been of one of the two B-26s reported lost by 322nd Bomb Group. This Group was attacking the rail bridges at Euskirchen when it was set upon by 20-30 German aircraft, of which about six were lost. *Oberfeldwebel* Gerhard Wilhelm and *Unteroffizier* Wichmann of IV./JG 3 were killed. Wichmann was flying the aircraft with the "Double Chevron" of the *Gruppekommandeur*, *Hauptmann* Weydenhammer. *Unteroffizier* Kröber died later from wounds sustained in combat.

For some seventy Marauders of the 387th and 394th Bomb Groups the target was the railway yards at Mayen. But before they got there several groups of German fighters dove on them. Here the losses were four aside, but these fighter units suffered further losses in intercepting a raid by medium bombers on the Moselle bridges between Cochem and Eller, where the Germans scored seven kills for the loss of eight aircraft.

JG 11's 9 Staffel lost its leader, *Oberleutnant* Herbert Planer, in combat over Mayen. Also shot down was "White 6," flown by *Unteroffizier* Pfaffinger. The remaining Staffeln of *Hauptmann* von Fassong's III./JG 11 were still engaged in combat between Bonn and the German frontier. Waves of bombers and fighter formations flying to and fro had for years been a daily event in the lives of the population of the area between Aachen and Cologne, but the drama that was enacted on December 23 over the bleak, snow-covered slopes of the Eifel looked like the first act of a tragedy. Never had these countryfolk seen so many aircraft drop out of the sky.

10. and 11./JG 11 became involved in an air battle over the Steinbach Dam, in which *Oberfähnrich* Bühmann was shot down. Bühmann bailed out of his stricken aircraft over Rheinbach. *Leutnant* Küke of 11 Staffel, which was led by *Hauptmann* Dähne, was shot down and killed near the same

Fighter Losses on December 23, 1944

Units Involved	Killed/ Missing	Wounded	Total Casualties	Aircraft	Locale
I/JG1	1	1	2	Fw 190 A-8	Bocholt
III/JG1		1	1	Bf 109 G-14	Dortmund, Wesel
			3		
I/JG2	2		2	Fw 190 A-8/D-9	Aachen, Bastogne
II/JG2	3	1	4	Bf 109 G-14	Marienberg
III/JG2	5		5	Fw 190 A-8/D-9	Meckenheim, Siegburg
			11		
I/JG3	1		1	Bf 109 G-14	Adenau, Meckenheim
III/JG3	1	1	2	Bf 109 G-14/K-4	St. Vith
IV/JG3	2	3	5	Fw 190 A-8	
			8		
I/JG4		1	1	Bf 109 G-14	
II/JG4	6		6	Fw 190 A-8	Nurburg, Roth
III/JG4	3	3	6	Bf 109 G-10/K-4	St. Vith, Trier
IV/JG4	3		3		
			16		
I/JG11	6	5	11	Fw 190 A-8	Adenau, Gillenfeld
II/JG11	3	3	6	Bf 109 G-14	Kaisersesch
III/JG11	7	3	10	Fw 190 A-87	Coblenz, Mayern, St. Vith
			27		
I/JG26	4	2	6	Fw 190 A-8	Duren, Cologne
II/JG26	1	1	2	Fw 190 D-9	Nettersheim
			8		
II/JG27	2		2	Bf 109 G-10/G-14	Bonn, Rhine-Main
III/JG27		1	1	Bf 109 K-4	Villip
IV/JG27	1		1	Bf 109 G-10	
			4		
II/JG53	1	2	3	bf 109 G-14 As	Rastatt, Wagshurst
III/JG53	1		1	Bf 109 G-14	Weissenburg
			4		
IV/JG54	2		2	Fw 190 A-8	Villip, St. Vith, Liege
I/JG77	6	2	8	Bf 109 G-14	Altenahr
III/JG77	2	5	7	Bf 109 K-4	Houverath, Lessenich, Neuenahr
			15		
Total Losses (Germany and Western Theatre)	63	35	98 (including 1 Staffel leader killed)		

village. Near the end of the war Dähne became commander of II./JG 1 and was killed in the crash of a Heinkel He 162 in April 1945. Two other members of the Staffel, *Feldwebeln* Borgenhagen and Schwarz, were wounded in combat somewhat further southwest, near Münstereifel.

Meanwhile 12./JG 11 must have encountered the enemy over the High Eifel in the triangle St. Vith-Prüm-Stadtkyll. It is presumed that *Major* Erich Putzka of the *Gruppenstab* JG 11 was shot down in his Fw 190 A-8 in this area of difficult terrain; his remains have never been found. The same applies to *Oberfeldwebel* Holland, last seen in a dogfight with around thirty Thunderbolts. *Oberfeldwebel* Titscher was also killed, having been shot down – according to his fellow pilots – by a Spitfire. This may well have been correct; the RAF carried out a daylight raid on Cologne at about this time on December 23 and the bombers did have a fighter escort.

Throughout the morning the skies between Aachen and Saarbrücken had been the scene of a ding-dong battle, the most intensive for weeks; but in the afternoon activity died down. The German fighter units were exhausted. Pilots who had baled out over the various zones of the action were trying to get back to their units, being taken off to nearby hospitals by the ground troops and the Eifel farmers, or even falling into Allied hands. Bodies were being recovered from shattered machines, and the countryfolk would gaze at the charred, twisted strips of scrap metal and the broken bodies within them and wonder what kind of sense it all made.

But meanwhile 9th US TAF had despatched a fresh force of over 200 twin-engine bombers with a Thunderbolt escort. It was shortly after midday when *Hauptmann* Köhler received orders for his III./JG 77. As the Gruppe took off its their base at Düsseldorf-Unterrath at about 1345, the pilots were hardly to know that not a single one of them would reach their destination round Bastogne. Heading south, the Messerschmitt Bf 109 K-4s first overflew Cologne, intending to turn west over the top of the Ahr Hills and make for the combat zone. And it was just over the Ahr valley that 11 and 12 Staffel were surprised by a pack of Allied fighters. 11 Staffel under *Leutnant* Hackler escaped with only two pilots wounded; but *Leutnant* Staroste would always remember the day the Americans carved up his 12 Staffel – eight pilots were killed or wounded. Among the wounded were *Leutnant* Ludwig as well as the *Unteroffiziere* Meyer and Reinberg. *Feldwebel* Rössner was shot down and killed near Houverath and *Unteroffizier* Walter Silwester fell over Altenahr. His aircraft, "Blue 12," crashed into a wood not far from the road to Gelsdorf/Meckenheim. One of the few pilots of III./JG 77 to bail out unwounded was *Leutnant* Unverzagt.

Scattered by the enemy pursuit, the German machines landed in ones and twos at airfields all over the place, and it was 1515 when the two Bf 109s of the Gruppe commander and his adjutant, *Oberleutnant* Kleber, touched down at Cologne-Wahn.

JG 53 "Pik As" (Ace of Spades) lost four pilots that day. *Unteroffizier* Zimmermann, who was last seen in the Rastatt area, was listed as missing in action, while *Leutnant* Westhoff was captured by the Americans near Weissenburg after being shot down by Thunderbolts over the front. *Unteroffiziere* Desaga and Krüger managed to bail out of their stricken G-14s. So one of the costliest days since the home air defense forces had been set up drew to its close. Despite involvement in innumerable encounters with a good number of kills to its credit, the fighter force had been unable to hamper the enemy's plan of attack. Thanks to its formidable fighter escort, US 8th Air Force was able to hold its losses to two four-engine bombers and fifteen fighters; but 9th US TAF lost 35-40 light and medium bombers, some of them accounted for by AA fire.

Of the 450-500 German fighter pilots who took part in the operations of December 23, 1944, records show 63 killed, missing or taken prisoner and 35 wounded. The Allied air forces, on the other hand, claimed 116 German fighters shot down and eleven unconfirmed.

Sunday, December 24, 1944

In I and II Jagdkorps, preparations to deal with a major Allied incursion went ahead on a scale not seen since the Allied landings. It was little short of a miracle that, less than twenty-four hours after its costly air battles in the West, the fighter force could resume its defensive operations with 700-800 machines at its disposal. It was largely thanks to the "men in black" of the ground staff that, after repeated sorties the day before, these machines stood ready on the tarmac in the morning. The measure of these men's achievement can be truly appreciated only by those who know how many Messerschmitts and Focke-Wulfs had returned with battle damage, engine faults or other technical defects, or had even been prevented by hydraulic failures from leaving the ground. Patching those machines up again in the few hours available called for a high sense of responsibility, unsparing effort and immense attention to detail.

The fighter force had good reason to draw itself up in such strength, for the bad weather of the preceding week had now finally cleared, and

December 24 dawned with a clear blue sky; cloud cover over Cologne, for instance, was only 1/10. It was not very hard to guess that the Allies would use this weather to put a stop to von Rundstedt's offensive once and for all. US 8th Air Force put 2,034 bombers into the air that morning – the largest single operation in its history. 1,400 bombers, with a 700 strong fighter escort, concentrated their bombs on eleven German airfields in the Giessen, Frankfurt and Darmstadt areas; the rest, supported by RAF and 9th US TAF formations, attacked communications targets, mainly railway installations between Trier and Euskirchen.

As the leading B-17 Flying Fortresses appeared over Germany, the last heavy bombers were just clearing the English coast – a veritable armada, under the command of Brigadier-General Frederic Castle. Headed by IV Gruppe, the former assault Gruppe, Jagdgeschwader 3 was one of the first German formations to close with the tight-packed Allied bombers. Behind every control column sat a pilot known to be well-versed in air defense; not a few of the rudders were well "notched." Once again the men of 13, 14 and 15 Staffeln were determined to give the Allies a really warm welcome.

The pilots of IV Gruppe spotted the leading bombers just in front of Liege. The American fighter escort was not yet in position, so the Focke-Wulfs were able to open the engagement with a frontal attack. Very soon four B-17s were plunging earthward in flames, and five others were so badly hit that they had to make forced landings. But meanwhile the Mustangs had appeared and were trying to force the attackers back. IV./JG 3 became involved in a really vicious dogfight. *Hauptmann* Wolfgang Kosse, leader of 13 Staffel, and *Oberfeldwebel* Egon Schulz broke away from the formation and have still never been traced. Five other pilots were shot down by the heavy bombers' gunners or the enemy fighter escort. All five – *Obergefreiter* Hirschfelder, *Feldwebel* Hopfensitz, *Unteroffizier* Kapteina, *Unteroffizier* Klose and *Feldwebel* Sommer – were taken prisoner. On this day Jagdgeschwader 3 had the largest number reported missing. Among them were two pilots of I Gruppe, including the *Kapitän* of 4 Staffel, Knight's Cross wearer *Leutnant* Franz Ruhl, and two pilots of III Gruppe.

However, one of the Flying Fortresses shot down was flown by Brig-Gen. Castle, one of the ablest commanders in the US 8th Air Force. Castle gave his crew the order to bale out, but by then it was too late for him to get clear himself and he dove to his death in the heavy bomber.

Heading east on a slightly zigzag course the formations pressed on and crossed the German frontier south of Aachen. JG 3 hung on to the enemy and shot down quite a few more bombers, and was joined by I./JG 27 and all three

Gruppen of Jagdgeschwader 6. Fierce fighting developed over the High Venn. More and more vapor trails sliced across the blue sky, the tragic beauty of their curves, rings, wave-patterns and whorls bearing witness to watchers on the ground of the progress of the fierce battle.

At 13,000 feet it was bitterly cold, and thus another hazard lay in wait for the young pilots – ice. No one knows how many pilots succumbed to icing, but it may well be that some of those reported missing were not in fact killed in action and that their remains lie hidden forever in the wild heathland and bogs of the Venn. Three of those who failed to return were members of I./JG 27, among them *Oberfähnrich* Max-Heinrich Klick, who was last seen hanging under his parachute. From JG 6 the leader of 10 Staffel, *Oberleutnant* Weyl, *Unteroffizier* Götz of 8 Staffel and *Oberfeldwebel* Heinz Schmidt of 4 Staffel were all reported missing. *Unteroffizier* Paul Borth was taken prisoner by the Americans near Aachen. *Hauptmann* Elstermann, leader of I Gruppe, lost three of his officers in this action: *Oberleutnant* Lyons, *Leutnant* Rieckhoff and *Leutnant* Starzacher.

To the north of Aachen and over the Ruhr, swarms of Spitfires, Typhoons and Tempests from 2 TAF were on patrol; the British also were surprised by the intensity of the German fighter force's operations that day. Their opponents, I and III./JG 1, two Gruppen of Jagdgeschwader 26, as well as three from Geschwader 27 and IV./JG 54, had in fact been tasked against the American bomber incursion and now had to abandon their original mission and take on the British. 193 Squadron suddenly spotted over fifty Messerschmitts and Focke-Wulfs in the process of shooting down one Hawker Typhoon and damaging another. This was probably IV./JG 27 and IV./JG 54. Ten British fighters which were just over West Münsterland and heard the contact over the RT turned to rush to the help of their friends, only to be engaged by German fighters coming at them out of the sun.

Other fighter units reported engagements between Malmedy and Eindhoven. Then, when further contact was made between the Rhine and the Dutch-German border, control of the German defensive operation seemed to be lost. Nobody knew any more where or with whom units were involved.

Not far from the Dutch border in the Nijmegen area the British shot down a machine of II./JG 27. One of the exploding cannon shells wounded the pilot, *Unteroffizier* Heumann, in the head. Heumann was delivered to the Luftwaffe field hospital at Dyk at about the same time as *Gefreiter* Welter, who had likewise been shot down and wounded. Between Maastricht and Cologne elements of III./JG 1 encountered four-engine bombers of the RAF with fighter escort. The Spitfires of 421 Squadron, RCAF, shot down two of the attackers. As III./JG 1 reported the loss of two pilots, the commander of III Gruppe, *Hauptmann* Erich Woitke, and *Leutnant* Schöne, who fell near Mönchengladbach, these were probably the two German fighters claimed by the Canadian squadron. *Hauptmann* Woitke was never found.

Eighteen aircraft of I./JG 26 took off at just before 1130 and engaged 60-80 Allied heavy bombers, which were on their return flight. The Gruppe shot down one Lightning against five losses. Three men were listed as missing, *Gefreiter* Gold crashed near Solingen and *Leutnant* Günther, the Gruppe's successful pilot that day, force-landed southwest of the Rhine with engine damage, sustaining injuries in the process. II Gruppe counted four losses. The loss of *Leutnant* Siegfried Benz was especially tragic. It is believed that a German fighter mistook his Fw 190 D-9 for a British Tempest and shot him down.

The action fought by Jagdgeschwader 77 was extremely dramatic, its I Gruppe taking heavy casualties from British and American fighters in an operation against 9th US TAF. In a short space of time the Geschwader lost a dozen Messerschmitts, with eight pilots killed and 1 missing. The machine of the *Kommodore*, *Major* Johannes Wiese, who had transferred from JG 52 to the Reich defense in autumn 1944, fell victim to the Browning machine-guns of a Spitfire. Wiese bailed out successfully, but his damaged parachute failed to deploy fully and he suffered serious injuries on striking the ground. *Hauptmann* Lothar Baumann, commander of I Gruppe, crashed with his Bf 109 G-14 in Luxembourg, north of Diekirch near Hoscheid. Today he is buried at Sandweiler Cemetery. The *Kapitän* of 2 Staffel, *Oberleutnant* Iring Englisch, died near Flamersheim, southeast of Euskirchen. Two members of his Staffel, *Unteroffiziere* Köberlein and Morgerauer, were shot down not far away, near Münstereifel. *Leutnant* Rolf von Kampen of 4 Staffel fell into the hands of the Americans; it was his 21st birthday. When he and his "Blue 2" failed to return from the area north of the Eifel, he was entered in the loss reports as missing. *Leutnant* von Kampen had escaped with his life, however. December 24 was a lucky day for him after all.

Across the Rhine, escorting Mustangs and Lightnings suddenly fanned out ahead of the bomber groups to screen the eastern flank of the US 8th Air Force raids on the Rhine-Main area; the Americans must have known they were getting into the operational area of those two well-tried formations, Jagdgeschwadern 300 and 301. The bomber force now split into two mass formations; one headed for the airfields of JG 4 and JG 11, while the other turned for JG 2's bases. Elements of I, II and III Gruppen, Jagdgeschwader

Fighter Losses on December 24, 1944

Units Involved	Killed/ Missing	Wounded	Total Casualties	Aircraft	Locale
I/JG1	1	1	2	Fw 190 A-8	Aachen
II/JG1	1		1	Fw 190 A-8	Monchen-Gladbach
III/JG1	2		2	Bf 109 G-14	St. Vith
			5		
II/JG2	3		3	Bf 109 G-14	Aachen, Bastogne
I/JG3	6		6	Bf 109 G-10	Ardennes-Eifel
III/JG3	4		4	Bf 109 G-14/K-4	Liege, St. Vith
IV/JG3	7		7	Fw 190 A-8/A-9	
			17		
I/JG4		1	1	Bf 109 G-14	Bopparo
II/JG4	2		2	Fw 190 A-8	Morfelden
III/JG4	1		1	Bf 109 G-10	Wiesbaden
			4		
I/JG6	9		9	Fw 190 A-8/A-9	Aachen, Eupen
II/JG6	2		2	Fw 190 A-8	Cologne, Liege
III/JG6	2		2	Bf 109 G-14	
			13		
I/JG11	2	1	3	Fw 190 A-8	Alzey, Trier
III/JG11	3	1	4	Fw 190 A-8	
			7		
I/JG26	4	1	5	Fw 190 A-8/A-9	Haltern, Liege
II/JG26	3	1	4	Fw 190 D-9	Malmedy, Rheine
			9		
I/JG27	4	1	5	Bf 109 G-14/K-4	Bochum, Bonn
II/JG27	1	1	2	Bf 109 G-10	Dyk, Hattingen
III/JG27		1	1	Bf 109 K-4	St. Vith
IV/JG27		2	2	Bf 109 G-10/G-14	
			10		
IV/JG53	1	1	2	Bf 109 G-14	Naustadt, Rottweil
IV/JG54	3	1	4	Fw 190 A-8/A-9	Liege, Setterich
I/JG77	9	1	10	Bf 109 G-14	Antweiler
III/JG77	1		1	Bf 109 K-4	Euskirchen, Hoscheid, Munstereifel
			11		
II/JG300	6	7	13	Fw 190 A-8	Eschwege, Fritzlar
III/JG300	2		2	Bf 109 G-10	Gottingen
IV/JG300	3		3	Bf 109 G-10AS	Hersfeld, Kassel, Ziegenhain
			18		
I/SG4	1		1	Fw 190 F-8	Bastogne
II/SG4	2		2	Fw 190 F-8	
			3		
Total Losses (Germany and Western Theatre)	85	21	106 (including 2 Gruppe commanders and 5 Staffel leaders killed or missing, 1 Geschwader commodore wounded)		

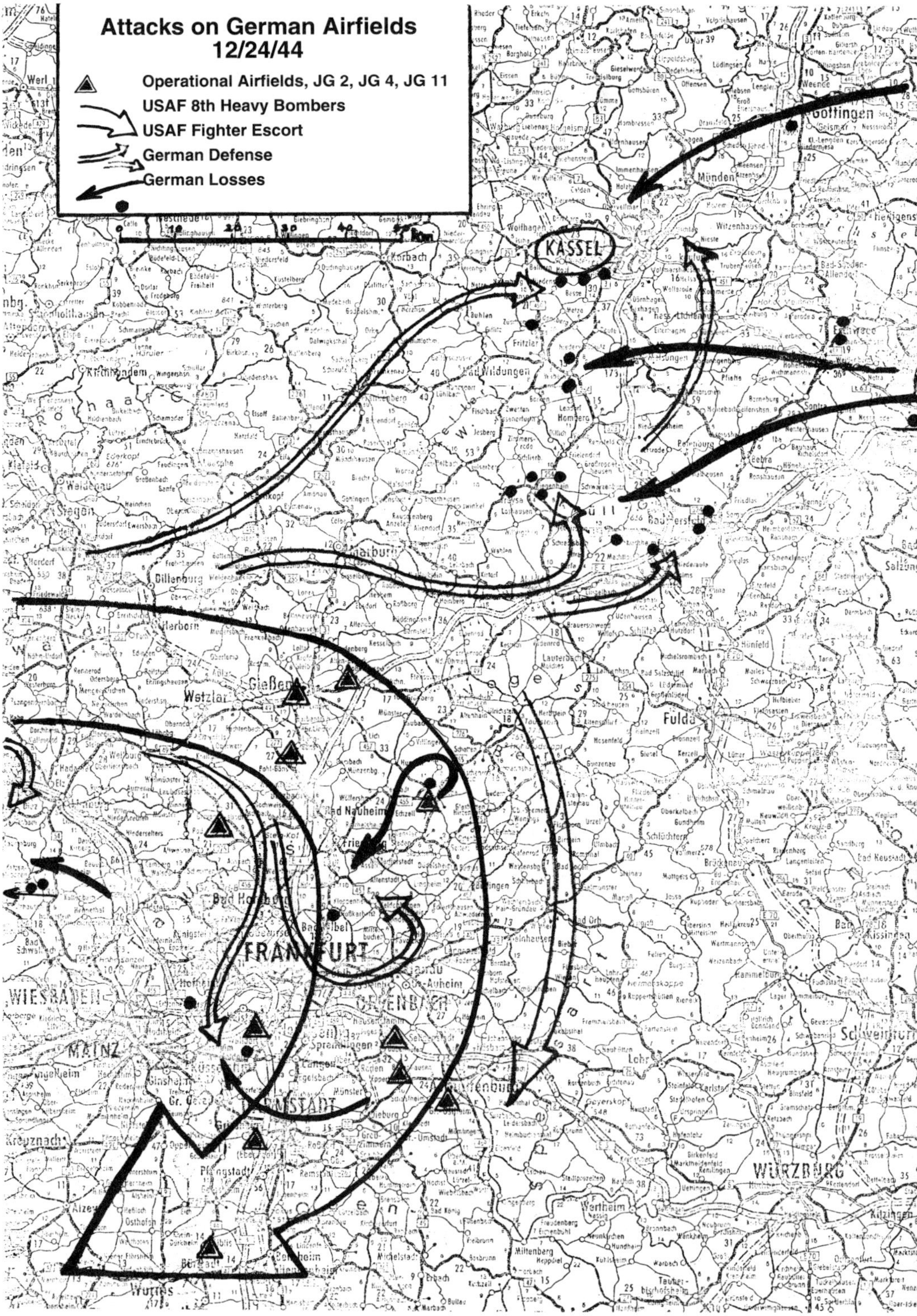
Attacks on German Airfields
12/24/44
Operational Airfields, JG 2, JG 4, JG 11
USAF 8th Heavy Bombers
USAF Fighter Escort
German Defense
German Losses
KASSEL
FRANKFURT
MAINZ
WIESBADEN
OFFENBACH
Göttingen
Münden
Fulda
Gießen
Wetzlar
Marburg
Bad Nauheim
Friedberg
Bad Homburg
Hanau
Darmstadt
Würzburg
Schweinfurt
Bad Kissingen
Siegen
Dillenburg
Herborn
Bad Wildungen
Fritzlar
Homberg
Korbach
Wertheim
Miltenberg

4, scrambled from their strips along the Frankfurt-Darmstadt autobahn to meet the Flying Fortresses in quadrants "*Paula-Quelle/Quelle-Quelle*" in the Mosell-Rhine triangle south of Coblenz. Almost on first contact two Focke-Wulfs from 5 Staffel were shot down. Both pilots, *Feldwebel* Erler and *Oberleutnant* Ullmann, were killed. *Unteroffizier* Ferchland of III Gruppe crashed near Erbenheim following air combat, while the Bf 109 G-14 of *Oberleutnant* Stark, leader of 3 Staffel, was shot down near Mörfelden. Stark bailed out virtually within sight of his base at Rhein-Main.

While bombs and strafing were ploughing up their runways at Biblis, Gross-Ostheim and Zellhausen, almost the whole of Jagdgeschwader 11 was involved with the Liberator formations of 2 (US) Air Division. Three pilots were killed in action. *Unteroffizier* Stöhr was killed in the attack on III Gruppe's airfield at Gross-Ostheim. *Major* Bischoff and *Fähnrich* Franz engaged a large number of Lightnings east of Trier. *Feldwebel* Horlacher crashed near Gross-Karben, north of Frankfurt/Main. *Leutnant* Richter and *Feldwebel* Schulirsch failed to return from the fighting over the Moselle. Neither they nor their Focke-Wulfs were ever found.

The second 8th Air Force bomber formation's target was five airfields in the general area of Giessen, mainly occupied by *Oberstleutnant* Bühligen's "Richthofen" Jagdgeschwader – Ettingshausen, Giessen, Merzhausen, Nidda, and Kirch-Göns. German fighter opposition was slight here; the Americans had already pinned down the bulk of the German fighter force west of the Rhine. JG 2 lost *Unteroffizier* Maier, killed in combat with Mustangs over Nidda, and the *Unteroffiziere* Kühn and Patzelt, both listed as missing in the western combat zone. *Unteroffizier* Löbering was killed in an air attack on Merzhausen airfield.

As the Americans had expected, the return flight over Northern Hesse encountered units of JG 300 and JG 301. Approaching from the direction of Thuringia, the German fighters attacked in several waves. As a result the battle extended from the Knüll Mountains to the Göttingen area.

Major Peters, who was forced to direct II./Sturm/JG 300's attack from the command post because of a leg wound, recorded the Gruppe's victories as well as its increasing losses. *Leutnant* Bretschneider, who was leading the entire "battle group" that day, ran into a superior Mustang pilot over the southern slopes of the Knüll Mountains. Following a bitter battle over Oberaula, Bretschneider's "*Raubautz* VII", an Fw 190 A-8 coded "Red 1," went down. At the time of his death Bretschneider, Knight's Cross wearer and leader of 5 Staffel, had 31 kills to his credit in only twenty missions, almost half of which had been scored flying night intercept missions in his single-engine fighter. With him fell five other pilots of II Gruppe. Five Messerschmitts of III and IV Gruppen were shot down in the area around Fritzlar; all of the pilots were killed. Over Uttershausen the pilots of 12 Staffel watched as *Leutnant* Günter Rudolph tried to bail out of his shot-up Bf 109 G-10. Rudolph managed to escape from the aircraft, but then his comrades were forced to watch as he plunged to earth like a stone after his parachute failed to open.

The great air battle came to an end. A few hours later, as darkness closed in on Christmas Eve, the fifth of the war, the German pilots could wish for no greater blessing than the coming of peace. No one yet knew the terrible price the day's operations had cost the German fighter force. It was not until later that the full extent of the disaster was realized: 85 fighter pilots killed, missing or captured, as well as 21 wounded. This meant the loss of 106 flying personnel. The Allies claimed the destruction of 125 German fighters and a further five probable.

The destruction of 44 heavy bombers bears witness to the intensity of the fighting and the determination of the German fighter pilots. But in the end all this could not hide the fact that the German fighter force could no longer carry out its mission of hampering Allied operations in the combat zone and over Germany and inflicting significant losses. And the fighter pilots' mistrust of their leadership continued to grow; for a long time now they had the feeling that they were being sacrificed to no good purpose.

Monday December 25, 1944

Christmas Day, 1944. The Ardennes offensive was nearing its climax; already the indications were there that the German troops could advance no further and that the Allies were beginning to firm up their defensive positions and even go over to the counterattack. By their massive operations against communications targets just behind the combat zone, the Allied air forces were succeeding in cutting the German lines of communication to the point where supplies were reaching the front line only with great difficulty if at all.

The German fighter pilots can hardly be held to blame for having only to a very limited extent accomplished their assigned task of tactical support for the advance; on the contrary they showed a magnificent fighting spirit in an unaccustomed role – and it cost them dearly. There was scarcely a single fighter unit that was not intercepted on its way to the target by overwhelmingly superior forces of Mustangs, Thunderbolts, Spitfires, Typhoons or Tempests and forced to give battle. Over this Christmas of 1944 the fighter force received its mortal blow; within a bare two weeks it was to be finally wiped out.

During the morning of December 25, Hawker Typhoons of 193 and 266 Squadrons 2nd TAF took off for low-level attacks in the area north of the Ruhr, while over Duisburg the Spitfires of 401 Squadron RCAF lay in wait for their prey. These units encountered German fighters and an air battle developed. Pieces of one of the shot-down Bf 109s struck the machine of British Squadron-Leader Everards and he was forced to bale out.

II./JG 26 had two casualties that day, *Feldwebel* Meindl, whose parachute failed to open, and *Feldwebel* Hoppe, who was killed near Dortmund in his "Brown 13." The Geschwader reported only two kills, two fewer than Jagdgeschwader 27, whose four Gruppen were dispersed over the whole western operational area. But JG 27 took a really punishing blow; with thirteen pilots lost it suffered the heaviest casualties of any formation that day.

The Bf 109 G-14s of I./JG 3 took off from their base at Paderborn. Their mission was providing air cover for the German armored forces near Liege. But they never got there. About noon they were attacked south of Bonn by a large force of Mustangs. Two of the American fighters maneuvered into position behind the machine of *Unteroffizier* Markl and put several bullets into his engine. The 3 Staffel pilot was forced to parachute from his damaged fighter and sustained back and knee injuries on landing near Tondorf. 4 Staffel lost two pilots in this action: *Gefreiter* Orth was killed near Merten and der Sieg, and *Feldwebel* Kühn was posted missing in action.

Southeast of Düren, Flight Lieutenant Sherk of 402 Squadron RCAF, flying a Spitfire, shot down a lone Fw 190. This was 125 Wing's 100th victory since the beginning of the invasion. The German pilot, whose parachute failed to open, may have been *Unteroffizier* Wolfgang Rosenow of 11./JG 11, whose Fw 190 A-8 was reported missing near Euskirchen.

Shortly after midday some pilots of 411 Squadron, Royal Canadian Air Force, spotted a lone Me 262, apparently approaching to land at Rheine airfield. The aircraft was 9K+MM of II./KG(J) 51, with *Oberleutnant* Lamle at the controls, on his way back from a sortie over Liege. He spotted the enemy fighters coming up on his tail but had already throttled back and lost too much speed to get away. He was shot down by Flight Lieutenant Boyle at about 1230 and was killed. That same afternoon the Canadians destroyed another Me 262. 403 Squadron intercepted a vic of these jet fighters near Eupen, and Squadron Leader Collier shot one down. The German pilot, *Feldwebel* Hans Meyer of I./KG(J) 51, was killed.

The Americans were heading for the German frontier when they were engaged over the High Venn by strong formations from Jagdgeschwadern 1 and 3. The whole of IV./JG 3, under its commander *Hauptmann* Hubert York Weydenhammer, was in the air that afternoon. Covered by the Messerschmitts of III./JG 1 the Germans broke into the bomber formations. The first Liberators were soon dropping out of the sky into the woods between Liege and St. Vith, and the fighters succeeded in shooting down a whole string of bombers, mainly from the 467th Bomb Group. But then their turn came, as 479th Fighter Group's Mustangs attacked from the rear and split the German battle group wide open. *Hauptmann* Weydenhammer was seen going in to attack a Liberator, but at that point the situation became confused. *Hauptmann* Weydenhammer disappeared, and with him *Feldwebel* Clässen, *Unteroffizier* Gaspers and *Oberfähnrich* Vaitl. According to Allied sources, the American fighter group engaged some 12-15 Focke-Wulfs, which were themselves attacking the Liberator formation. They shot two German fighters down, literally chasing a Fw 190 right into the ground. Presumably at least one of the missing pilots from IV Gruppe, among them the Gruppe commander, was killed in these two aircraft. Two of the Gruppe's pilots, *Leutnant* Mebesius and *Unteroffizier* Wagner, came down over Belgium and were taken prisoner by the Americans. *Feldwebel* Hoffmann on the other hand managed to dive clear of the fighters only to be caught in Allied flak, and landed back at Cologne-Wahn with his Fw 190 like a sieve.

With eleven casualties, Jagdgeschwader 1 could scarcely be said to have come through this mission unscathed. *Oberleutnant* Bilfinger, leader of 10 Staffel, was killed over Meckenheim in combat while engaging the heavy bombers. It is likely that he, like the two other pilots of 11 Staffel, *Feldwebel* Sperling and *Unteroffizier* Zinnen, were shot down by enemy fighters, as the 352nd Fighter Group claimed a number of victories over German fighters in the Bonn area. Major Preddy, commanding the 352nd Mustang Group, one of the American fighter aces, scored his 26th and 27th kills that day. But he himself did not return to base; he was hit by his own side's flak while crossing the front and was killed when he crashed near Liege. The same thing happened to Lieut. Bouchier of the 479th Fighter Group, but he landed safely by parachute.

Numerous small groups of twin-engine bombers from 9th US TAF flew 629 sorties against the road and rail network behind the battle line, concentrating on the area between Cologne and Coblenz. Against them Luftflotte Headquarters West sent in III./JG 6, I and III./JG 11, all of JG 27, IV./JG 54 and I./JG 77. The fact that they frequently met British fighters instead of the Americans they expected, or vice versa, serves to characterize the scale and scope of Allied air operations over Western Germany at that time.

The Bf 109 G-14s of III./JG 6 from the Oldenburg area encountered Allied escort fighters between Cologne and Düren and were split up. *Unteroffizier* Scherf was shot down and killed near Bergheim as 12 Staffel attempted to escape north along the Erft. *Unteroffizier* Radke was wounded in the same area. A small number of Messerschmitts of 9 Staffel took off at 1059 and ran into a hornet's nest in the Cologne area; *Leutnant* Siegfried Dönch and *Obergefreiter* Werner failed to return. The Gruppe also had the misfortune to run into the Typhoons of 193 Squadron near Quackenbrück. The British claimed the destruction of a Focke-Wulf, and it is almost certain that this was the Fw 190 A-8 of *Oberleutnant* Paris of the *Gruppenstab.* Paris suffered serious injuries, from which he died two months later on February 9, 1945. A Messerschmitt was shot down over Bergisch-Gladbach and crashed into a swampy field in Paffrath at about 1130. Only small pieces of the pilot's body and his parachute were found, preventing identification. To this day the name of the pilot killed near Paffrath is unknown.

IV./JG 54 had also suffered extraordinarily high losses in the defensive actions of December 1944, which saw the Gruppe decimated. South of Cologne the Gruppe tried to fight off the numerous Allied fighters, but to no avail. *Leutnant* Franke was shot down and killed over Heckenbach near Kempenich, *Oberfähnrich* Ernst Hoffmann was still aboard his A-8 when it smashed into the ground near Walberberg, a few kilometers south of Brühl, *Oberfeldwebel* Eugen Lude was shot down near the edge of a forest near Duisdorf, and twenty-four-year-old *Fähnrich* Erwin Schommert died over Jammelshofen on the High Acht and was buried in the village. Only a fraction of the scattered Gruppe's aircraft landed back at Vörden. Eight pilots had been killed.

I./JG 77 reported two losses between Cologne and Bonn, while III./JG 11 lost four pilots in the same area. Further south elements of I./JG 11 encountered Allied fighters over the Eifel, losing the Fw 190 A-8s of

Fighter Losses on December 25, 1944

Units Involved	Killed/ Missing	Wounded	Total Casualties	Aircraft	Locale
II/JG1	1	1	2	Fw 190 A-8	Hohes, Venn
III/JG1	7	2	9	Bf 109 G-10/G-14	Liege, Marche
			11		
I/JG3	2	1	3	Bf 109 G-14	Liege, St. Vith
III/JG3	1		1	Bf 109 G-14	
IV/JG3	7		7	Fw 190 A-8	
			11		
III/JG6	4	1	5	Bf 109 G-14	Cologne, Quakenbruck
I/JG11	2		2	Fw 190 A-8	Bitburg, Euskirchen
III/JG11	4		4	Fw 190 A-8	Siegburg
			6		
II/JG26	2		2	Fw 190 D-9	Dortmund, Furstenau
III/JG26	1		1	Bf 109 K-4	Horneburg
			3		
I/JG27	1	2	3	Bf 109 G-10/G-14	Aachen, Adenau
II/JG27	2	4	6	Bf 109 G-10/G-14	Malmedy, Mayen
III/JG27	1		1	Bf 109 K-4	Neuenahr
IV/JG27	2	1	3	Bf 109 G-10/G-14	Nurburgring
			13		
II/JG53	2		2	Bf 109 G-14	Hochspeyer
III/JG53	1		1	Bf 109 G-14	Oberharmersbach
			3		
IV.JG54	8		8	Fw 190 A-8/A-9	Jammelshofeh, Kempenich
I/JG77	1	1	2	Bf 109 G-14	Ollheim
Total Losses (Germany and Western Theatre)	49	13	62 (including 1 Gruppe commander and 1 Staffel leader killed, or missing, 1 Gruppe commander wounded)		

Unteroffiziere Holzinger and Weismüller. The two pilots were initially reported missing in action, but it was later discovered that both had been killed in quadrant "*Quelle-Otto-4*" near Densborn and Usch.

On the following day the supreme Headquarters communique read:

> "Yesterday German fighter units again intercepted strong enemy formations and prevented them from bombing their intended targets." What the populace was not told was that on 25 December the German fighter force once again lost over 60 aircraft with more than 40 pilots killed.

Tuesday, December 26, 1944

> "26.12.44. Very cold. The Americans and British appeared only in limited strength, and the intensity of our own operations was diminished.
>
> II./JG 1 had the day's heaviest losses. Eight pilots failed to return and were reported missing. The Gruppe was involved in dogfights round Bastogne.
>
> Fifteen "long-noses" from I./JG 26 under the command of *Oblt.* Hartigs took off at 1058 and became involved with Mustangs over Belgium. *Oblt.* Hartigs (4 Staffel.) and *Uffz.* Schöndorf (1 Staffel.) were taken prisoner near Carlsbourg. One victory by *Ofw.* Schwarz reported a kill, but *Flieger* Bergmeier and *Unteroffiziere* Grad and Sattler were killed in action.
>
> JG 27 also had six pilots killed in the Liege area.
>
> In the southwest, II./JG 53 had contact with an American incursion in the Stuttgart area. *Hptm.* Meimberg, the Gruppe leader, was shot down and baled out over Schaichhof. *Oblt.* Ludolf met a tragic end at Rutesheim; he jumped when too low, and the parachute did not have time to deploy fully. *Gefreiter* Ruland (8 Staffel) was wounded and made a belly-landing near Flacht. *Gefreiter* Meermann (6 Staffel) was shot down and killed east of Wimsheim.
>
> Schlachtgeschwader 4 (Fw 190 F-8s) lost four pilots, including Staffelkapitäne *Hptm.* Jungclaussen (3 Staffel) and *Hptm.* Schürmer (I Staffel) were killed in action north of the Soon Woods. *Ofw.* Weinreich and *Ofw.* Zumkeller are missing."

Wednesday, December 27, 1944

After twelve days of winter warfare the Western Allies succeeded in breaking out of the encircled and bitterly contested town of Bastogne and in bringing the German offensive to a halt once and for all. The German troops had reached the limit of their penetration. Their spearheads were in front of Dinant, within sight of the Meuse; but they lacked the strength to push further ahead, and their losses were many times greater than had been expected.

The cold, clear winter weather held, and yet again the Allies superior forces dominated the airspace over the combat zone. In addition over 1,000 heavy bombers from US 8th Air Force flew into the Rhineland to bomb communications targets in the Coblenz area; and once more the swarms of Mustangs fanned out far ahead of the bombers to screen their northern flank.

Hauptmann Ehlers and his I Gruppe of Jagdgeschwader 1 took off to support German forces in the Dinant area. But just west of Mayen, in the Eifel, they became involved in a large-scale air battle and lost nine pilots. At the head of the list stood *Hauptmann* Hans Ehlers' name; he crashed in his Focke-Wulf "White 20" near Bereborn, at the foot of the 2,200 feet Hochkels. *Unteroffizier* Schiller of 1 Staffel was shot down by Mustangs of the 364th FG as the dogfight began over the High Acht, and the Fw 190 A-8 of *Feldwebel* Wolf Oswald of 3 Staffel went down over the Nürburgring auto race track. *Leutnant* Birnbaum was killed at about the same time near Antweiler on the Ahr, while *Unteroffizier* Schaumberg of 2 Staffel set course for Coblenz, but was forced to make a forced landing on the west side of the Rhine near Bensdorf. Three pilots were missing after the mission: *Feldwebel* Heribert Mehl of 1 Staffel, *Leutnant* Gottfried Just, the leader of 2./JG 1, and *Oberleutnant* Pörschel of 4./JG 1. *Oberleutnant* Millers of 1 Staffel lay wounded in a hospital in Adenau. The Geschwader had thus lost a total of fifteen pilots that day.

II./JG 2 took part in the same operation but escaped with two wounded. *Unteroffizier* Trefzer bailed out at Wershofen, north of Antweiler, after a dogfight with some twenty Mustangs; and *Fahnenjunker* Alfred Richter put his Bf 109 G-14 down in a forced landing about twenty miles away, near Brühl.

Jagdgeschwader 27 was again tasked to provide air cover over the leading infantry, and this time most of them managed to get through to the

Bastogne area. *Leutnant* Beckmann, whose 4 Staffel was flying top cover, suddenly spotted two P-38 Lightnings and shot one down. As the American fighter disappeared from view southeast of Bastogne, the Staffel met a bunch of Mustangs, two of which closed on the Staffel leader in a pincer movement. Beckmann's wingman, *Unteroffizier* Karl-Heinz Klempau, was already hanging beneath his parachute, his Messerschmitt having been shot down over the High Eifel. Now *Leutnant* Beckmann's G-14 was hit in the rudder, and he too had to reach for his rip-cord. However I Gruppe only lost two killed, one of whom, *Unteroffizier* Sauter, was despatched by Flight Lieutenant Fox of 412 Spitfire Squadron (Royal Canadian Air Force) near Rheine airfield. JG 27's other losses were two wounded from II Gruppe and one from IV Gruppe. *Feldwebel* Bürger, a member of 13 Staffel, was initially listed as missing, but later returned with minor injuries. He had been forced to abandon his machine, "White 4," a few kilometers west of Düren. As 411 Squadron RCAF claimed three Messerschmitts shot down near Düren, one of their victims must have been *Feldwebel* Düren. Fighter-bombers of 440 Squadron RCAF attacking targets in the St. Vith area came upon three Messerschmitts, one of which was shot down by Flight-Lieutenant Jenvey. It is possible that this was the aircraft of the *Staffelkapitän* of 7./JG 27, *Leutnant* Gernot Stein, who was last seen in this area. *Gefreiter* Leitner of 6./JG 27, who was listed as missing between Rheine and Aachen, may have fallen victim to Flight-Lieutenant Malloy during an encounter between Tempests of 274 Squadron and a formation of eight Messerschmitts over the Lower Rhine.

Around 1300 Thunderbolts of 9th US TAF and RAF Tempests of No 486 Squadron came upon a German fighter formation east of Münster, and for the first time in quite a while elements of Ill./JG 54 found themselves in action. It was *Leutnant* Crump's 10 Staffel and *Oberleutnant* Dortenmann's 11 Staffel. Straightaway the British picked on the "long-nosed" Fw 190s and shot down four aircraft from 10 Staffel for the loss of one Tempest, the four kills being credited to Flying Officers Tanner, Taylor-Cannon, Smith and Short. Two of the downed German pilots, *Oberleutnant* Breger and *Feldwebel* Dähn, fell near Telgte and Everswinkel, the other two were wounded over Münster-Handorf. 12 Staffel lost one aircraft; its pilot, *Feldwebel* Hutz, was shot down and killed by a Thunderbolt.

Generally speaking the American 9th TAF seemed to be out in strength again that day, their Thunderbolts being involved in almost every contact. It even came about that No. 137 Squadron's Typhoons were set upon by an

American fighter formation, but this scrap ended without loss. With its continuous ground support operations of December 26-27, 9th US TAF played no small part in the defeat of the Ardennes offensive. On these two days 9th TAF recorded seventy kills for a loss of 39 twin-engine bombers, most of them shot down by German AA.

Jagdgeschwader 3 "*Udet*", on the other hand, was having a costly day. I, III and IV Gruppen were involved between Cologne and the Ahr Mountains with American and British fighters which were waiting over the combat zone in overwhelming numbers. Some of this fighting overlapped the action of Jagdgeschwader 1 whose squadrons were over the Eifel at the same time but rather further to the south. 14 Staffel lost its leader when *Leutnant* Glaubig went down in his "Black 9" near Antweiler, the victim of a small group of Thunderbolts. With the loss of *Leutnant* Rennewanz of 15 Staffel and *Oberfähnrich* Büchsenmann of 16 Staffel, both of whom were listed as missing in the St. Vith area, IV./JG 3 finished the day with five pilots lost.

III Gruppe, which encountered American fighters south of Cologne, suffered similar losses; *Unteroffizier* Kaudela was wounded and *Gefreiter* Stump killed. Two other pilots became involved in a hopeless battle with about ten Thunderbolts. There was no escape for "Yellow 13" with *Unteroffizier* Aigner and "Black 8" with *Obergefreiter* Hirschmann. Both pilots have been listed as missing in action since.

On December 27, the well-known and much feared "St. Vith area of operations" also claimed a further toll from Jagdgeschwader 27. Elements of II./JG 77 and IV./JG 54 which were attached to the main force, also felt the Allied fighter-bombers' deadly sting. Three pilots from 14./JG 54 failed to return to their base at Vörden and were reported missing. Among them was another experienced leader, *Leutnant* Alfred Budde. The other two pilots were *Leutnant* Baur-Bargehr and *Oberleutnant* Drexler.

But although the air battle did not always look hopeless and few chances were missed to give the Allies a bloody nose, the duel in the sky was sheer hell for most of the German fighter pilots. JG 27 alone scored ten kills on December 27. Many of the wingmen found it more and more difficult and often impossible to cover their formation leader in a tight dogfight. And many leaders were no longer in a position to keep an eye on the green pilots and stop them making ill-considered moves in the heat of battle.

Ground staff as well, the mechanics and technicians on the airfields, were stretched to the limit and beyond, and one began to wonder how long

Fighter Losses on December 27, 1944

Units Involved	Killed/ Missing	Wounded	Total Casualties	Aircraft	Locale
I/JG1	8	4	12	Fw 190 A-8	Bastogne
II/JG1	1	1	2	Fw 190 A-78	Dinant-Vielsalm
III/JG1	1		1	Bf 109 G-14	Mayen, Munstereifel
			15		
II/JG2		2	2	Bf 109 G-14	Bruhl
I/JG3	3		3	Bf 109 G-10/G-14	Antweiler, Liege
III/JG3	4	1	5	Bf 109 G-14	Malmedy
IV/JG3	5		5	Fw 190 A-8/A-9	Marche, St. Vith
			13		
I/JG27	2	1	3	Bf 109 G-14/K-4	Bastogne
II/JG27	2	1	3	Bf 109 G-10/G-14	High Eifel
IV/JG27	1	1	2	Bf 109 G-10	Rheine, St. Vith
			8		
III/JG53		1	1	Bf 109 G-14	Kirrlach
IV/JG53		1	1	Bf 109 G-14	Schonaich
			2		
III/JG54	3	2	5	Fw 190 D-9	Munster, Telgte
IV/JG54	4		4	Fw 190 A-8	St. Vith, High Eifel
			9		
II/JG77	1		1	Bf 109 G-14	Eupen, St. Vith
Total Losses (Germany and Western Theatre)	36	14	50 (including 1 Gruppe commander and 4 Staffel leaders killed or missing)		

they could carry on. Their devotion to duty received no mention in the operational reports, but they worked continuously right round the clock. It was only through their efforts that the pilots were able to take off on the next mission.

But what was the use of it all? In the last analysis the Allies overwhelming strength was increasingly calling the tune.

Friday, December 29, 1944

At its base situated northeast of the village of Varrelbusch on the Cloppenburg-Friesoythe railway line every available machine stood ready for the first Gruppe-size operation since December 25, when this unit had officially been placed under command of JG 26. In all, almost seventy Focke-Wulf 190 D-9s were to take over the job of providing takeoff and landing cover for the Me 262s of KG(J) 51 based at Rheine. Together with elements of Jagdgeschwader 6 from the Oldenburg area and a Staffel from IV./JG 27 from Achmer, III./JG 54 was ordered to engage all low-flying Allied aircraft astride the Dortmund-Ems and Mittelland Canals. 3rd Jagddivision at Wiedenbrück was to provide radio direction ("Y-Führung").[2] This was to prove the last major operation in which III./JG 54 was to take part. For the express order from Jagddivision control center to commit the Gruppe by Staffeln proved completely misguided, with the result that the whole operation failed and ended in catastrophe – just as the Staffel leaders had predicted. Seventeen pilots were killed and three injured: it was a Black Friday indeed for III Gruppe, Jagdgeschwader 54.

First into the air, at about 0900, was *Oberleutnant* Crump with his 10 Staffel. 9, 11 and 12 Staffeln followed at intervals of about an hour. One thing which is not clear is why the fighter pilots were not properly briefed on the actual air situation and the real strength of the Allied fighters. For as they were approaching the area of operations, numerous Allied fighter formations were dominating the airspace over the Tecklenburg area and the whole of Münsterland. Under these circumstances it was a serious command error to send units into the air Staffel by Staffel and so present the Allies with a chance to intercept them one at a time and destroy them one at a time. The problem may have been that certain ground control centers tended not to react on the scale the situation called for and to direct the course of operations speedily enough for the formation commander in the air, who had to read the situation instantly and make split-second decisions. And this air defense operation of December 29, 1944 was clearly no exception.

Just as the second sub-unit to go, 9 Staffel, reached the area Lingen-Rheine, they were taken by surprise by the Spitfires of 411 Squadron RCAF, flying from Heesch in Holland. The German pilots in their Focke-Wulfs barely had time to defend themselves. The *Staffelkapitän, Leutnant* Heilmann, did everything he could to get his pilots up above the altitude of only 6,500 feet that had been ordered, but in vain. *Unteroffizier* Busch and *Unteroffizier*

Reichardt were shot down, their "Doras" crashing near Lingen. *Unteroffizier* Fernau and his "White 6" came down only a few kilometers to the southeast, near Messingen, and *Leutnant* Bartak was shot down by the Spitfires just short of the German border near Bentheim. *Fähnrich* Schmauser and *Unteroffizier* Toepler also fell to the guns of the enemy fighters over the Ems between Rheine and Lingen.

Six pilots killed and many parachute jumps – no wonder the *Gruppenkommandeur, Hauptmann* Robert Weiss, stared helplessly out over the field as, instead of the 9 Staffel he expected, only the odd machine came in. It didn't take him long to make up his mind. He took off with the *Stabsschwarm* for the combat zone to find out the situation for himself. 11 Staffel too was now airborne, with *Leutnant* Prager standing in as its leader.

It was about noon, and the Dortmund-Ems canal was to the Germans' right as the Fw 190s approached quadrant "*Friedrich-Quelle*." Suddenly a large formation of Spitfires came into view. This time the Germans were able to use their height to advantage and dive on the enemy aircraft; but then some Typhoon formations appeared out of nowhere down below the Spitfires, and the Germans were heavily outnumbered. A dogfight developed over Lengerich, near Lingen, and ended with *Feldwebel* Neersen and *Oberleutnant* Schreiner being shot down. In the course of the battle the *Gruppenkommandeur*, Knight's Cross wearer *Hauptmann* Weiss, was shot down and killed in a fight with several Spitfires. By this time 11 Staffel had become widely scattered, and its aircraft were hunted down and forced to give battle to the Allied fighters. *Oberfeldwebel* Wilhelm Philipp was shot down west of Nordhorn. Philipp sustained serious injuries bailing out of his burning "Yellow 6." Meanwhile the rest of the Staffel attempted to escape to the south. Two more pilots were killed, however: *Feldwebel* Kreisel over Nienborg and *Unteroffizier* Rupp near Vreden.

The Allied forces involved, 331 and 401 (RCAF) Squadrons with Spitfires and 168 and 439 (RCAF) Squadrons with Typhoons, reported a total of nine confirmed kills and two unconfirmed for a loss of six aircraft. Among 439 Squadron's victories was an Fw 190 A-8, which was probably the machine which came down behind the Dutch border near the Oldenzaal canal. The Focke-Wulf's pilot, *Unteroffizier* Wolfgang Miebach of III./JG 6, was killed.

Influenced by what had gone before, *Oberleutnant* Dortenmann's 12 Staffel scrambled from Varrelbusch and climbed straight to 20,000 feet. It was about noon when these further twelve Fw 190 D-9s set course for

Münster and made contact between the Dümmersee and the Ems, most probably with the Tempests of 3 and 56 Squadrons flying from Volkel. In this encounter the flight lost only one pilot, *Unteroffizier* Seibert, while *Unteroffizier* Zessin baled out wounded from his "Red 12." The evidence strongly suggests that 7 Staffel of Jagdgeschwader 6 was also involved, for the British shot down *Unteroffizier* Schneider's A-8 near Wallenhorst. The two British units together lost four Tempests; *Feldwebel* Steinkamp of 13./JG 27 scored a double, and one further kill was credited to 11 Staffel.

Three Messerschmitts of 13./JG 27 were lost in air combat near Alsstätte. Two of the pilots, *Fähnrich* Ferdinand Miebach and *Feldwebel* Patan, were killed, and the other, *Unteroffizier* Thormählen, was wounded.

Since the parts played in the day's operations by fighter units of both sides frequently overlapped and fighting continued almost uninterrupted from 0900 to 1500, it is impossible to say precisely which units opposed one another. Although one can determine in broad terms which units were involved and which made or may have made contact with one another, the operational area was too widespread to be sure that other units were not also involved in a particular engagement. On top of this comes the problem – one which does not only apply to December 29 – that gaps and errors in detailed reporting led to misunderstandings; and these in turn make a proper evaluation of debriefing reports and other documentation extremely difficult. The Allies were apt to apply a pretty broad brush to their location reports, so that for instance "in the Enschede area" may well in fact mean "over the Teutoburger Wald." In the absence of an opportunity to reconstruct the course of events by means of matching statements and other supporting evidence, this lack of precise locations may significantly distort a detailed account of this kind. Again, it was not only the German pilots who were subject to optical illusions in the matter of aircraft recognition. With Fw 190s and Bf 109s alongside each other in almost every encounter, a British or American pilot might well report a kill on a Focke-Wulf instead of a Messerschmitt; likewise the Germans could not always tell Spitfires, Typhoons and Tempests apart, and in the heat of battle they could hardly be expected to. Thus one can only seek to establish whether the total kills and losses can be matched up.

On this basis, the balance-sheet for the operations of December 29 reads as follows. For a loss of eleven fighters, 2 TAF scored 31 kills in all. Flight Lieutenant Audet of 411 Squadron RCAF shot down five German fighters. German reports give a loss of twenty pilots from JG 6, JG 27 and JG 54; but

In mid-1944 the newly formed "Sturmverbände" (Assault Geschwader) of the fighter force succeeded in achieving an above average success rate, and thus gave a fresh impulse to home air defense. The picture shows members of 10.(Sturm)/JG 3 gathered round their Staffel leader, Oblt. Weik (back to camera) at Illesheim in July 1944. From Left to right: unknown, unknown, Fw. Brand, Uffz. Volz, Uffz. Vohl, Fw. Ehrhard, Ogfr. Kott, Uffz. Trittler, Oblt. Weik, Lt. Hagena, unknown.

A Focke-Wulf 190 A-8 of II./JG 1, just after takeoff.

Enemy bomber forces have been reported. Day-fighter pilots at cockpit readiness and about to scramble. Here the pilots must rely on their trusty mechanics.

A pair of Bf 109Gs from I./JG 27 scrambles.

From other airfields as well, Messerschmitts are taking off to intercept heavy bomber formations.

Boeing B-17G "Flying Fortresses" of the 447th Bomber Group, US 8th Air Force. Almost every day German fighters took on these American bombers in close formation in their efforts to ward off attacks on Germany.

An Fw 190 D-9 attacking through a bomber formation just avoids the falling bombs from an American bomber.

Time and again German fighters broke through the barrier of American fighter escorts to get at the bomber packs. This shows the giant tail unit of a B-17G from 384th Bomber Group which was shot sown and made a forced landing.

Vapor trails in the blue sky depict the course of bitter air combat between German fighters and the intruding enemy.

Flames streaming from it, an American bomber plunges downwards. This time a score for the AA gunners at Merseburg — central Germany, November 2, 1944.

Photographed from the nose window of a "Flying Fortress", a pair of Messerschmitts dives clear after a frontal attack on an American bomber formation.

Landing after combat. On the airfields the return of the Messerschmitts and Focke-Wulfs from operations is eagerly awaited. But lack of fuel, technical faults or battle damage force not a few to land elsewhere.

From the summer of 1944 onwards, allied air superiority mounted steadily. German losses in air defense rose from week to week and sad pictures like these became a daily event. Often there is only a tiny crater to mark the end of a fighter pilot and his machine.

No account of fighter operations would be complete without a mention of the ground staff, the "men in black", for without them the best of fighter pilots would never have achieved success. But, thanks to the tireless work of the mechanics, even the greenest young pilot soon gained confidence in his machine.

Thunderbolts. This American aircraft was the heaviest single-engine fighter built during World War II. It was used in the European theatre as a fighter-bomber by the 9th US TAF, while the fighter units of the US 8th Air Force were steadily being converted to the Mustang. Its 6-8 half-inch (12.7mm) Browning machine-guns gave the Thunderbolt massive firepower under which many a German fighter met its end.

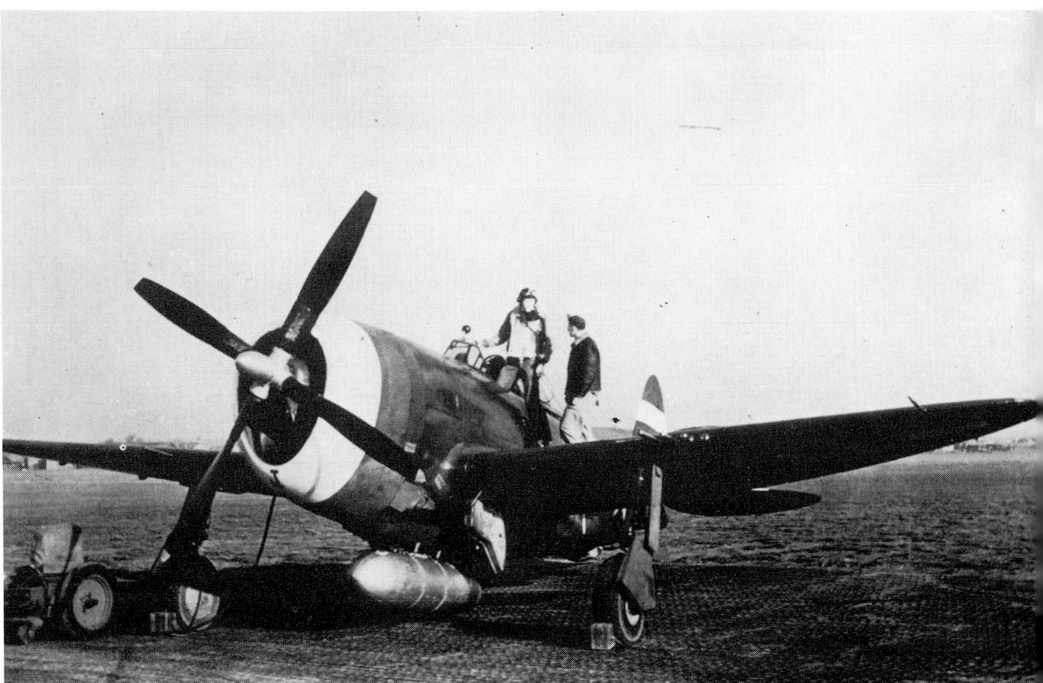

The Royal Air Force's red, white and blue roundel on the fuselage spells danger! From autumn 1944 the 2nd TAF, equipped with the three types of aircraft shown above (Spitfire IX, Typhoon IB and Tempest V) was flying almost daily operations over North Germany to draw the German Air Force to battle.

Three pilots of III./JG 3 "Udet" safely returned to base, are given a first quick debriefing by their squadron commander, Hptm. Dahl.

With the introduction of the Fw 190 D-9, yet another new type came off the production line into the first-line units. Pilots considered this aircraft, second only to the Me 262, the best that the Luftwaffe had to offer. The D-9's climb rate and top speed of almost 700 kph made it a match for, and in some respects superior to all types of enemy fighters.

German fighter stations were one of the top priorities on the Allies' target lists. The photograph shows Twenthe airfield after a raid in mid-November 1944. At the turn of 1944/45 I./JG 1 as well as various night fighter units were based there.

A German Jagdstaffel in autumn 1944 — 11. Staffel/JG 53, probably taken at Kirrlach. The flight leader, Lt. Landt, is sitting on the Bf 109 G-14. Of the eight senior NCOs standing, three had been killed and three wounded by mid-March 1945. From left to right: Uffz. Sommerhoff (wounded 11/18/44), Uffz. Tesarik (killed 3/14/45), Fw. Scheer, Uffz. Fröschmann, Uffz. Dröge (killed 3/14/45), Uffz. Gröbke (killed 3/17/45), Fw. Plettner (wounded 1/1/45), Uffz. Maier? (wounded 1/10/45).

Ofw. Heinrich Bartels, killed in action on December 23, 1944. With 99 victories to his credit, Bartels was a veritable mentor to the young pilots of IV./JG 27 (Replacement). He used to pass on his experience in a way that quickly instilled confidence.

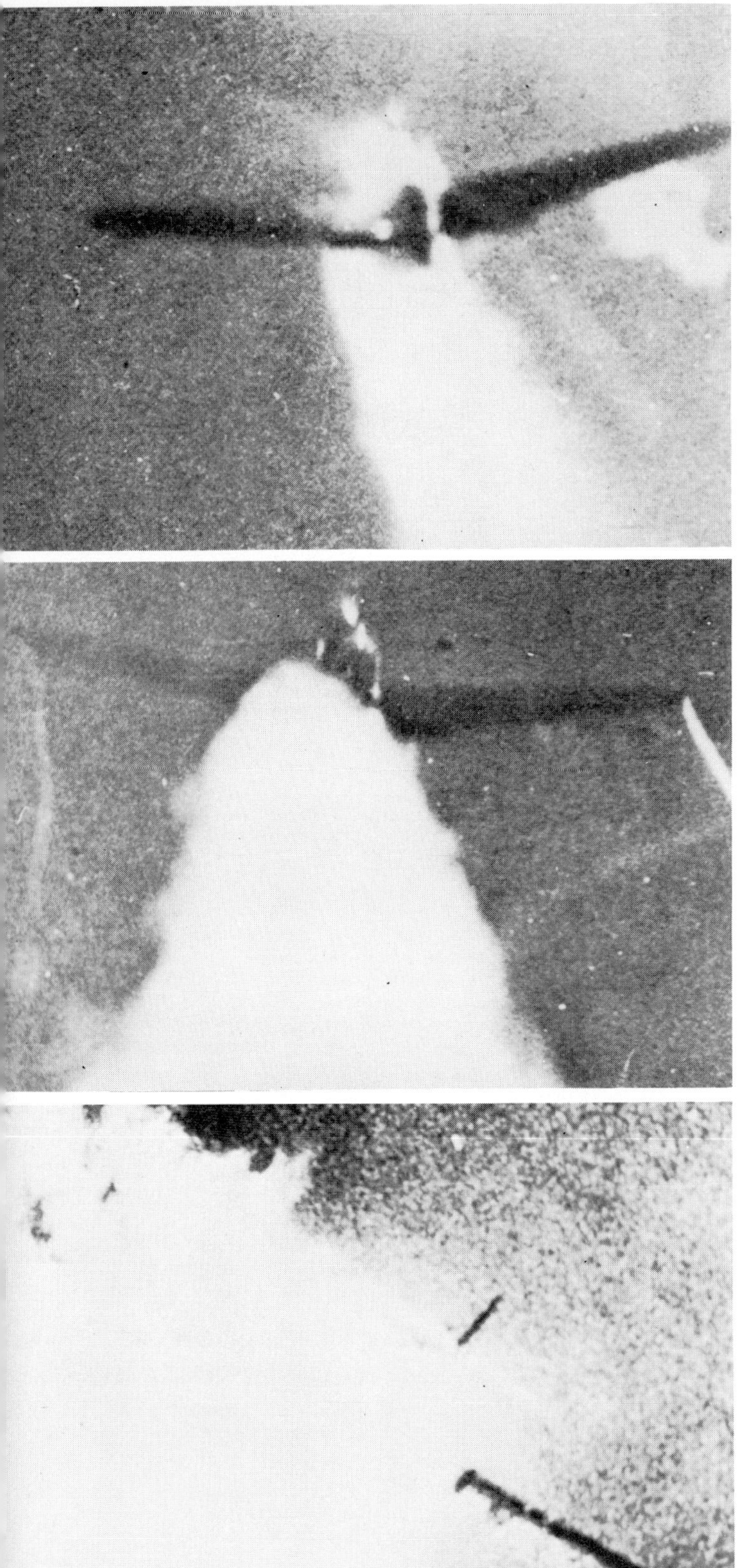

The gun camera of a Mustang captures the shooting down of a Messerschmitt Bf 109G. In the Ardennes offensive, the German fighter force took incredibly heavy losses. In the five days from December 23-27, 1944, over 260 pilots were killed, captured or missing.

Oberstlt. Bühligen, the last commander of JG 2 "Richthofen", is one of the few German fighter pilots to have achieved over 100 kills against the Allies in the West. The photograph shows Bühligen at Cherbourg in 1943, when he was commanding II./JG 2.

As the scale of bombing raids on Germany steadily mounted and German defense failed to come up with the hoped for successes, reproaches of cowardice on the part of fighter pilots began to make themselves heard in the highest Luftwaffe circles. In his capacity as Director of Fighters, Gen.-Lt. Galland firmly stood up for his pilots, to the point where his sharp criticisms led to his falling out of favor and being relieved of his command. Only in the last few weeks of the war — far too late — was he allowed to set up a special jet fighter unit, "Jagdverband 44" (JV 44). This brought local successes, but they came too late to have any significant influence on the course of events.Oberstlt. Michalski, shown here in his early days as a Leutnant with 4. Staffel/JG 53, commanded JG 4 and led it against the Belgian airfield of Le Culot on New Year's Day, 1945. The attack went awry and the unit suffered the heaviest rate of pilot losses of the day.

the lost machines of pilots who baled out unwounded must be added to these, so there is no reason to doubt the Allied figures.

In any event the German Air Force took a painful blow, for the losses amounted to roughly a third of the aircraft committed – a sacrifice which could have been avoided by better operational planning. But the most severe loss of the day was without doubt the death of a battle-hardened formation leader – twenty-four year-old *Hauptmann* Robert Weiss, who had commanded III./JG 54 since July 1944 and had 121 kills to his credit. *Oberleutnant* Bellaire, who had taken off with Weiss in the *Stabsschwarm*, was shot down and killed about two kilometers northwest of Vreden over the small village of Köckelwick.

Sunday, December 31, 1944

On December 30, US 8th Air Force heavy bombers had raided communications centers round Kassel, Mannheim and Kaiserslautern, and now it was the fuel industry's turn. This last day of 1944, a rugged year of war, saw yet another major air battle in the North German skies – a battle which cost the Americans 39 heavy bombers and Jagdgeschwader 1 twenty pilots killed, four missing and ten wounded. Among the German casualties were one Gruppe commander and 2 Staffel leaders, and the loss of these experienced men weighed especially heavy.

The bomber force of some 1,300 machines flew in over North Germany with the Hamburg-Harburg refineries and the hydrogenation plant at Misburg as its targets; it need scarcely be said that an escort of several fighter groups accompanied the Flying Fortresses. This massive incursion was met by the two "Reich" Geschwader, JG 300 and JG 301, with a total of 14 Staffeln. Two were equipped with Bf 109s and the rest Fw 190 A-8s, A-9s and the odd D-9, a total of 150-190 machines of which at least forty were to be lost.

Gruppenstab of III./JG 300 and 10 Staffel hoped to intercept the bombers around Langenhagen to the north of Hanover; but the Messerschmitts met the Allied fighter escort instead. The battle that followed cost III Gruppe the life of its commander, *Major* Hans-Karl Kamp; his machine, which bore the commander's chevrons on its fuselage, was shot down in flames.

10 Staffel lost *Unteroffizier* Ferdinand Dyk between the villages of Kaltenweide and Bissendorf near Altenhorst.

Meanwhile 1st Jagddivsion had scrambled the whole of II./JG 300 (the assault Gruppe) and directed them to quadrant "*Dora-Theodor*" from the south, directly in front of the leading formations of the mighty stream of bombers. As they were going into a frontal attack, the speckled grey Focke-Wulfs with the red-brown *Reichsverteidigung* bands on their fuselages were attacked from above by the fighter escort. The "air battle of Rotenburg" was under way. But one American bomber after another went down; the lead formation, 3rd Air Division, itself lost fourteen B-17s, half of them from 100th Bomb Group; and the Hamburg anti-aircraft guns accounted for ten more.

But this duel to the death over Rotenburg, near Bremen, took its toll of the German fighter force too. The first two assault fighters to go were shot down near Unterstedt, to the southwest of Rotenburg; *Feldwebel* Rudolf Müller and *Feldwebel* Kurt Schoepp were killed. 7 and 8 Staffeln each reported one pilot missing, quite possibly after crashing into the peatbogs of Borschelsmoor or Great Lohmoor. 8 Staffel suffered worst, with three losses. *Feldwebel* Arnezeder was killed and *Unteroffizier* Hieke wounded. *Leutnant* Norbert Graziadei, leader of 5 Staffel, was wounded over Rotenburg when his "Red 14" was hit by enemy fighters.

It was the US 78th and 364th Fighter Groups who made things most difficult for the German fighters as they tried to stick with the bombers and go on shooting them down. But meanwhile all three Gruppen of Jagdgeschwader 301 were flying in from the Salzwedel area, and elements of them soon reached the battle area and joined in. They too scored some kills on the heavy bombers, but themselves lost four machines including the "Red 19" flown by the leader of 10 Staffel, *Oberleutnant* Stahl. Stahl was wounded, as was Staffel comrade *Feldwebel* Penzin. *Unteroffizier* Hillert parachuted from the third machine, an Fw 190 A-8, but the fourth, "White 1", took its pilot, *Gefreiter* Marschik to his death.

The other formations simply never got through to the Rotenburg area, being intercepted and pinned down by the Americans. Three further pilots of JG 301 were shot down and killed, and one, *Fähnrich* Leopold of 2 Staffel, was wounded and bailed out.

The battle formed a second focus on the right flank of the bomber formations, southeast of Hamburg. There, astride the Elbe, American fighters in strength blocked off the attack by 6, 8, 11 and 12./JG 301. At about the same time the Flying Fortresses, their bomb-doors already open, turned sharply to the northwest and ran in on their target. When *Oberleutnant* Herzog led his 11 Staffel off from Stendal that morning, he can scarcely have

Fighter Losses on December 31, 1944

Units Involved	Killed/ Missing	Wounded	Total Casualties	Aircraft	Locale
II/JG1	3	1	4	Fw 190 A-8	Emsdetten, Mesum
I/JG2	1		1	Fw 190 D-9	Coblenz
III/JG4	2		2	Bf 109 K-4	Bad Durkheim
IV/JG4	2		2	Bf 109 G-14	Bastogne, Eisenberg
			4		
I/JG6	1		1	Fw 190 A-8	Oldenzaal
III/JG54		1	1	Fw 190 D-9	Limburg
IV/JG54	1		1	Fw 190 A-8	Osnabruck, Munster
III/JG77	3		3	Bf 109 K-4	Hemer, Munster
II/JG300	6	3	9	Fw 190 A-8	Altenhorst, Hoya
III/JG300	2		2	Bf 109 G-10	Rotenburg, Unterstedt
			11		
I/JG301	1	3	4	Fw 190 A-9/R11	Boitzenburg
II/JG301	7	1	8	Fw 190 A-9/R11	Fassberg
III/JG301	8	3	11	Fw 190 A-8	Luneberg, Riepe, Soltau
			23		
Total Losses (Germany and Western Theatre)	37	12	49 (including 1 Gruppe commander and 3 Staffel leaders killed, 1 Gruppe commander and 2 Staffel leaders wounded)		

imagined that he was about to lose four pilots. 11 Staffel crossed the big bend of the Elbe at Hitzacker and pressed on towards the Hamburg-Berlin railway line, where they came face to face with the Americans. *Feldwebel* Ernst Otto was shot down just beyond Lübtheen Forest. He crashed to his death in his Focke-Wulf "Yellow 4" near Düssin. About ten kilometers farther west, near Blücher, *Feldwebel* Karl Rienth was shot down and killed. "Black 18," piloted by twenty-two-year-old *Unteroffizier* Rolf Burghardt, has never been found. *Unteroffizier* Franz Leeb managed to bail out of his blazing Fw

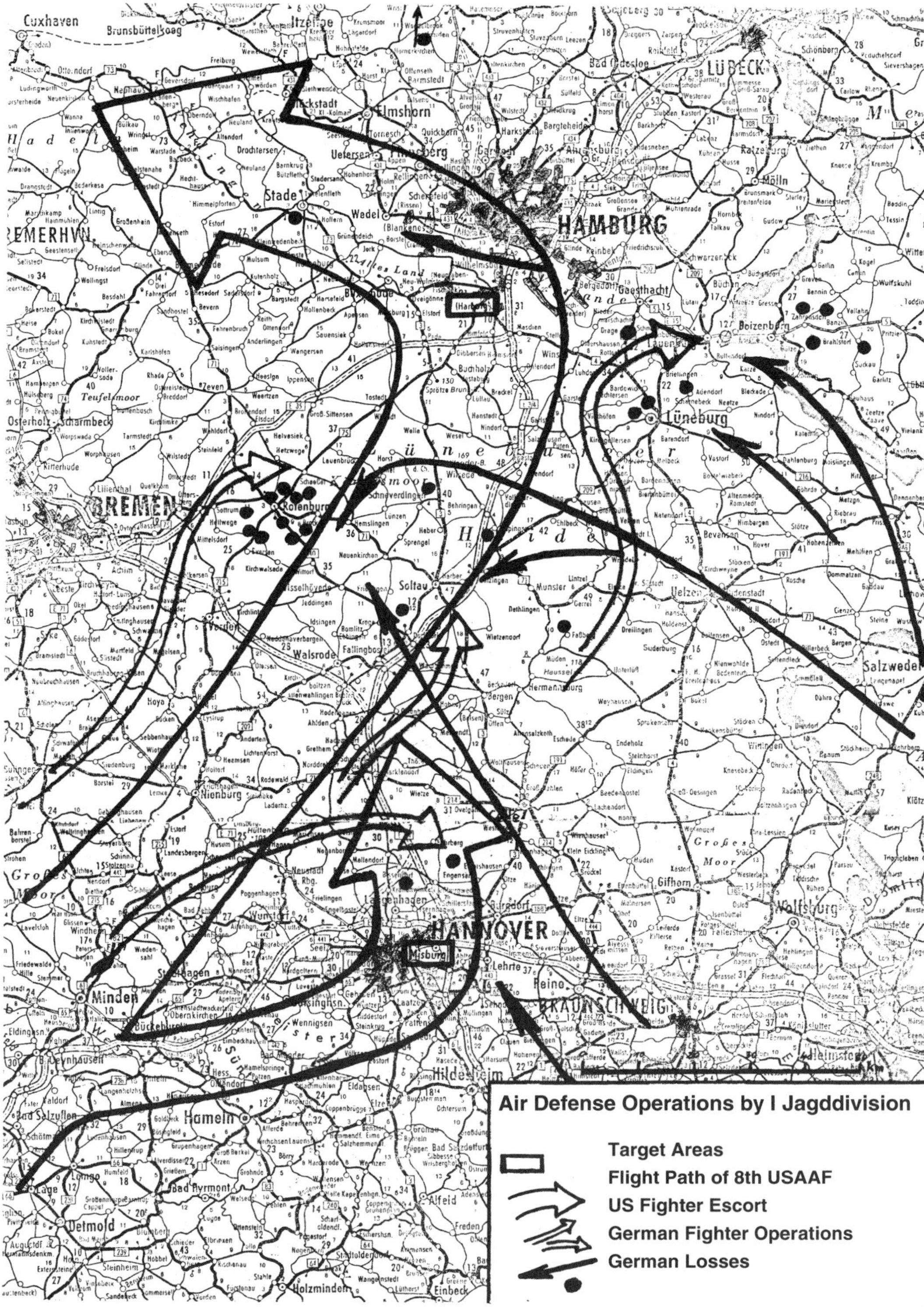
Air Defense Operations by I Jagddivision
Target Areas
Flight Path of 8th USAAF
US Fighter Escort
German Fighter Operations
German Losses
Hamburg
Hannover
Bremen
Lüneburg
Soltau
Misburg
Harburg

190 A-9, which crashed in Winsener Marsch near Eichholz. However *Oberleutnant* Walter, leader of the Staffel, was shot down and killed near Reichsstrasse 5. There was another parachute in the sky, after the *Kommandeur* of II./JG 301, *Hauptmann* Nölter, abandoned his badly shot-up "Dora 9."

In ones and twos the Germans went on trying to follow the bomber formation, which had meanwhile vanished into the midday haze and was headed for home. This pursuit cost 10 Staffel yet another casualty, the Americans shooting down *Leutnant* Max Müller near Stade. Thus 10 and 11 Staffel lost four pilots each on December 31 – six killed, one missing and one wounded.

But apart from several missions over the front, the bulk of the German air defense fighter units stayed on the ground on December 31; every available machine was required for the large-scale fighter operation planned for the following day – a special task of which only a very few pilots had any inkling. 6./JG 1, for instance, was still smarting from a skirmish with Typhoons of 137 Squadron RAF, in which three of their pilots had been killed in action over Emsdetten and Mesum. During the morning Spitfires from 411, 416 and 422 RCAF Squadrons were again making things hot over Münsterland, where they encountered about fifteen Messerschmitts, probably from III./JG 27. The Canadians attacked at once and scored four kills. III./JG 77 lost *Leutnant* Eck and *Oberfähnrich* von Rath killed in action. A single Focke-Wulf, the machine of *Oberfähnrich* Kraass of 14./JG 54, was shot down between Münster and Osnabrück by Flying-Officer Tapley.

Sector Control Middle Rhine at Darmstadt had scrambled two Staffeln of Jagdgeschwader 4 from the Rhine-Main area and directed them into the Palatinate to counter American fighter-bombers. This operation cost 16 Staffel two pilots – *Oberleutnant* Hans Schleef, the Staffel leader, with at least 98 kills to his credit, and *Unteroffizier* Klein.

Both Messerschmitts crashed in the area around Bad Dürkheim and exploded on impact. Farther north, near Eisenberg, 9 Staffel lost a Bf 109 K-4. The pilot, *Unteroffizier* Schwagerick, was still aboard the aircraft when it smashed into the ground. *Unteroffizier* Georg Schwarze of 12 Staffel failed to return to Egelsbach, raising the loss total to four pilots.

When at last the roar of battle faded from the skies and the BMW, Jumo and Daimler-Benz engines were silent, many a pilot was drawing up a mental balance-sheet. One does not know the outcome of their ponderings; no doubt their differing approaches, outlooks, imaginations and powers of expression led to a variety of answers. But it is safe to assume that the question in the forefront of their minds was whether there was any sense in carrying on the struggle. Nor can one tell how many gave way to such thoughts. After the long weeks of bitter, hopeless struggle, many a fighter pilot was looking forward to celebrating New Year's Eve 1945 by looking on the wine when it was red and so forgetting for a few hours at least the futility and the horror of it all, the daily toll in lives and the uncertainty over his own fate – to drowning his sorrows in fact. They were certainly in for a rude shock.

Early in the evening all passes were cancelled and all drink was forbidden. Before them stood the most demanding, sweeping operation to be flown by German fighter pilots in the whole of the War, and one that was to prove the costliest – Operation "Bodenplatte!"

Review of December

Even more than the preceding month, the past weeks had demonstrated the British and American pilots' superior mastery of operational flying in the foulest of weathers. The result was, that on most days of December the home air defense fighter pilots were again faced with superior numbers wherever they turned.

Moreover the Allies succeeded in gaining not only the initiative on the fronts but along with it control of the rear areas; as a result the month was marked by disruption of the communications system and destruction of air force installations. Thus in this last month of 1944, in bombing raids on as many as eighty airfields, 129 machines were destroyed on the ground and a further 140 damaged. In the last four days of the month the Allied air forces flew 5,500 heavy bomber sorties over Germany; I Jagdkorps shot down 63 bombers' and 23 escort fighters for the loss of 128 fighters. In the same period, according to *Generalmajor* Grabmann, AA artillery accounted for almost three times as many Allied aircraft. It follows that the German day-fighters could no longer be claimed to offer an effective defense.

The losses were devastating. From the beginning of the month to the opening of the German Ardennes offensive on December 16, 136 fighter pilots failed to return. In the four days from December 19-22, the figure was "only" 83. But in the week or so from December 23-31, the fighter units lost 316 pilots killed or missing, quite apart from the wounded. Over Christmas alone, Luftflotte Headquarters West and the units attached to it for the Ardennes offensive suffered over 260 aircrew casualties. On these figures it would appear that German fighter force casualties for December 1944 amounted to 500 pilots killed or missing, 35 taken prisoner and 194 wounded.

In face of attrition on this scale, it is remarkable to say the least that Operation "Bodenplatte", planned for New Year's Day, could take place at all. But, as few would now gainsay, the outcome of the War had long since been decided. It was of little help that the Luftwaffe High Command at last seemed to have appreciated that the Luftwaffe was no longer capable of influencing the course of events. The fighter pilots had become a forlorn hope, and their outstanding achievements will probably never receive the credit they deserve.

Notes

[1]Of which some 650 were serviceable.

[2]VHF R/T ground-air control with Wireless Set FuG 16 ZY (38.5 – 42.3 Mcs band). The ground station measured the slant range to the airborne transmitter and thus determined the accurate location of friendly aircraft. These figures were processed together with the location and height of the Allied units, so that the fighters could be directed onto the enemy aircraft with precision. Conversely, of course, friendly aircraft could be guided back to their various bases ("air defense fighter net" – "*Reichsjägerwelle*").

III

TAKEOFF AT DAWN
Operation "Bodenplatte"

Operation "Bodenplatte"

January 1, 1945

When the fighters' "Big Blow" planned for early November failed to come to fruition and the forces initially intended for it were cut to pieces supporting the Ardennes offensive, that seemed to be the end of the matter. Few people indeed still believed in the possibility of a mass operation by the Luftwaffe. But towards the end of December Headquarters, II Jagdkorps received a directive ordering them to mount a large-scale operation, to be carried out in the early morning of a day as yet unnamed. All available day fighters were to be committed to low-level attacks on the Allied air forces' ground organization in Holland, Belgium and France. The intention of Luftwaffe Headquarters Germany was effectively to take out the Allied fighter forces based on the Continent. They saw this as the only way to break the Allied fighter superiority once and for all, and thus to regain a position from which to mount a more effective defense against the bomber hordes. The aim of the operation was thus: to regain control of Western airspace, lost since the Allied landings.

The plan for Operation "Bodenplatte", one of the most controversial in the history of the German fighter force, could only have been born of desperation. Pilots were sent on an operation which failed to achieve its aim – and was bound to fail, for the fighter force had already been bled white. For months the pilots had felt themselves misjudged and had to carry this moral burden through their hopeless battles. To begin with it was Hitler who, faced with streams of Allied bombers pouring unhindered into Germany, repeatedly questioned the operational fitness of the fighter defense. Then the Commander-in-Chief of the Luftwaffe joined in with his accusations, which culminated in his announcing that the fighter force was manned entirely by cowards.

Göring's first meeting with the commanders of the day and night fighter forces at the beginning of November had borne little fruit. One side demanded greater efforts and better results, while the other – for the thousandth time – tried to put across the facts which underlay the real reasons for the "failures" – inadequate pilot reinforcements, lack of equipment and spares, and understrength, decimated fighter units.

True, the fighter pilots' appeals did not go wholly unheard. But the repeatedly called-for major and decisive operation amounted in fact to the senseless frittering away of the resources assembled for it, in battles over Germany and the Western theater. Back in autumn 1944 a massive counterstroke of the kind envisaged by Galland would indeed have stood a very good chance of succeeding. The estimated loss of as many as 400 German aircraft was seen as acceptable provided that at least the same number of bombers was destroyed. But in the meantime the losses in home air defense units had risen far above this figure without making any perceptible impression on the Allies. And by the time 1944 drew to its close the moment for the "Big Blow" was long past.

Yet it was only then that the Luftwaffe High Command, reacting like a wounded stag at bay, concocted a plan intended to change the situation at one stroke, a carefully drawn-up plan but one that was finally to tear the heart out of the remnants of the fighter force – Operation "Bodenplatte." Appointed to lead it was *Generalmajor* Peltz. As commander of II Jagdkorps he was responsible for air operations in the Ardennes offensive, thus usurping the role of *General der Jagdflieger* Galland, who had been sent into the desert, so to speak.

As a spell of bad weather had been deliberately chosen for the launching of the Arrny's counter-offensive, there was no choice but to hold the Air Force's operation over until the weather cleared. This happened towards the end of December. The plan lay under extreme security restrictions, but the small circle of those in the know were aware that "Bodenplatte" was to take place in the early morning of January 1, 1945.

Even today it is still widely supposed that the morning of New Year's Day was chosen for the operation simply because it was hoped that the general celebrations would impair the alertness of the Allied defense. Although this factor could not but operate in the undertaking's favor, the supposition was in fact a false one. Choice of the date for "Bodenplatte" was

Organization on January 1, 1945

Operation "Bodenplatte"

Luftflotte Headquarters West (Schmid)

Limburg

II Jagdkorps (Peltz)

Flammersfeld

3 Jagddivision	**Number of Gruppen**	**Targets**
Wiedenbruck		
Jagdgeschwader 1	3	St. Denis-Westrem (Belgium)
Jagdgeschwader 3	3	Eindhoven (Holland)
Jagdgeschwader 6	3	Volkel (Holland)
Jagdgeschwader 26	3	Brussels-Evère (Belgium)
with under command		
III/JG54	1	Brussels-Grimbergen (Belgium)
Jagdgeschwader 27	4	Brussels-Melsbrök (Belgium)
with under command		
IV/JG54	1	
Jagdgeschwader 77	3	Antwerp-Deurne (Belgium)
Middle Rhine Fighter Sector (Handrick)		
DARMSTADT		
Jagdgeschwader 2	3	St. Trond (Belgium)
Jagdgeschwader 4	3	Le Culot (Belgium)
Jagdgeschwader 11	3	Asch (Belgium)
Jagddivision 5 (Hantschel)		
KARLSRUHE		
Jagdgeschwader 53	3	Metz-Frescaty (France)

Elements of the following units also took part in the operation:
Einsatzstaffel/JG 104 (under command JG 26)
SG 4 (Close Support) (under command of JG2)
Kampfgeschwader 51 (Fighters)
Einsatzstaffel KG (J) 76 (under III.Gruppe)

Sources indicate that the pathfinder aircraft were drawn from the following night fighter units among others:

5./NJG 1
7./NJG1
9./NJG1
4./NJG3
10./NJG3
II/NJG 101

based wholly on the weather, and Monday, January 1, 1945 happened to be the first occasion on which conditions were suitable.

The outline plan for "Bodenplatte" had already come up at the December meeting of all Jagddivision commanders concerned. "Maintaining complete radio silence up to the moment of attack, all Geschwader will fly low over the frontier simultaneously in the early hours of the morning, to take the enemy air forces by surprise and catch them on the ground." Outward and return flight paths were laid down and all relevant navigational data was entered on the pilots' operation maps – but only on the other side of the German frontier, so that if a marked map fell into enemy hands, the bases of the various units could not be directly identified.

II Jagdkorps directed: "The Geschwader will receive air photos of the targets allotted to them and will use these at their briefings to take every pilot through the operation in detail." But such meticulous preparation was not always achieved, for to prevent the Allies learning of the operation in advance most briefings were not held until just before take-off and, in the short time available, many commanders were happy if they managed to get the bare essentials across to their pilots. When "Bodenplatte" got under way, there were still many who did not know what it was all about. They were thinking in terms of a reconnaissance in force over the front line or were content just to follow their leader.

So the fighter pilots got their instructions in briefings that ranged from the sparse in detail to, in a few instances, extravagant exhortations aimed at boosting morale by recalling the heroic fighter tradition, and by references to Führer and country and to what the German people expected of them. But these fighter pilots had already given of their best in courage and readiness to sacrifice themselves. The commanders who gave vent to such pathetic appeals either had not been on the operations of Christmas 1944 or happened to be giving their briefing in a higher headquarters operations room. Or perhaps they deliberately tried that January morning to paint their pilots a false picture.

In fact the pilots' morale was impressively high – far higher than could be expected after weeks of hard fighting and heavy casualties. In all units most of the men showed high confidence; the younger and less experienced in particular were enthusiastic about the plan and were convinced that they would be just as successful in taking the Allies by surprise and inflicting a damaging blow as their ground forces had been on December 16. They were not to know that the success of two weeks back had almost played itself out and that today's operation was doomed to failure before it even started. They had no real idea of the broader picture and, as always, the enemy was underestimated. It is true that never before that January morning had so many fighters stood on the tarmac ready for takeoff – but the bottom of the barrel had been scraped. In fact some 900[1] aircraft stood waiting to carry the German Jagdwaffe on its flight to destruction.

One or two night fighters were allotted to each Geschwader to guide it on a prearranged course over the front lines. These pathfinder aircraft then turned away and did not themselves take part in the operation. And the pilots received one other important instruction: "Look out for 'golden rain.'" This referred to marker flares used as additional navigational aids for the fighter pilots and to warn ground troops and the forward area anti-aircraft guns[2] of a low-level flight across the front by German fighters. But the use of "golden rain" was planned mainly for the area of the Middle Rhine Fighter Sector.

"But what will happen if 'golden rain' doesn't work for some reason or other? What if our AA gunners don't know it's us over their heads?" Whomever asked this question can scarcely have guessed that it would provide the heading for a tragic chapter in the history of the German fighter force.

•

German anti-aircraft was to play a disastrous part in "Bodenplatte" and, unintentionally of course, to make a substantial contribution to German fighter losses. At the turn of 1944/45 Luftflotte Headquarters West had under its command about 267 heavy and 277 medium or light flak batteries, and in addition to this there were 100 naval flak batteries on the Dutch North Sea coast. The path of most of the attacking formations lay over the sector of 16th Flak Division, with its fire control center at Doetinchem some fifteen miles east of Arnhem. This anti-aircraft unit, commanded by *Generalmajor* Deutsch, was over fifty batteries strong.

Again, the "Bodenplatte" briefing had said: "To achieve maximum surprise the plan is to attack all target airfields simultaneously, or as near simultaneous as possible" – an instruction that unfortunately did not quite work out and thus paved the way for a disaster.

The 16th Flak Division was indeed informed of the operation, but the passage of information was totally inadequate. Only a fraction of the batteries knew the times at which the German fighters were due to overfly their positions and free-fire zones. And then, when for one reason or another – a sudden ground mist on the field, having to wait for their pathfinders, or delays in forming up – the take-off of some Geschwader or Gruppe was delayed, nobody thought to pass the revised timings to the flak gunners. When strong fighter forces approached at the wrong times, the gunners took them for enemy aircraft and let fly at them. The results were catastrophic. Any aircraft that the Allies didn't manage to shoot down were knocked out of the sky by German batteries – to the tune, it is estimated, of about 100 machines.

But this still lay in the future. Now ten Jagdgeschwadern with a total of 33 Gruppen were standing waiting for the order to go. Under every machine hung a 65 gallon drop-tank. Just before takeoff the pilots received their final orders: "Mission Hermann, 1.1.1945, time 0920."

The codeword "Hermann" signified time of attack and this therefore meant that all units were to go into the attack on the Allied airfields at twenty past nine.

The weather in the operational area was more or less as forecast; by and large the sky was clear to overcast, with rather heavier cloud cover over the Belgium-Dutch border; visibility was ideal and the pilots had no need to worry about rain. But despite this the operation did not get under way on time; in many areas, especially in northwest Germany, an unexpected ground mist suddenly came up, causing delays in take-off with the disastrous consequences described above.

But even if this large-scale operation did not always achieve the hoped-for degree of surprise, the Allies could scarcely have reckoned with a mass attack by the Luftwaffe, least of all on New Year's morning 1945. The Luftwaffe succeeded in causing considerable confusion and inflicting substantial damage, most of all in the 2nd TAF area, that is in the British sector of the front. Many of the British, and of the Americans too, were at that first moment hardly in a state to produce an instant defensive reaction. But as the initial shock wore off, strong and increasing counter-action on their part weakened or frustrated every low-level attack. It was not until after the end of the War that the Germans fully realized that a number of Allied airfields – including some of those listed as primary targets such as Antwerp, Le Culot or Volkel – were untouched or were engaged only by a few machines. Other fields, among them Knocke and Ophoven, were attacked during Operation "Bodenplatte", because they were listed as secondary targets or were mistaken for the allotted target. And thanks to inadequate

Airfield		Allied Code No.	Effectiveness of Attack*
Antwerp-Deurne	(Belgium)	B-70	3
Asch	(Belgium)	Y-29	2
Brussels-Evère	(Belgium)	B-56	1
Brussels-Melsbrök	(Belgium)	B-60	2
Eindhoven	(Holland)	B-78	1
Ghent/St. Denis-Westrem	(Belgium)	B-61	1
Gilze-Rijen	(Holland)	B-77	4
Heesch	(Holland)	B-88	4
Knocke	(Belgium)		4
Le Culot	(Belgium)	A-89	3
Maldegem	(Belgium)	B-65	1
Metz-Frescaty	(France)	Y-34	2
Ophoven	(Belgium)	Y-32	4
St. Trond	(Belgium)	A-92	2
Volkel	(Holland)	B-80	3
Wönsdrecht	(Holland)	B-79	4
Ursel	(Belgium)	B-67	2
and Probably:			
Beauvechain	(Belgium)		
Helmond	(Holland)		
Grave	(Holland)		

*1 = Successful
2 = moderately successful
3 = not attcked/only intermittently attacked
4 = attacked by mistake/as opportunity target. No effect.

aerial reconnaissance it happened on occasion that a strong fighter force attacked an airfield, Grimbergen for instance, only to find it unoccupied except for a few machines.

There are conflicting data on the losses suffered by the Allies that New Year's morning. The British figures are 144 Allied aircraft destroyed and 84 damaged, while American sources report 134 total losses and 62 damaged beyond repair. These figures look very low and may well in fact not represent the overall losses by those in 2nd TAF and 9th US TAF areas respectively.

The German Air Force High Command report on "Bodenplatte", dated

Allied Aircraft Losses Caused by Operation "Bodenplatte"				
Source	**Destroyed on Ground**	**Shot Down**	**Total Destroyed**	**+Damaged**
German				
OKW communique 1/2/45	400	79	479	100
Situation Report 1/2/45			507	
OKL Report 1/27/45	402	65 (+12)	467 (+12)	114
Bartz, Clostermann,				
Feuchter,			800	
Galland			400	
Allied:				
RAF (2 TAF)			144	84
USAAF			196	
			150*	50

*30 USAAF, 120 RAF

January 27, 1945, states that photo-reconnaissance of eight airfields showed 279 machines destroyed on the ground (239 single-engine, 21 twin-engine and 19 four-engine). This probably does not tell the whole story, and on top of it the German fighters shot down 65-75 Allied aircraft. Thus visual reconnaissance reports on seven other airfields give a total of 123 machines (113 single-engine). The above figures do not include the 114 damaged aircraft observed on all these airfields.

The inescapable point is that the Allies lost five hundred aircraft at a stroke – a loss that they were certainly able to make good in something under a fortnight. And it caused scarcely a ripple in Allied aircrew strength. For the Luftwaffe it was a very different story.

Details of German losses follow the accounts of individual units' parts in the operation.

Bases of II Jagdkorps
Operation "Bodenplatte"

Unit/Sub-Unit	Aircraft	Location
JG1 (*Oberstlt.* Ihlefeld)		
I Gruppe (*Hptm.* Hackbarth i.V.)	Fw 190 A-8	Twenthe
II Gruppe (*Hptm.* Staiger)	Fw 190 A-8	Drope
III Gruppe	Bf 109 G-14	Rheine
JG2 (*Oberstlt.* Bühligen)		
I Gruppe (*Hptm.* Hrdlicka)	Fw 190 A-8/A-9	Merzhausen
II Gruppe (*Hptm.* Schröder)	Bf 109 G-14/K-4	Nidda, Ettingshausen
III Gruppe (*Hptm.* Lemke)	Fw 190 D-9	Altenstadt
JG3 (*Oberstlt.* Bär)		
I Gruppe (*Oblt.* Seidl i.V.)	Bf 109 G-10/G-14	Paderborn
III Gruppe (*Hptm.* Langer)	Bf 109 G-14/K-4	Lippspringe
IV Gruppe	Fw 190 A-8	Gutersloh
JG4 (*Major* Michalski)		
I Gruppe (*Hptm.* Steinmann)	Bf 109 G-14/K-4	Darmstadt-Greisheim
II Gruppe (*Major* Schröder)	Fw 190 A-8	Babenhausen
IV Gruppe (*Hptm.* Laube)	Bf 109 G-14/K-4	Rhine-Main
JG6 (*Oberstlt.* Kogler)		
I Gruppe (*Hptm.* Elstermann)	Fw 190 A-8	Delmenhorst
II Gruppe (*Hptm.* Naumann)	Fw 190 A-8	Quakenbruck, Vechta
III Gruppe (*Major* Kühle)	Bf 109 G-10/G-14	Bissel
JG11 (*Major* Specht)		
I Gruppe (*Hptm.* Kirchmayr)	Fw 190 A-8	Darmstadt-Greisheim
II Gruppe (*Hptm.* Leonhardt)	Bf 109 G-14/K-4	Zellhausen
III Gruppe (*Hptm.* v.Fassong)	Fw 190 A-8	Gross-Ostheim
JG26 (*Oberstlt.* Priller)		
I Gruppe (*Major* Borris)	Fw 190 D-9	Furstenau
II Gruppe (*Major* Hackl)	Fw 190 D-9	Nordhorn
III Gruppe (*Hptm.* Krupinski)	Bf 109 G-14/K-4	Plantlunne
JG27 (*Major* Franzisket)		
I Gruppe (*Hptm.* Schade)	Bf 109 G-14/K-4	Rheine
II Gruppe (*Hptm.* Hoyer i.V.)	Bf 109 G-14	Rheine
III Gruppe (*Hptm.* Clade)	Bf 109 K-4	Hesepe
IV Gruppe (*Hptm.* Dudeck)	Bf 109 G-10	Achmer
JG53 (*Oberstlt.* Bennemann)		
II Gruppe (*Major* Meimberg)	Bf 109 G-14/K-4	Malmsheim
III Gruppe (*Major.*Götz)	Bf 109 G-14	Kirrlach
IV Gruppe (*Hptm.*Müer)	Bf 109 G-14	St Echterdingen

JG54 (*Oblt.* Dortenmann i.V.)		
III Gruppe (*Oblt.* Dortenmann i.V.)	Fw 190 D-9	Furstenau
IV Gruppe	Fw 190 A-8/A-9	Vorden
JG77 (*Major* Leie)		
I Gruppe	Bf 109 G-14	Dortmund
II Gruppe	Bf 109 K-4	Bonninghardt
III Gruppe (*Hptm.* Köhler)	Bf 109 K-4	Dusseldorf-Lohausen
Schlachtgeschwader 4 (*Oberstlt.* Druschel)		
III Gruppe	Fw 190 F-8	Cologne-Wahn
Einsatzstaffel/JG104	Fw 190 D-9	Fürstenau
KG (J) 51 (*Hptm.* Unrau)	Me 262A	Rheine
Einsatzstaffel III./KG (J) 76 (*Hptm.* Lukesch)	Ar 234B	Münster-Handorf

The Sacrificial Flight of Jagdgeschwader 1

Barely ten miles from the German frontier, in the triangle Oldenzaal-Hengelo-Enschede, lies the airfield of Twenthe, which I Gruppe of Jagdgeschwader 1 had shared with *Hauptmann* Rath's I./NJG 2 since being transferred there in mid-December 1944. On New Year's Eve they still knew no details of the following morning's major operation, but they smelled a rat because everyone was confined to quarters. When *Hauptmann* Hackbarth gave them the details of "Bodenplatte" at his briefing on the morning of January 1, they felt easier in their minds. At least the outward flight would be safe enough, most of them reckoned, because they would be flying mainly over ground held by their own troops. They were to come in over the sea to attack their target, Maldegem airfield about 10 miles east of Bruges.

Two Ju 88s were to serve as pathfinders. The first *Schwarm* was airborne at 0730. There are woods to the east and south of the field, and they swung to port onto the line of the railway and the arrow-straight Hengelo-Oldenzaal

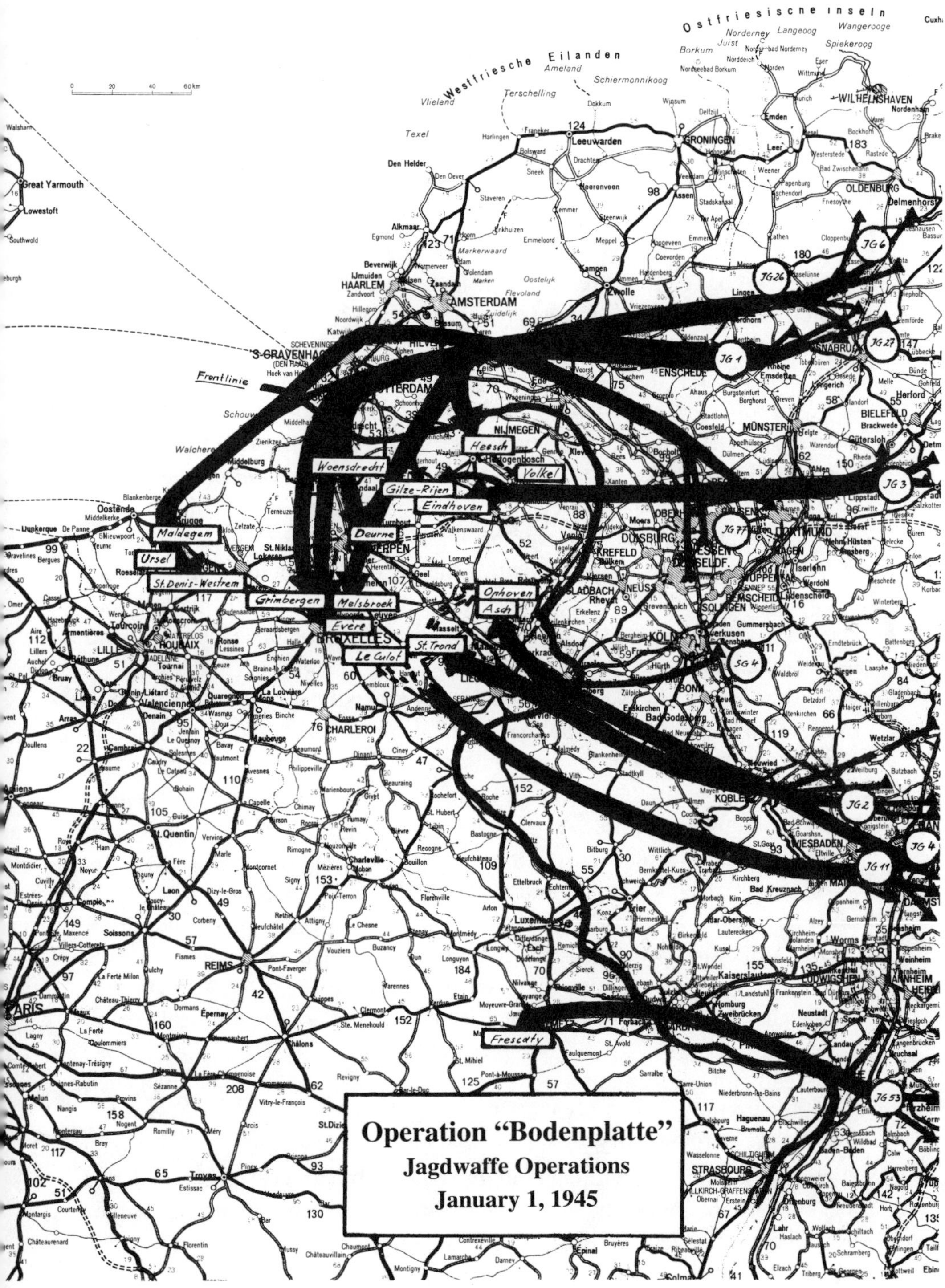

Operation "Bodenplatte"
Jagdwaffe Operations
January 1, 1945

road before setting course for the southern tip of the Zuider Zee. They were followed at a few minutes' interval by the Messerschmitts of III Gruppe from Rheine, which was to join them in the attack on Maldegem – some 55 aircraft in all, led by Hauptmann Hackbarth in his Fw 190 A-8 and the rest of I *Gruppenstab.*

However the outward flight was not to prove so easy as they had thought, for the pilots in I Gruppe's four Staffeln were scarcely to know that the German AA had not been fully briefed on German fighter movements. Large fighter formations like this, especially if they were still flying low in the coastal area, were bound to be hostile – so the gunners reasoned: By the time they realized their mistake, it was in most cases too late.

Unteroffizier Comtesse of 1 Staffel and *Unteroffizier* Kilian of 3 Staffel were the first to die in this operation; but south of Rotterdam the flak brought down a third machine, 3 Staffel's "Yellow 15." Its pilot, *Unteroffizier* Heinz Böhmer, did his best to fly east along the Old Maas and regain friendly territory, but the Focke-Wulf went in at Strijen, about eight miles southeast of Dordrecht. I Gruppe's pilots could scarcely contain their anger with their comrades in the anti-aircraft batteries, for they had no idea of the circumstances. At this moment the temptation to break radio silence was great; but it was maintained.

Now they had the North Sea coast just north of the Hague ahead of them; the sea looked leaden and uninviting in the grey light of dawn. In a few minutes the leaders were over the Island of Schouwen; still the enemy did not seem to have spotted them, for there was no sign of defensive action so far. Despite this the whole formation looked rather disorderly; the loss of three pilots had been unsettling, but fortunately nobody lost his nerve.

Between Blankenberge and Knokke the Focke-Wulfs turned south towards Bruges and then headed east again. Over Bruges five aircraft of 4 Staffel broke formation and headed on southward. *Oberleutnant* Meinhoff with this tiny force had gone off to see if there were any worthwhile targets on the airstrip some six miles south of Maldegem between Knesselare and Ursel.

Meanwhile the remainder of I Gruppe and elements of III Gruppe went in to attack Maldegem. They had planned to make five runs, but something went wrong with this idea. It later emerged that in the general confusion a number of aircraft had without realizing it tagged on to II Gruppe, which had meanwhile appeared on the scene, and these pilots suddenly found themselves back over the St. Denis-Westrem field. III Gruppe's Messerschmitts reached

Maldegem without interference. However, they found it difficult to spot targets on the ground and so made a strafing run in the hope of hitting something. So it came about that Maldegem did not receive the full weight of the attack; but eleven parked Spitfires of 485 Squadron RAF were set on fire and two others damaged, leaving this squadron with only five serviceable aircraft.

After the attack III Gruppe turned away to the north to start its homeward flight. The unit had lost two machines, the pilots, *Leutnant* Guha and *Fahnenjunkerfeldwebel* Wichard, being taken prisoner by the British. In a few minutes, they reckoned, they would all be safely back over their own lines. But fate had decided otherwise. No one knows whether *Feldwebel* Wilhelm Kraüter's machine was hit by flak or fell to an enemy fighter; whatever it was may have happened back over Maldegem. In any case "Green 23" suddenly plunged straight down and smashed into the ground near Dirksland on Overflakkee Island.

Neither German nor Allied sources reveal whether the diversionary attack on Ursel was successful. In any event *Unteroffizier* Fritzsche was shot down by enemy AA before reaching the target and captured by the British. The flight leader, *Oberleutnant* Meinhoff, also failed to get back to Twenthe. "Red 8", which he was flying on this sortie, was hit by flak on the way home and crashed, Meinhoff's body being found near Breda.

Just after 0900 the Focke-Wulfs of II./JG 1 roared in from the southwest over the St. Denis-Westrem field. After taking off from Drope, to the north of Rheine, the thirty machines at first followed almost the same flight path as the other two Gruppen. Then they broke up into Staffeln and flew between the Leie and the Schelde, both these rivers leading them on to the airfield, situated to the south of Ghent. It was a long time since the Flemish had seen a German aircraft, and at first they took them for Spitfire squadrons flying back into St. Denis-Westrem after an operation. But the Jagdgeschwader 1 pilots knew that their attack would not take the enemy completely by surprise, for the widespread dogfights over the Maldegem area could scarcely have passed unnoticed.

Stationed at St. Denis-Westrem were three Polish squadrons of 131 Wing RAF. All three were airborne – in more senses than one – in the early hours of January 1, 1945. 302 Squadron was the first back, landing with its tanks almost dry right into its own flak and the hail of bullets from the German fighters' guns. For the German attack struck at the very moment the Spitfires were taxying in or about to touch down. One Spitfire crashed after being hit by flak and the JG 1 aircraft destroyed a further nine. Fires blazed up all over the airfield.

Two German fighters went down just near the field. One was that of the *Kommandeur* of I./JG 1, whose target was actually Maldegem. *Hauptmann* Georg Hackbarth, victor in thirty air combats, fell near Ghent on this New Year's morning. The second Focke-Wulf, "Blue 5" of 5 Staffel, crashed at the edge of the village of Zwijnaarde. The pilot, Latvian volunteer Harrys Klints, was thrown clear on impact. *Feldwebel* Klints, who with five other officers of the "Latvian Army Fighter Aviation" had been assigned to various fighter units of the Luftwaffe in October 1944, and who at the end of December was the last of the Latvian volunteers still in action, was killed. Several years later he was buried at Lommel cemetery.

When the German attack on St. Denis-Westrem began, the Allies immediately recalled the two other squadrons. Only a few minutes after the first Spitfires had landed in the German fighters' fire, 308 Squadron was closing in on the airfield from the northeast. The Polish pilots were about twelve miles from Ghent when they spotted the first Focke-Wulfs over Kokeren; they quickly shot down four of the German fighters. Among the downed pilots were two of 5 Staffel: *Unteroffizier* Ardner, who bailed out and was picked up by the English, and *Leutnant* von Johannides, who was killed. Also shot down and killed in this battle was *Feldwebel* Paul Mayr of 8 Staffel.

As the Spitfires reached their smoke-shrouded base, JG 1 was just making another low-level run. Six parked fighters belonging to 317 Squadron went up in flames; *Feldwebel* Fritz Hofmann of 3 Staffel destroyed a four-engine machine standing on the edge of the field and in that very instant was himself hit by the airfield's light AA. His sortie ended in a prison camp.

As his comrades had not had time to watch Hofmann crash, he was initially listed as missing. The Germans had no time for further runs, for they had their work cut out keeping the Spitfires off their tails. The British were gradually gaining the upper hand, and a vicious dogfight now flared up over Ghent and the rolling plains of East Flanders.

•

"I must get out!" – a voice suddenly came up loud and clear on the radio; and the pilots in their Focke-Wulfs winced. Those who had not got a dogfight on their hands at the moment tried to spot the machine they presumed to be

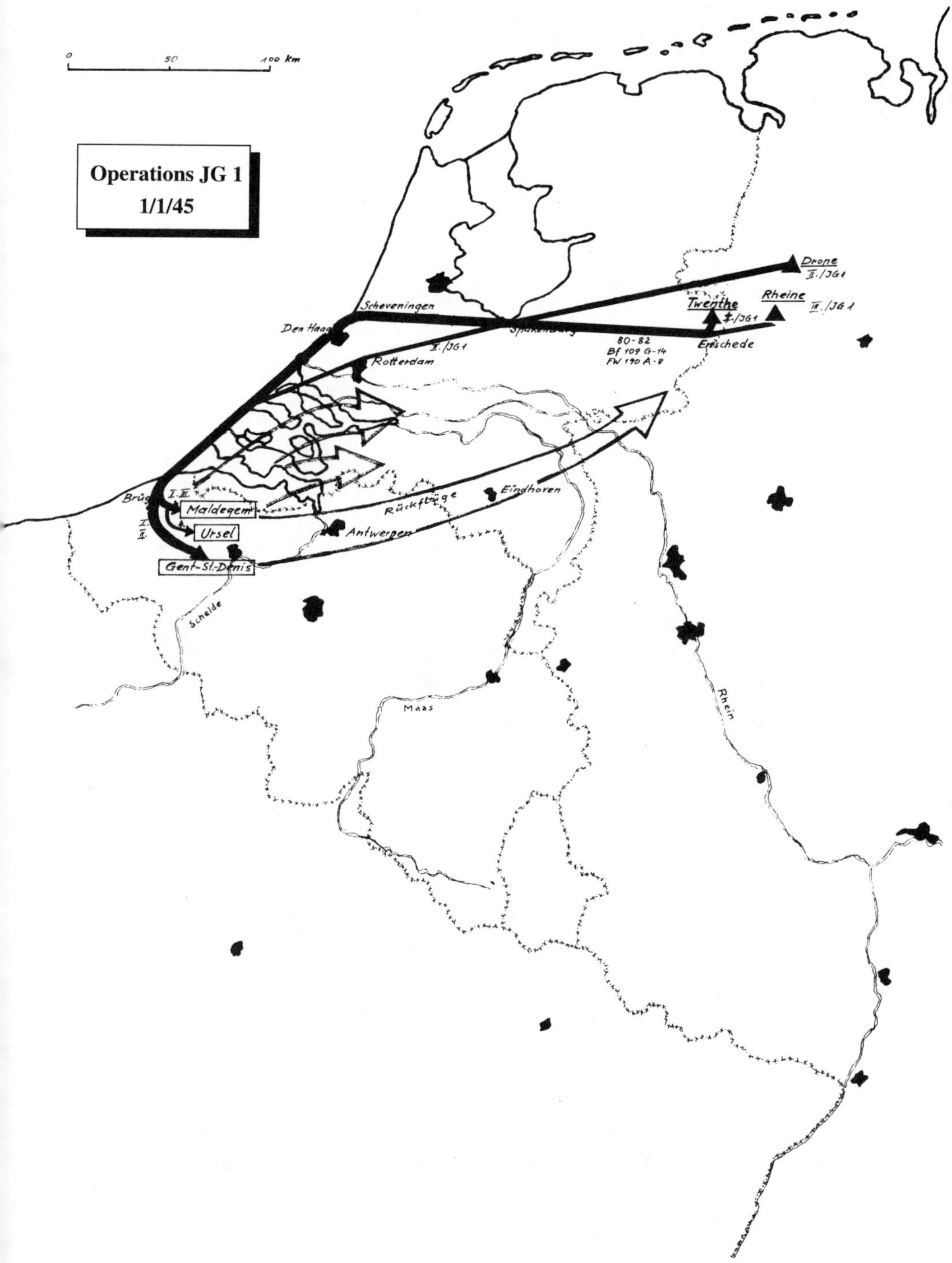

Operations JG 1
1/1/45
0
50
100 km
Drone
II./JG1
Rheine
III./JG1
Twenthe
I./JG1
Scheveningen
Den Haag
80-82
Bf 109 G-14
FW 190 A-8
Enschede
Rotterdam
Eindhoven
Rückflüge
Maldegem
Ursel
Antwerpen
Gent-St.-Denis
Schelde
Maas
Rhein

plunging earthward. No one seemed to know quite what to do. Was radio silence still in effect? The events of the past fifteen minutes had made anything of that kind worse than pointless. No one knew whose mouth had uttered this desperate call or whether the pilot was still in a position to bail out. Only one thing was clear – the number of German machines going down was mounting steadily. *Leutnant* Swoboda's 5 Staffel was already down to half strength after losing five pilots.

Polish Spitfire pilots Stanowski and Breyner despatched two Focke-Wulfs each, and Flight-Lieutenant Chojnacki, after destroying another Fw 190, was himself shot down and killed. After a duel over Ghent a Focke-Wulf went down to crash in the riverside depots of the Schelde, but in the heat of battle no one could make out its tactical sign.

At last the mission was over, one which had cost JG 1 twenty-four pilots. Six of them were in Allied hands, and the fate of four remains unresolved. Allied records show that the wreckage of nineteen German aircraft was found in the general area of Ghent. Even though the Allies losses in material exceeded those of Jagdgeschwader 1, with 32 Spitfires destroyed in all, eighteen of them on St. Denis-Westrem, his casualties were minimal. Only one pilot each from 308 and 317 Squadrons was killed in action.

Oberst Ihlefeld, *Kommodore* of Jagdgeschwader 1, made no secret of his bitterness. He too had guessed well enough how a desperate mission of this kind was bound to end. There can be no doubt that lack of quality and quantity in pilot reinforcements and over-hasty mounting of the operation were the reasons why, of the Jagdgeschwader 1 aircraft which took off on Operation "Bodenplatte", one third was sacrificed to no good purpose.

The End of Jagdgeschwader 2 "Richtofen"

On the northern slopes of the Taunus, a bare twenty miles as the crow flies from Frankfurt-on-Main and looking south onto the Usingen-Idstein road, lies Merzhausen airfield, where I Gruppe, Jagdgeschwader 2 "*Richthofen*", had been stationed since the beginning of October 1944. On January 1, it was still dark when the pilots of all four Staffeln left their billets in Altweilnau, Niederlauken and Wilhelmsdorf for the short journey to the airfield.

The briefing was soon over. The Staffel leaders themselves had only been told the target in the small hours, and there was little time left to explain the concept of the operation to the thirty pilots. So the watchword was: "Simply follow me and stay close!"

Slowly the trucks carrying the pilots in their black leather flying-suits pulled onto the airstrip. Feelings were mixed; some were still muttering darkly about missing their New Year's party. Despite everything, a few had managed to have a drink or two; others seemed more cheerful, even high-spirited. They only realized how this operation was once again going to stretch their flying skill to the limit to the extent that they recalled how every sortie of the past few weeks had turned into a dogfight with no quarter given, in which in the end they had to resign themselves to the Allies monstrous superiority. But "Bodenplatte" was to exceed their worst fears, although the whole operation could in fact have been a success – if the fighter force had been properly and methodically prepared for it.

In other Gruppen the picture was the same; there too the "couldn't care less" attitude would soon disappear, when just an hour later Jagdgeschwader 2 crossed the Ardennes front. A complete Jagdgeschwader, and a famous one rich in tradition at that, was doomed to defeat even before it ever reached the target. It was to prove of little avail that the Jagdgeschwader flew over 90 strong, or that I and III Gruppen were equipped with the Focke-Wulf Fw 190 D-9, some of them straight off the line and still lacking their tactical markings.

Hauptmann Hrdlicka complied with his orders, and it was only just before the operation began that he opened the sealed envelope he had received on the evening of December 23. It contained the operation instruction for the Richthofen Geschwader which up to that moment had remained secret:

> "Take-off 0800. Form up over quadrants '*Paula-Quelle* 4 and 5' and wait for II and III Gruppen to join. Target: St. Trond airfield (Belgium). Attack to be carried out in conjunction with Schlachtgeschwader 4 (*Oberst* Druschel)."

The inertia starters whirred softly. The mechanics stood back. The Jumo engines with all their 1,770hp sprang into life, to be throttled back and then run up. Soon the machines were rolling along the perimeter taxiway. In the grey half-light I Gruppe took off, throwing up clouds of snow from the runway behind them. The airfield was so large that the woods surrounding it caused them no problem. The "long noses" took off southward and straightaway turned west; to port the Grosser Feldberg fell away astern, and over Camberg the squadron set course for the designated assembly area over Coblenz.

From Nidda airfield, running from southwest to northeast along the stream of the same name, the Messerschmitts of II Gruppe under *Hauptmann* Schröder were lifting off, while the rest of the Jagdgeschwader took off from Ettingshausen and Altenstadt. Between Giessen and Frankfurt the whole formation turned west to follow up I Gruppe. For Jagdgeschwader 2 Operation "Bodenplatte" had begun.

Ten minutes later the Staffeln of III Gruppe, flying from Wetzlar and Weilburg, reached the Westerwald – when suddenly black smoke began to pour from the engine cowling of *Unteroffizier* Altpeter's D-9, blinding the pilot. Seconds later, almost before the others had time to see what was happening, the engine was in flames. The others wanted to call him up and tell him to bale out, but that would have broken radio silence. *Unteroffizier* Fritz Altpeter of 11./JG 2 did not bale out; he crashed to his death in his "Yellow 4" near Dierdorf to become Jagdgeschwader 2's first casualty of the New Year. Having formed up over the Rhine-Moselle triangle, the formations spread out and flew on west-northwest towards the High Eifel; from there they would head northwest to the line of the Meuse. Between Aachen and Liege they would be joined by the formation made up of elements of Schlachtgeschwader 4, flying from the Cologne and Bonn fields under *Oberst* Alfred Druschel, holder of the Knight's Cross with Oak Leaves and Swords.

Druschel took off from Cologne-Wahn with the Focke-Wulf F-8s[3] of III./SG 4. Between Düren and Zülpich he set course for Aachen, the first German city to be captured by the Allies. Even before they joined up with the machines of the *Richthofen* Geschwader, the ground-attack aircraft came under fire from light and heavy AA. This claimed four of their pilots, One of these F-8s was piloted by *Oberst* Druschel. All that is known is that he was hit and must have come down somewhere south of Aachen. The fate of this *Geschwaderkommodore* from Wiesbaden remains a mystery, and his name is still on the register of missing in action.

Jagdgeschwader 2 was also greeted by heavy anti-aircraft fire over the front, and likewise suffered losses. *Unteroffizier* Dost was shot down and killed, while *Unteroffizier* Breitweg was taken prisoner. 4 Staffel lost half its pilots that day. *Unteroffizier* Optenhostert was shot down by German anti-aircraft fire and killed, but fellow Staffel member *Unteroffizier* Wilkens, as well as *Feldwebel* Hohenberg, who was initially reported missing, fell into enemy hands.

Meanwhile the Jagdgeschwader's leading formations were approaching their target. St. Trond was familiar ground to the Germans. During the past year II and IV Gruppen of NJG 1 and I Gruppe of NJG 3 had alternately been based there. As late as October 1944, the night-fighter ace *Major* Wolfgang Schnaufer, known to the British as the "Ghost of St. Trond", was still operating from here with his IV./NJG 1 Night against incursions by RAF Bomber Command. The field itself, the hangars and the camouflage were just the same; only the occupants and the code number had changed – A-92 instead of 309. And now there stood on it, parked in long lines, the Thunderbolts of the 48th and 404th Fighter Groups, 9th US TAF.

As the German fighters began their low-level attacks, the airfield's antiaircraft defenses opened up with a withering fire. Allied pilots already airborne on operational sorties had warned by radio of the approach of a strong German fighter force. This sealed Jagdgeschwader 2's fate. Almost every Staffel lost some aircraft, and the attack on St. Trond was the last ever seen or heard of many a pilot. 12 Staffel lost "Blue 1" with *Unteroffizier* Adolf Redlich, then the Messerschmitt of *Unteroffizier* Bollwerk of 5./JG 2 was shot down. *Leutnant* Werner Edelhoff of the *Gruppenstab* was brought down and taken prisoner near St. Trond. II Gruppe emerged relatively unscathed with two killed, but returned to base without its commander. *Hauptmann* Georg Schröder survived the crash but was captured. For the Geschwader this was naturally a painful blow, as good COs had become something of a rarity in the fighter force.

But the German pilots were not altogether unsuccessful, even if the American fighters they had set on fire and destroyed on the ground represented only a small proportion of St. Trond's aircraft strength. And still ahead of them lay the return flight, which took Jagdgeschwader 2 in a wide sweep to the north, recrossing the German frontier near Venlo.

The machines turned back toward the east. It was then that 10 Staffel lost its sixth pilot; *Leutnant* Christfried Clemens came down with his Fw 190 D-9 near Mierlo. Two of the Geschwader's Staffeln, the 4th and 10th, had been decimated, losing half their strength. As January 1, 1945 drew to a close, one of the most experienced and successful Geschwader in the whole German fighter force had received a mortal blow. The losses amounted to some 40% of the force committed to the operation – 23 pilots killed or missing, ten taken prisoner and four wounded.

It was to be at least a fortnight before *Richthofen* Geschwader would again be in a position to mount a major defensive operation.

Success at Eindhoven

A lone Fw 190 A-9 stood on the tarmac at Störmede to carry *Oberstleutnant* Bär, commander of Jagdgeschwader 3 "*Udet*", to join his I Gruppe at Paderborn. Störmede was home ground to this battle-hardened commander for, before moving there from Effurt-Bindersleben with *Stab* JG 3 at the end of November 1944, he had been based at Störmede. It was from there that Bär, at the time with II Gruppe, Jagdgeschwader 1, had flown on April 22, 1944 to chalk up his 200th kill by shooting down a Liberator. Since then the war in the air had exacted such a high toll in lives that the only way out was an operation designed to destroy a large proportion of the Allied fighter forces on the ground and so weaken the German fighters' "Number One Threat." That was why *Oberstleutnant* Bär, like the other Geschwader commanders, was about to go over the forthcoming mission with his Gruppe commanders so that they could then brief their Gruppen.

There had been a preliminary briefing on the afternoon or evening of December 31, at which the pilots of the Jagdgeschwader had been told something of Operation "Bodenplatte", although security had prevented them being told the details. At Paderborn *Oberleutnant* Seidel, the acting CO of I Gruppe, gave his 30 or so pilots a run-down on their mission. *Hauptmann* Langer was doing the same for his III Gruppe and *Leutnant* Müller, 16 Staffel leader and acting CO, for IV Gruppe, the former *Sturmgruppe*.

In Jagdgeschwader 3 too, passes were withdrawn and alcohol forbidden as soon as the briefing ended, and the only thing left for the pilots to do was to go to bed. But on the airfields activity was intense. The army of ground crews worked without pause to get the slender Messerschmitts and the potent Focke-Wulfs ready for the morning's big show. On Luftflotte orders, the FuG 25 identification-friend-or-foe (IFF) set had to be stripped out of every aircraft on security grounds.

Reveille sounded in pitch darkness. About 0700 there was a further briefing at which the pilots received their final orders. Only now were they handed the marked maps showing courses and fixes. And only now were they told the actual target: "This is the airfield west of Eindhoven. It is swarming with Spitfires. So watch out for any Spitfires which may be already airborne and over the target zone!"

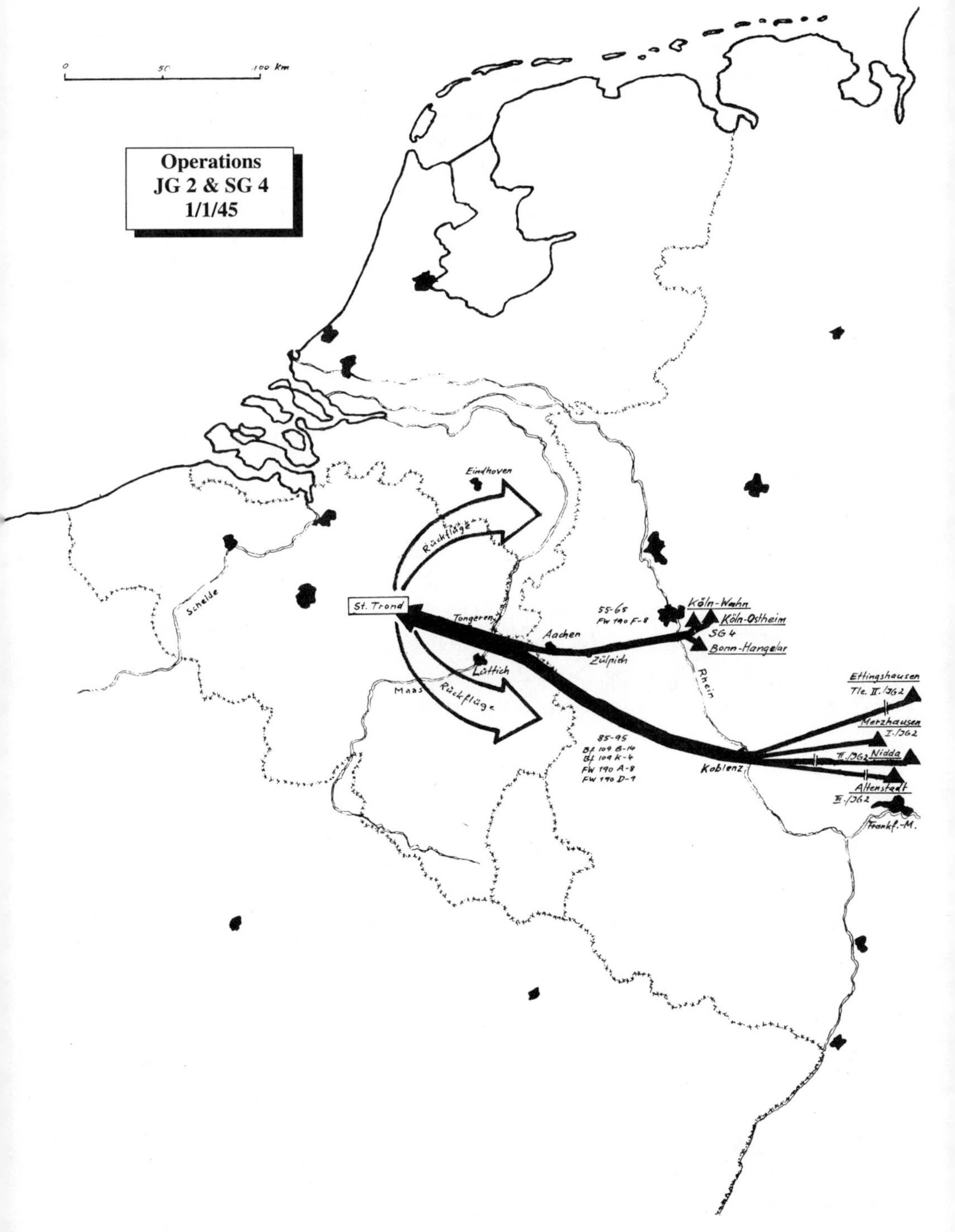
Operations
JG 2 & SG 4
1/1/45
0
50
100 km
Eindhoven
Rückflüge
St. Trond
Tongeren
Aachen
Lüttich
Maas
Rückflüge
Schelde
55-65
FW 190 F-8
Köln-Wahn
Köln-Ostheim
SG 4
Bonn-Hangelar
Zülpich
Rhein
85-95
Bf 109 G-14
Bf 109 K-4
FW 190 A-8
FW 190 D-9
Koblenz
Ettingshausen
Tle. II./JG2
Merzhausen
I./JG2
II./JG2
Nidda
Altenstadt
III./JG2
Frankf.-M.

An hour later all was ready. At 0830 *Oberstleutnant* Bär took off from Paderborn with the *Geschwaderstab* and I Gruppe. At the same moment fifteen Messerschmitts from 10, 11 and 12 Staffeln were airborne from Lippspringe. At Gütersloh *Leutnant* Müller roared down the runway with his command flight, followed by six more flights from IV Gruppe. "Assemble in quadrants 'Konrad-Richard two, three, five and six,'" ran the order just before takeoff, or radio silence was in effect as soon as the men climbed into their aircraft.

The Jagdgeschwader formed up over Lippstadt and headed off west at treetop height, the machines down to between 50 and 150 feet. They were on a set course and a Ju 88 pathfinder was to lead Jagdgeschwader 3 across the Rhine into Holland. Unaccustomed peace reigned in the fighters' narrow cockpits – no voices, no orders. The other aircraft in the formation were still only silhouettes, but it was good to see him there, for everyone felt this to be no mere run-of-the-mill operation. Even the "old hands" were feeling a little nervous.

In extended formation – with about 200 yards between individual Staffeln – the machines flew over the north edge of the Ruhr, passed their first fix at Dorsten and crossed the Dutch frontier about fifteen miles north of Venlo. The time to target was about twenty minutes, and below them lay the flat plain of Brabant with the town of Helmond to the south. Over the Sonse Heath the formation turned south to make a wide sweep round Eindhoven and come in from the southwest over the airfield, which lay between the Eindhoven-Tilburg road and the village of Zeelst.

From maps captured by the British it seems that a small element of the Geschwader broke away from the main force before the attack and flew on west for a surprise attack on the field at Gilze-Rijen. Unfortunately, it has not been established which sub-unit this was; and as some aircraft of Jagdgeschwader 27 were also assigned to attack this strip, the aircraft reported by the British as destroyed cannot be identified. The airfield anti-aircraft guns alone shot down five aircraft, including an Me 262, which may possibly have belonged to KG(J) 51, although no corresponding casualty report can be traced.

The Allies suddenly realized that an unusually strong attack was under way. In the AA positions the gun crews doubled to their guns and tried to break up the German formations by intensive fire. Jagdgeschwader 3 lost a number of machines from Flak as it approached the target, some of their pilots being captured. One of the first to fall was *Oberfähnrich* Uwe Naumann and his "Yellow 1" of 11 Staffel.

Meanwhile the Eindhoven had also been alerted, but too late to take any really effective countermeasures. The RAF fighter units stationed there on January 1, 1945 were:

137 (Typhoon) Squadron
168 (Typhoon) Squadron
181 (Typhoon) Squadron
182 (Typhoon) Squadron
247 (Typhoon) Squadron
400 (Spitfire) Squadron RCAF
414 (Spitfire) Squadron RCAF
430 (Spitfire) Squadron RCAF
438 (Typhoon) Squadron RCAF
439 (Typhoon) Squadron RCAF
440 (Typhoon) Squadron RCAF

Two Typhoon squadrons had taken off earlier that morning, one on weather reconnaissance and the other on an armed reconnaissance patrol. Another formation was about to scramble, and Flight Lieutenant Gibbons' Typhoon was just lifting off as the attack struck. Gibbons managed to bag a Focke-Wulf before he was himself shot down, still over the airfield, by three Bf 109s. The pilot of the shot-down German machine must have been *Feldwebel* Leipholz of 14 Staffel.

0910. More Allied fighters tried to take off, but they had about fifty German fighters overhead, and the first pair of Typhoons, flown by Flight Lieutenant Wilson and Flight Sergeant Burrows, were destroyed practically while still on the ground. The base was taken completely by surprise, but after the first few low-level runs the attacking aircraft came under well-aimed fire from the base anti-aircraft defenses, making further formation runs impossible. Despite this the German pilots saw that they had gained surprise and made the most of it. The Typhoons and Spitfires, all drawn up in rows, made such a wonderful target that it was almost impossible to miss. As their machines swung in again, *Oberstleutnant* Bär's A-9 set two Typhoons on fire, giving him his 204th kill. Fires were blazing all over the place. On a second run against some Mitchell bombers parked on the edge of the field, one of the I Gruppe pilots hit a fuel truck, which went up in an orange-colored mushroom cloud.

The Spitfire squadrons suffered losses too. Five machines from 400 RCAF Squadron went up in flames, one of them from a German machine crashing into it, and four others were severely damaged. But it was the

Typhoons which suffered worst. After the attack, 438 Squadron reported only two aircraft undamaged, while 440 Squadron only had two aircraft left at all, both of them severely damaged; and the four squadrons of 124 Wing could muster only 24 aircraft between them. Thus, in addition to a large number of Spitfires, 2nd TAF lost the equivalent of a complete squadron of Typhoons.

Meanwhile the Allied fighters which had already been on a sortie that morning were coming back in, and they joined the party without further ado. Squadron Leader Wonnacott spotted about twenty Messerschmitts pulling out of their run over Eindhoven and shot two of them down. 10./JG 3 had already lost its leader, *Leutnant* Hans-Ulrich Jung, to anti-aircraft fire near Helmond, and now the "Yellow 6" of the *Kapitän* of 12 Staffel, *Oberleutnant* Graf von Treuberg went down in flames and is still missing. Immediately after shooting down a Spitfire which was right on the tail of a crashing Bf 109, *Oberfeldwebel* Hameister was attacked by a second Spitfire. The *Oberfeldwebel*'s "Green 7", in which he had taken off this day on his first mission with JG 3, caught fire and Hameister was forced to make a crash-landing. Not until next morning was he captured by British troops.

After an attack lasting more than twenty minutes, the last German machines turned away to the east. At Eindhoven they left behind a pile of ruins. Aircraft still burning, burnt-out vehicles of every kind, twisted sheet steel, and scrapmetal!

But the Jagdgeschwader 3 pilots now began a long and dangerous flight home. To the west of Helmond 15 Staffel met four Typhoons of 439 RCAF Squadron returning from their weather reconnaissance, accompanied by two Spitfires. The resulting scrap lasted about five minutes and cost several Focke-Wulfs. *Unteroffizier* Gerhard Schmidt, flying "Yellow 12", had already destroyed two Spitfires on the ground at Eindhoven. Now he shot down the Typhoon flown by Flight Lieutenant Angelin, but was himself hit and forced to make an emergency landing. Soon afterward the *Unteroffizier* was taken prisoner.

Battle damage or shortage of fuel prevented a number of machines from reaching their home base. Flak and dogfights had split up the formations badly; singly, in pairs or in small groups the pilots took the shortest route east. Although radio silence was supposed to be maintained until landing, emergency calls or short messages were to be heard on air now and then. Following the attack *Unteroffizier* Grell strayed south into the Cologne area in his "Yellow 12." Suddenly he found himself facing several enemy

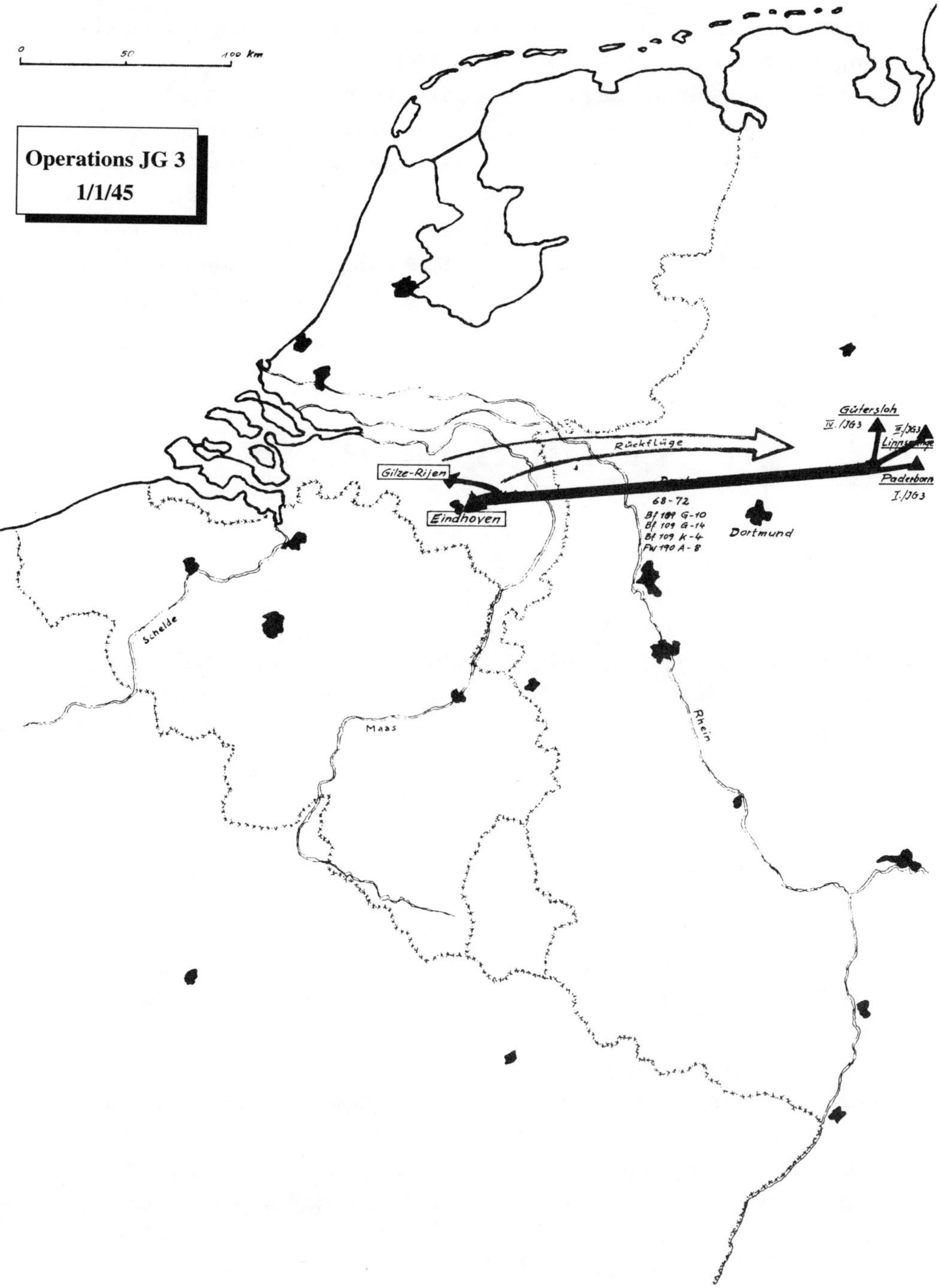

Operations JG 3
1/1/45

fighters, which sent the lone Focke-Wulf of 15./JG 3 down in flames. Grell was killed.

All in all the attack on Eindhoven airfield must be reckoned as one of the most successful in the whole of Operation "Bodenplatte", although it cost Jagdgeschwader 3 "Udet" ten pilots killed or missing and six taken prisoner, a loss-rate of some 22%. At Eindhoven Allied 2nd TAF lost a complete Canadian Typhoon squadron, a substantial number of Spitfires and the lives of 25 pilots. On the German side those missing in addition to Graf von Treuberg were *Unteroffizier* Horst Schöne of 3 Staffel and *Unteroffizier* Alois Schmidt of 16 Staffel.

A Total Failure

At Babenhausen, II./JG 4's base, the "Bodenplatte" briefing was held comparatively early. By 1800 on December 31, *Major* Schröder had called his men together to go over the route for the next morning's mission with them. *Oberleutnant* Siller and the handful of pilots from his 6 Staffel came over by road from Darmstadt-Griesheim, where they had landed with I Gruppe after their previous sortie. Now the mystery of the Ju 88 that had flown in to Babenhausen was resolved. The twin-engine night fighter ("What's he doing here?", was one pilot's comment) had been sitting on the field for several hours with the armored Focke-Wulfs taking off and landing past it. Its crew couldn't understand the strange markings on these aircraft, for the Fw 190 A-8s of this unit, the *Sturmgruppe*, all wore the black-white-black fuselage band of the *Reichsverteidigung* on their fuselages.

Stab and IV./JG 4, with about forty Messerschmitts, were based on the old Rhine-Main airship field; its giant hangars had been demolished at the beginning of the French campaign to enlarge the field for use by units of the Luftwaffe. On the morning of January 1, only half of the Bf 109s were serviceable, although the ground staff had been working on them all night. In ones and twos the pilots went over to the airfield from their billets in Sprendlingen to get their final orders from the commander of Jagdgeschwader 4, *Major* Michalski. Studying the aerial photos at the briefing, the pilots saw a comparatively large airfield occupied by about 100 American Thunderbolts as well as some medium and heavy bombers. "Mission – low-level attack on Le Culot airfield. The Geschwader is to form up over Bingen."

Much the same was happening in *Major* Steinmann's I Gruppe at Darmstadt-Griesheim, which was to commit some ten machines to "Bodenplatte." So Jagdgeschwader 4 stood ready for the attack on Le Culot – codeword "Hermann." For reasons which have never been fully explained, this operation was a total failure. As happened in Jagdgeschwader 6's operation too, it can only have been a navigational error which left the target airfield, Le Culot, completely unscathed and put Jagdgeschwader 4's machines into a completely different area. But that was still to come.

The controllers' flags dropped as dawn broke. The pathfinder aircraft was already airborne and had switched on its navigation lights to allow the fighter formations to home on it. About 0810 II Gruppe formed up over Babenhausen and hung around waiting for the Focke-Wulfs of 6 Staffel; but these were in fact already on the way with I Gruppe and did not join II Gruppe until Bingen.

From Bingen, Jagdgeschwader 4, led by its commander, flew on over the Hunsrück, and in ten minutes or less they had reached the first fix marked on the pilots' maps, over Bullay on the Moselle. On they went towards Prüm in the Eifel, their second fix, reaching it at about 0840 just as the first rays of the sun lit up their machines.

From there they should have been over Le Culot in less than half-an-hour, but airfield Allied code number A89, north of Wavre and some ten miles from Brussels, was never attacked on January 1. What happened? We cannot ask the commander, *Major* Michalski, for he was killed in an auto accident just after the War. Neither his staff nor the pilots of the three Gruppen taking part can offer any explanation for the plan's having gone awry. But they were convinced they were over Le Culot. All airfields, especially Allied, look very alike in a snow-covered landscape. From its briefing on the air photos, Jagdgeschwader 4 was looking for a field full of Thunderbolts but Le Culot was not the only one used by this type of aircraft. US 9th TAF had P-47 units stationed at St. Trond and, in the northeast corner of Belgium, at Ophoven.

Several formations found no Allied airfield at all and joined up with other fighter units, taking them for elements of their own units. The sky was full of German aircraft that morning. And so some alternative targets must have been taken on, wherever they may have lain. Some elements of Jagdgeschwader 4 which had completely lost contact went over to strafing troop concentrations on the roads round Bastogne – which of itself suffices to show how widely they had become scattered.

But once again it was anti-aircraft fire that was the Germans' main problem – and the Allied shooting was good. Every Gruppe and every Staffel took losses. *Feldwebel* Franz Schneider of 4./Jg 4 went down and was not seen again. 5 Staffel reported *Unteroffizier* Erich Keller missing, *Unteroffizier* Diercks killed and *Oberfähnrich* Peschel shot down.

II Gruppe, or at least most of it, attacked an airfield that looked absolutely identical to St. Culot, with the same mass of Thunderbolts that the air photos had showed. But this was in fact St. Trond, the *Richthofen* Geschwader's allotted target. The flak was already coming up and there was no time for a detailed check. Within seconds the fate of one Focke-Wulf had been sealed. "White 11" flown by *Gefreiter* Walter Wagner took a hit which left the pilot no choice but to make a forced landing. In fact the damage was not severe, and Wagner had no difficulty in putting his machine down, which he did, just to be on the safe side, right in the middle of the enemy airfield. It was only when the Americans took him prisoner that he learnt that it wasn't Le Culot after all. But the 404th Fighter Group got their hands on an almost intact Fw 190 A-8.

Other elements of IV Gruppe pressed on westward and engaged an airfield that was also full of Thunderbolts with a few four-engine machines thrown in. 15 Staffel lost four Messerschmitts from flak. *Feldwebel* Berg was listed as missing, *Oberfähnrich* Horst Grüner was killed. *Unteroffizier* Schmidt and *Oberfähnrich* Russow were captured. It turned out that the airfield they had attacked was Melsbroek. Another Bf 109, damaged by anti-aircraft fire, crash-landed near Liege.

The Jagdgeschwader, now completely split up and having failed utterly in its mission, turned for home. Whether Jagdgeschwader 4 had in the general confusion also attacked the Ophoven airfield has never been confirmed and remains a supposition. All that is clear is that elements of Jagdgeschwader 4 overflew southern Holland and lost at least five more pilots in the process. 5 Staffel lost *Oberfähnrich* Franz Schaar, who fell near Helden, raising its total losses to six. Only a few miles farther and Helden would have been across the Maas and over friendly territory. "White 2", flown by *Unteroffizier* Anetzhuber, also went missing on the return flight. This was the second pilot lost by 13 Staffel; *Unteroffizier* Holtkötter had been shot down earlier. It was later discovered that Anetzhuber had died southeast of Helmond.

The final victim of this operation was *Unteroffizier* Güldenpfennig of 7 Staffel, who lost his life near Venray. *Leutnant* Morio, also of 7 Staffel,

Operations JG 4
1/1/45

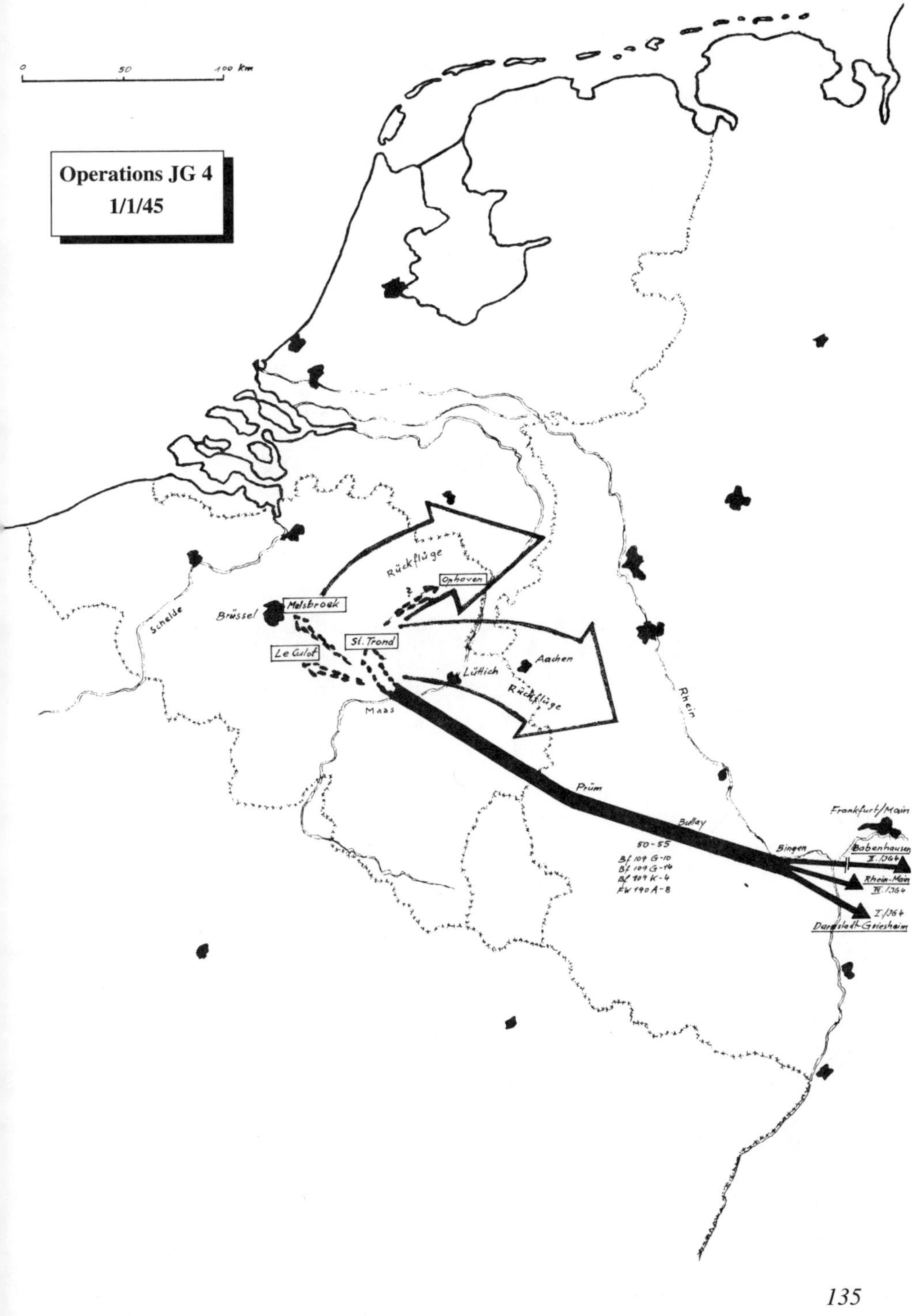

managed to get his flak-damaged Fw 190 across the front, finally making a forced landing near Wesel. Morio was injured in the process. At the end of April the *Leutnant* was listed as missing after failing to return from a mission over central Germany. Morio in fact survived.

In about four hours Operation "Bodenplatte" was over for JG 4. Only thirty of the 55 machines which had taken off remained. Seventeen pilots were killed or missing, and six fell into enemy hands. II Gruppe suffered worst, reporting fewer than ten Focke-Wulfs serviceable on the evening of January 1; the former *Sturmgruppe* had ceased to exist.

The Mission Against Volkel Miscarries

As late as mid-December 1944 *Oberstleutnant* Johann Kogler was the only one in the whole of Jagdgeschwader 6 to know of the plan for a major Luftwaffe operation against the Allied fighter bases in the West. He had passed this information on to his Gruppe commanders at the appointed time, but neither they, nor for that matter II Jagdkorps or Luftflotte Headquarters West had been told at that stage the exact date on which the operation was to take place. Nor had targets and target data been issued. All that they knew was that it would be as soon as possible and that it would be launched in the early morning on a day when the weather conditions were suitable. Before the right day came the fighter force had been half bled to death supporting the Ardennes Offensive. The weather only cleared in the last days of the year, and on December 31 the operation order was issued. Jagdgeschwader 6's target was Volkel in Holland.

The pilots were briefed by Gruppe and were thus able to familiarize themselves with the target airfield with the aid of a model. "There's really nothing that can go wrong", thought *Major* Kühle, and he was quite happy about the way he had briefed his men in III Gruppe. There was nothing left now except to make sure that his "Gustavs" were correctly armed and fully fuelled.

The Ju 88 that was to lead the Jagdgeschwader on the prescribed course into Holland and up to the southern tip of the Zuider See was already circling over Quakenbrück before the fighter formations were airborne. On the fields at Bissel, Delmenhorst, Quakenbrück and Vechta the controllers' lamps were flashing cleared for take-off. The first *Schwarm* of 3 Staffel was just taxying, and *Leutnant* Bauer in the Staffel's lead aircraft was already airborne, when "Yellow l" flown by *Oberleutnant* Pfleiderer suddenly lost speed and plunged into the trees ringing the Delmenhorst airfield. The pilot was killed. The takeoff by the other machines went ahead uninterrupted, but the *Oberleutnant*'s death even before the operation was under way was a bad omen. Jagdgeschwader 6 was to lose ten of its officers that day, among them six unit leaders – an unimaginable loss of command talent within a single Geschwader.

The formations assembled over Quakenbrück as planned and headed westward. II Gruppe under *Hauptmann* Naumann was in the lead, followed by *Major* Kühle's III Gruppe, with *Hauptmann* Trost's I Gruppe from Delmenhorst bringing up the rear – about seventy machines in all, flying at 500 feet. As they flew, the men were going over the whole plan in their heads, checking grid references and changes of heading and learning the compass bearings by heart. They knew that this mission was something special, for it was a long time since so large a force had been committed to a single operation. Every serviceable machine was airborne, but not every pilot had the requisite operational experience – something they were going to need in full measure before the day was out. Over Volkel, *Major* Kühle with III Gruppe was to fly top cover, while I Gruppe led the attack. Then *Hauptmann* Naumann was to bring II Gruppe in from the south as a second wave and, when his Focke-Wulfs were clear, III Gruppe was to drop down for the Geschwader's third run over the airfield. Or that was the idea. But the Geschwader was still headed westward for the Zuider See.

Jagdgeschwader 6 had been formed in summer or autumn 1944 from Zerstörergeschwader 26, and a good number of the older, more experienced Zerstörer fighter pilots were still flying with it. Among them was *Feldwebel* Karl Schubert of I Gruppe, who recalls Jagdgeschwader 6's first casualty on January 1 as follows:

> "I was leading a *Schwarm*, but I can't remember in which Staffel it was. After we got airborne from Delmenhorst we headed for the Zuider See. Right over its southern tip *Oberfeldwebel* Walter Jung went down. We assumed he must have collided with another machine. Nothing was heard from

> *Ofw*. Jung. His machine apparently crashed and burned in a meadow beside the lake. After the operation was over I landed back at Twenthe with I Gruppe, Jagdgeschwader 1 and the enemy air activity was so intense I couldn't fly on to Delmenhorst till the evening."

The night fighter allotted to Jagdgeschwader 6 as pathfinder was now over Spakenburg. The planned course ran south from here down to Veghel, then east and thence onto Volkel. But the pathfinder made a navigational error and flew straight on past the turning point, with the result that the whole Geschwader got much too far over to the west. No one can recall just who spotted the mistake first, but in any case only a few of Jagdgeschwader 6's aircraft ever reached Volkel. Some others found themselves over Eindhoven in the curtain of flak put up to welcome the *Udet* Geschwader but the bulk of the Geschwader went in on quite a different airfield, only about 10 miles northwest of Volkel on the Hertogenbosch-Njimegen road. This was Heesch, Allied code number B-88, and on it were stationed all five Spitfire squadrons of 126 Wing, 2nd TAF. At 0914, 401 Squadron's machines were out on the runway when the first Messerschmitts and Focke-Wulfs came roaring over the field at treetop height. Once again the surprise did not last long. The airfield defenses let loose with everything they had at the machines as they swooped down from all sides; the gunners had never seen so many German aircraft in the air at once.

A few moments later 401 RCAF Squadron scrambled right into the middle of the attack, shooting down five German machines – four Bf 109s and one Fw 190 of which Flight Lieutenant Cameron himself claimed three.

The bark of light flak, the rattle of machine-guns, the savage wail of engines on full boost and explosions on the ground provided the incidental music for the German low-level attack – punctuated by the thump of aircraft exploding on impact, for the attackers did not go unscathed.

When the attack went in on Heesch, two squadrons of Spitfires were already airborne on an operation, one in the Venlo area where it became involved in a scrap with a large force of Focke-Wulfs, and the other heading for Twenthe. The second of these, 411 RCAF Squadron, was just between the Maas and the Waal when the Germans attacked Heesch; it turned back straightaway and quickly made an interception, in which Flight Lieutenant Audet shot down two Focke-Wulfs. One of these must have been "Blue 13", an Fw 190 A-8 of 14 Staffel flown by *Unteroffizier* Karl Fries, which was

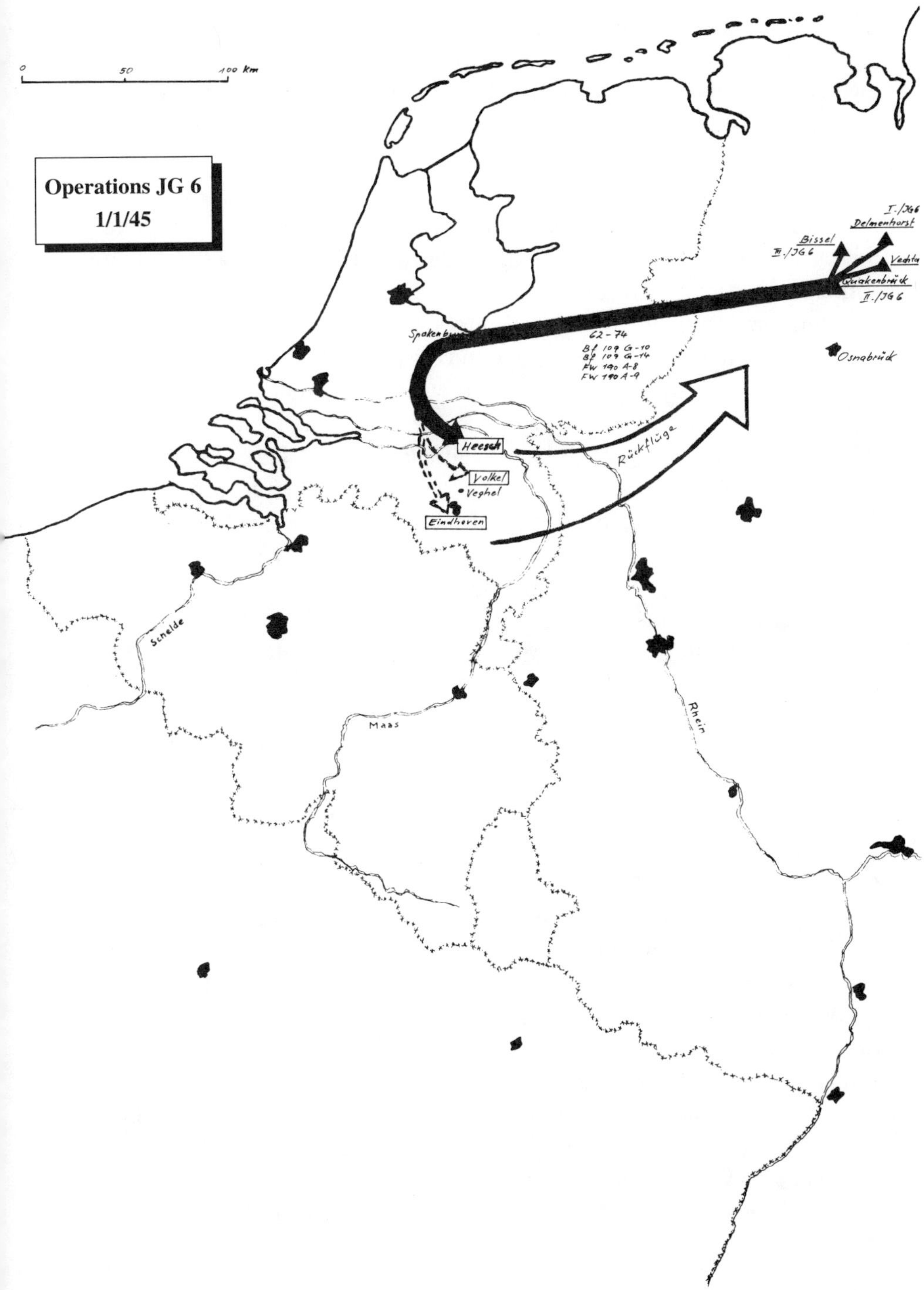
Operations JG 6
1/1/45
0 50 100 km
I./JG6
Delmenhorst
Bissel
III./JG 6
Vechta
Quakenbrück
II./JG 6
62 - 74
Bf 109 G-10
Bf 109 G-14
Fw 190 A-8
Fw 190 A-9
Osnabrück
Heesch
Volkel
Veghel
Eindhoven
Rückflüge
Schelde
Maas
Rhein

shot down in the same area, near Nijmegen.

442 Squadron accounted for three Messerschmitts as it returned from its mission to find the party over its base in full swing. Flight Lieutenant Gordon was hit by his own flak and made a crash-landing in his Spitfire. British sources indicate that 126 Wing scored 24 confirmed kills on January 1, for the loss of just one Spitfire.

Meanwhile it became clear that the German operation had completely miscarried. The individual units of Jagdgeschwader 6 had become badly split up and were now trying to concentrate again as best they could. They flew back and forth over the flat countryside, diving onto various airfields under the impression that they had found the right target. Any semblance to a plan had gone by the board, and the allotted target, Volkel airfield, remained untouched. Stationed there were the lethal Tempests, two squadrons of which had just taken off on a surveillance patrol.[4] Three German machines, probably the only ones actually to reach Volkel, were reported shot down after a brief skirmish. "Red 5", the aircraft of the *Kapitän* of 5 Staffel, *Hauptmann* Norbert Katz, crashed right on the airfield; Katz was killed. A few miles farther southwest fellow 5 Staffel member *Leutnant* Grabmeier crashed near the small village of Erp. A third fighter, the Bf 109 G-10 flown by *Unteroffizier* Betz of 12 Staffel, went down near Veghel, taking its pilot to his death.

The rest were already on their way home. Some of them were chased by Allied fighters, but *Feldwebel* Schubert managed to shoot down one of these British machines, a Typhoon, to the north of Venlo. The Jagdgeschwader, now completely split up, headed east on a wide front. Missing were its *Kommodore*, the *Kommandeur* of III Gruppe and the *Kapitän* of 2 Staffel. Only much later was it learnt that *Oberstleutnant* Kogler and *Hauptmann* Trost were in Allied hands. *Major* Helmut Kühle however was killed.

With Volkel completely unscathed and the scale of damage even at Heesch no more than light, the loss of a third of the aircraft sent in by Jagdgeschwader 6 seemed a very heavy price to pay. It remains a hypothetical question whether things would have turned out better if the wing had followed the correct, specified course. Maybe then Volkel would have been taken on, and maybe it would have been destroyed; on the other hand the Tempests might have taken an even heavier toll. In any event controversy continues to rage about the whole of this New Year's Day operation; but no blame can ever be laid at the door of the German fighter pilots.

The Tragedy Over Asch

At about the same time as *Gefreiter* Böhm and his friends in 9 Staffel were walking across to the briefing room at Gross Ostheim, Col. John C. Meyer, at the Belgian airfield of Asch, had just been trying to get an operation ordered during the night cancelled. The 352nd US Fighter Group, which had moved across from England to Field Y-29 (Asch) at the end of December, was tasked on January 1st for a wide-ranging fighter escort mission, accompanying strong bomber forces from US 8th Air Force to the Kassel and Coblenz-Trier areas. However, Asch was so near to the front that Meyer was unhappy about this and suggested that he should fly a patrol programme instead. Finally he got permission to send up small patrols of Mustangs.

Col. Meyer and his pilots were of course not to know that Asch airfield, about ten miles north of the Albert Canal, was on the German fighters' target list for that day. No more could *Gefreiter* Böhm imagine that only an hour or so later he would be in a dogfight with this American officer; in fact he had never even heard of Asch airfield.

Oberleutnant Fiedler, adjutant III./JG 11, had first learned of the major air operation just before the launching of the Ardennes offensive, when *Hauptmann* von Fassong had held a secret briefing for his unit leaders on the II Jagdkorps plan. *Hauptmann* von Fassong, Knight's Cross, from Kassel, had been CO of III Gruppe since March 1944. For all the 100 or more kills to his credit, this was to be his last sortie; indeed the whole of his squadron was to suffer an appalling blood-letting, for just under half the pilots who took off never returned.

Meanwhile however, the men of the *Geschwaderstab* and the three Gruppen of Jagdgeschwader 11 were preparing for takeoff. A Ju 188 was already waiting at Gross Ostheim to lead the formation across the front line somewhere near Limbourg. On the other side of the hill, Colonel Meyer, with twelve Mustangs of the 487th Squadron, was also getting ready for his mission. Meyer, one of the top American fighter aces, had decided to revisit old haunts and comb the St. Vith area for enemy fighters. But things didn't work out quite that way.

Oberleutnant Fiedler, who had been injured on December 23 when he had to make a forced landing with engine trouble, had only rejoined his squadron on December 31st and was now to fly with them on this New

Year's Day venture. A new machine, "Yellow 9", stood waiting for him on the tarmac.

0830! The whole of III Gruppe took off and then formed up south of Aschaffenburg before *Hauptmann* von Fassong turned in astern of the pathfinder aircraft and headed west. Here, too, of course there was strict radio silence. The Focke-Wulfs, flying low, were approaching Frankfurt on Main when the slim silhouettes of 25-30 Messerschmitts loomed up to starboard. It was II./JG 11 from Zellhausen. And somewhere up ahead must be the *Geschwaderstab* and elements of I Gruppe. The whole formation was now headed by two Ju 188s, and behind them *Oberstleutnant* Günther Specht in his Fw 190 A-9. Specht, from Silesia, had started the War as a *Zerstörer* pilot, then joined JG 11 in 1943 and assumed command of it in April 1944; he now ranked as one of the outstanding commanders in the *Reichsverteidigung*.

The pilots were more than two-thirds of the way to their target when flak started to come up. Jagdgeschwader 11 was now roughly over Aachen, in enemy-held territory. Suddenly, *Oberleutnant* Fiedler's Focke-Wulf was hit, and the adjutant was struck in the head by splinters. He could feel consciousness slipping away; down and down he sank. He still has no idea how he managed a forced landing; nor can he recall foreign soldiers pulling him clear of the wreck and giving him first aid. He came round to find himself in British hands. The second victim was *Unteroffizier* Noreisch, flying "Black 10." It is not clear whether Noreisch was shot down by flak or fighters as the German formations were attacked by several Thunderbolts at about the same time.

The German fighters flew north along the Maas. They passed over Emael, then Kanne, Vroenhoven and Veldvezelt, names famous from May 1940. This was where the Luftwaffe had launched its first attack in the West, and it was now about to deliver its last blow in the same area. Jagdgeschwader 11 was only a few minutes short of its target. The snow-covered heathland round Asch lay under heavy ground-mist, which somewhat impaired the visibility, but allowed the German machines' low-profile approach over fields and woods to remain undetected up to the last moment. The Allied forces on Y29 had no idea what was about to hit them.

Stationed at Asch at this time were four Spitfire units from 2nd TAF, 41, 130, 350 and 610 Squadrons, and with them the 352nd US Fighter Group, mentioned above, from US 8th Air Force and the 366th Fighter Group from 9th US TAF. One unit, 41 Squadron, was airborne on an armed reconnaissance over the Eifel at the time of the attack.

Led by Colonel Meyer in "Petie II", twelve Mustangs were taxiing for takeoff on the Belgian airfield. It was 0940 as the P-51 roared down the runway. Just before he lifted off, Meyer suddenly saw the puffs of Flak – and then he noticed a machine towards him, a low-flying Focke-Wulf. Before the Americans realized what was going on, more fighters wearing the Black Cross appeared over the field. Meyer could not break off his run and instinctively opened fire on the approaching Germans. But *Gefreiter* Böhm in his "White 3" did not seem to notice the enemy fighters and held course for the twin-engine C-47 Skytrain[5] transports parked on the field. But the Browning bursts had struck home; in a flash the Focke-Wulf exploded on impact just by one of these transports, taking its brave pilot with it. Nothing like scoring a kill during take-off!

The airfield was now under running attack, but despite this the rest of the Mustangs, together with some Thunderbolts and the odd Spitfire from 610 Squadron managed to get off and give battle. The ground-mist had still not lifted and many pilots had difficulty in telling friend from foe. Flight Lieutenant Gaze in his Spitfire had just shot down a Focke-Wulf when he saw his squadron set upon by several Mustangs, who must have taken them for Messerschmitts. But no harm was done.

Now it was II Gruppe's Messerschmitts sweeping in, then again the Focke-Wulfs of the other two formations. "Attention, target identified. Attack by *Schwarm.*" Again and again Jagdgeschwader 11 machines formed up for another run over Asch airfield. Parked aircraft, buildings and vehicles were hit. But the Geschwader paid a heavy price indeed for what later turned out to have been only slight damage. The operation had already cost eight pilots. *Obergefreiter* Sistenich of 1 Staffel, *Feldwebel* Schwarz and *Feldwebel* Kraschinski of 7 Staffel and *Gefreiter* Böhm of 9 Staffel were all killed. *Oberleutnant* August Engel of 8 Staffel was also shot down and killed over Asch. The rest had fallen elsewhere or were missing. But the mission was not yet over.

Staffelkapitän Leutnant Georg Füreder, whose 5./JG 11 was the only unit of II Gruppe to come through the day unscathed, gave the following account of the attack:

> "After the briefing, held late in the evening of the day before, neither the pilots nor anyone else who had been present were allowed to leave the airfield. My Staffel was billeted in Klein-

Krotzenburg. We took off later than planned because of the weather (fog), and I think this did much to impair the success of the operation. The Gruppe took station in the Geschwader formation and set course for the target, following the two Ju 188 pathfinders. We flew low, and the pathfinders relieved us of all navigational chores up to their breakaway point. This was the Maas. One of the Ju 188s behaved like any good bellwether and before breaking away turned his machine-guns on an enemy AA position on a bridge. He was a good shot.

I didn't notice whether any of the aircraft in our formation were hit by our own or enemy flak on the way in, but I seem to remember someone coming up on the air saying they had been hit just before we got to the target. In front of the target we pulled up and fanned out to port and starboard; then we had a quick look at it and went in with our guns.

I pulled up fairly straight and made my run almost without having to change heading. My approach angle was too steep for the Thunderbolts, most of which were parked on the eastern half of the field, so I drew a bead on four or five twin-engine machines over in the northwest corner and then pulled out in a tight 180 degree turn to take on the Thunderbolts on the east side. I pulled up level when a burst of tracer whistled round my ears. I thought at first it was flak coming up from astern, but then saw to my astonishment that I had two Thunderbolts sitting on my tail. One was letting me have it with everything he had, but he was pulling to much lead. I pulled sharply up to port to evade and his fire passed astern of me. My pursuer and his wingman gave up, went into a powerdive and headed off west. I turned westward too and to begin with I made to go after them, holding my height. But then I broke away and made a final run over the field, roughly southward. At this instant I could see no more aircraft over or near to the airfield. The southern half of the field was covered in black smoke, pluming up from burning aircraft. I didn't try to see how many aircraft had been hit on the ground. I made my final run a bit higher because of the smoke, but still had to fly through the pall over the southern half of the field. But in all the hullabaloo not even the best of pilots could see for instance where the Geschwader commander had gone, and so on, once the first run was over."

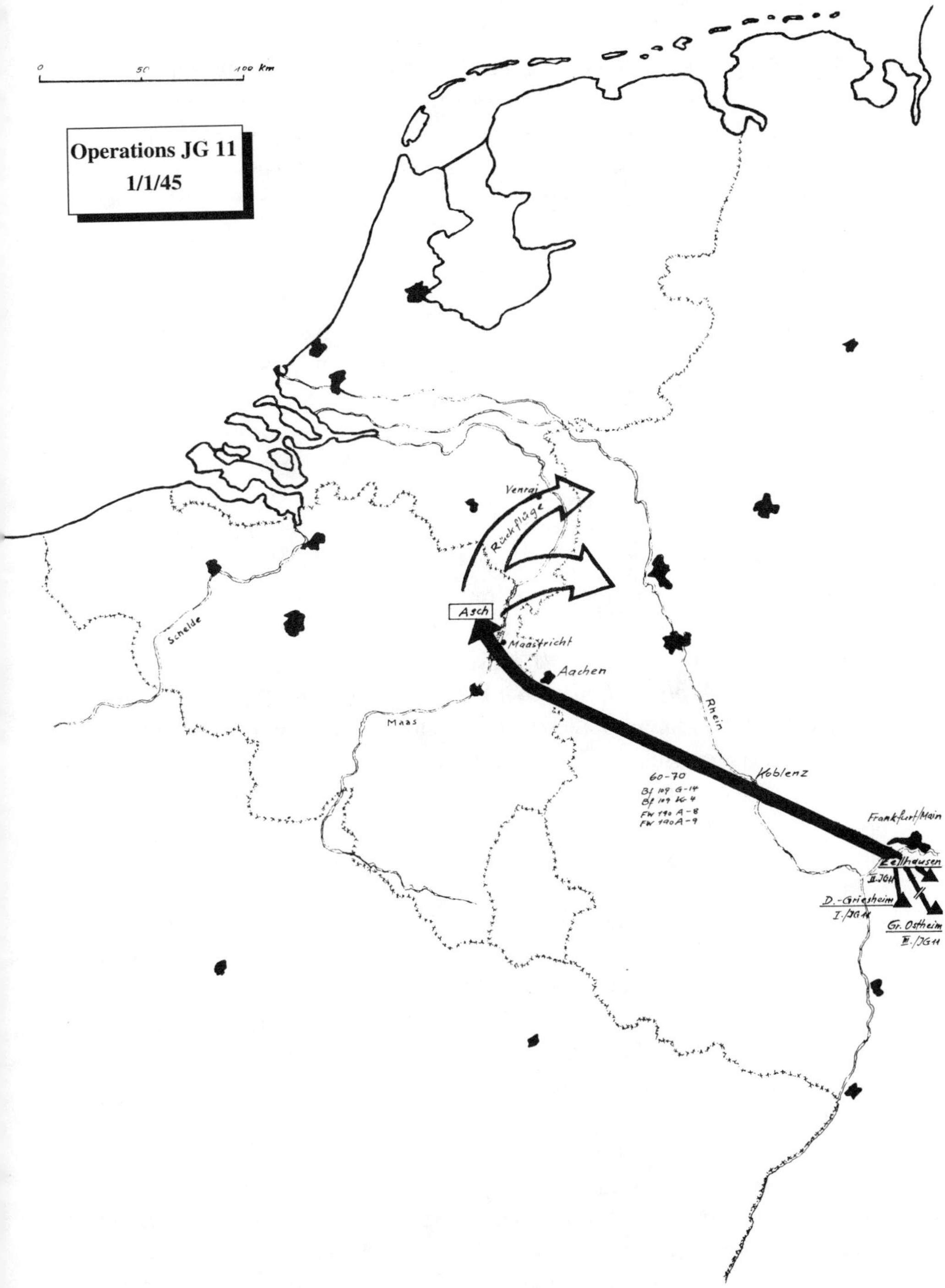
0
50
100 km
Operations JG 11
1/1/45
Venraij
Rückflüge
Asch
Maastricht
Aachen
Schelde
Maas
Rhein
Koblenz
60-70
Bf 109 G-14
Bf 109 K-4
FW 190 A-8
FW 190 A-9
Frankfurt/Main
Zellhausen
II./JG11
D.-Griesheim
I./JG11
Gr. Ostheim
III./JG11

The pilots of III./JG 11 were waiting for a signal to break off the attack. When they didn't have Allied fighters on their tails, they looked around for their CO's machine – and finally saw it away to the south of Asch in a dogfight with two Thunderbolts. *Hauptmann* von Fassong has not been seen or heard of since. At this stage the men of JG 11 did not yet know that they had lost their commander. Like that of nine other pilots, the fate of *Oberstleutnant* Specht remains uncertain. III Gruppe alone reported six pilots missing, among them *Major* Vowinkel of the *Gruppenstab*.

A bare three quarters of an hour after the attack had begun, the scream of engines and the rattle of machine-guns died away over Asch. The fighter formations, or rather what was left of them, headed for home. They flew north to begin with and then east across Belgium. But the enemy was still hot on their heels, and Col. Meyer dispatched yet another Focke-Wulf to chalk up his 24th kill.

Two more pilots fell before they were able to reach their own lines. *Feldwebel* Reschke and *Unteroffizier* Barion were both shot down near Venray. And where *Oberfeldwebel* Franz Meindl and his "Blue 11" had got to, none of his comrades of 11 Staffel could say. The same applied to *Unteroffizier* Kurt Nüssle of 9./JG 11, who was later reported missing in action by *Staffelkapitän Hauptmann* Funck. Funck himself was killed five days later over Kirchheimbolanden during an action against heavy bombers.

In addition to damaging buildings of airfield Y-29, Jagdgeschwader 11 destroyed seven British fighters from 350 Squadron on the ground and damaged three others from 130 Squadron. Several Dakotas were also destroyed. Four Mustangs of the 352nd Fighter Group were shot down in dogfights, but all their pilots survived. But Jagdgeschwader 11 losses were substantially greater, amounting to almost 40% of the aircraft committed; and twelve of the pilots have still never been traced. On this occasion Allied claims and German figures virtually matched. The 352nd Fighter Group reported 23 kills on German fighters, the P-47s claimed four, and the British pilots one. This adds up to 28 machines out of the total reported lost by Jagdgeschwader 11, which also of course included some shot down by Allied AA.

It was less than three hours later when the first machines came in to land at their bases east and south of Frankfurt. Many pilots only got back much later after having had to make an intermediate landing because of lack of fuel or battle damage. Almost every machine showed signs of hits.

When *Major* Jürgen Harder, a very experienced officer, handed over I./

JG 53 and came to take over Jagdgeschwader 11, he found very little left of this famous unit, which had played such an outstanding role in home air defense. And with the deaths of *Oberstleutnant* Specht and *Hauptmann* von Fassong, January 1, 1945 had cost the fighter force two more talented unit commanders.

JG 26 and the Brussels Airfields

Handrup airstrip, near Fürstenau, was a hive of activity – nothing unusual since *Oberstleutnant* Priller had settled in there with the *Geschwaderstab* and I Gruppe of Jagdgeschwader 26 "*Schlageter*."[6] The "long noses" were up almost every day fighting it out with the British, who were always on the prowl over North Germany shooting up railway engines, supply barges on the rivers and canals and Luftwaffe aircraft on the ground and in the air. *Major* Borris, commanding I./JG 26, had lost sixteen pilots since they had first landed at Fürstenau on November 24, 1944.

The arrival of three Focke-Wulfs from Achmer on the afternoon of December 31 attracted little attention. It was *Feldwebel* Dietrich with two instructors from the Operational Staffel of Jagdgeschwader 104, normally stationed at Fürth, near Nuremberg. Just as darkness fell a further twenty "Dora 9s" flew in – III./JG 54 from Varrelbusch. All these aircraft, were to join I./JG 26 for Operation "Bodenplatte." And they were scarcely on the ground when the briefings began.

Major Borris gave out the target to the sixty pilots; it was Grimbergen airfield, north of Brussels and just to the west of Vilvoorde. "Operation maps will not be issued until tomorrow morning. Takeoff 0815, when the two Junkers pathfinders are airborne. Form up over the field."

By 0600 the pilots were on the field and picking up their map folders. The marked maps showed that the first leg of their flight was direct to Spakenburg at the south tip of the Zuider See. The second change of course was near Rotterdam, and from there the formation would turn south and head for the Schelde estuary.

It was 0814 and still half dark when the takeoff signals flashed. The whole battle group took off with *Oberstleutnant* Priller at its head. Several engines were reluctant to start, and it took them almost twenty minutes to get airborne from Fürstenau. But finally all 67 Focke-Wulfs were away: 47 machines of the *Geschwaderstab* and I./JG 26, 17 machines of III./JG 54 and three Fw 190 D-9s of the Operational Staffel of JG 104. As they were flying at only 150-500 feet, they had to make sure they kept a good interval between aircraft; and it was a well strung-out formation of fighters that headed for the Zuider See.

Feldwebel Karlheinz Hartmann of 4 Staffel was barely able to hide his excitement. He had been with JG 26 barely two weeks, and this was his first mission with the Gruppe. Unfortunately, he had missed the briefing and simply followed his formation leader, unaware of the true significance of the day's operation. He could not know that he would be in Allied captivity an hour later, after being shot down by flak over Grimbergen and bailing out.

Between Utrecht and Rotterdam the formations found themselves in some vicious flak, which brought down the 2 Staffel leader, *Oberleutnant* Franz Kunz. His "Black 1" came down near Polsbroek. For Kunz, who suffered serious injuries in this incident, Operation "Bodenplatte" was over. West of Rotterdam the remaining formations turned south. Once again they ran into flak and suffered losses. One machine of III./JG 54 was damaged so badly that its pilot, *Unteroffizier* Kroll, had to make a forced landing. He, too, was pulled from the wreck of his aircraft with serious injuries. Only a short time earlier, *Obergefreiter* Niessen of 3 Staffel had also been forced to make an emergency landing after his aircraft was damaged by anti-aircraft fire. Another Focke-Wulf, that of one of the instructors of JG 104, was hit in the auxiliary fuel tank, which, fortunately, he was able to jettison.

These losses naturally led to the German formation becoming rather split up. The pilots were getting angry because their own AA gunners down below showed no signs of ceasing their fire. At about this stage the formation crossed the front lines. It is uncertain whether it was German or Allied flak which brought down "Black 3" flown by *Obergefreiter* Vogel. The Focke-Wulf veered off to the west and crashed on Walcheren Island. The pilot was killed.

The machines now reached the mouth of the Schelde, where more heavy anti-aircraft fire was awaiting them. *Oberfeldwebel* Eckert of 11./JG 11 was shot down and killed, and Steinkamp's machine was hit in the wing roots and engine. He tried to nurse it back to his own lines, but lost control and had to bail out into captivity.

Another to be taken prisoner by the British was *Obergefreiter* Dieter Krägeloh of 3./JG 26. This is his story:

> "Our New Year's Eve party was cut short by a briefing. We went across to the field early the next morning. My machine wouldn't start at first. Finally I got airborne and joined up with the nearest flight. We flew low. Some night fighters guided us as far as Holland. Over the Schelde estuary we got above a British warship and suffered our first losses. Two machines near me caught fire and ditched. My crate was still under control and didn't seem to be losing fuel, so I flew on. Then a bunch of Spitfires suddenly came up on our tail. My prop (a wooden one) was shot away; the engine over-revved and nearly shook itself from its mountings. So I shut the engine down and decided to try a forced landing. I was too low to bale out. Luckily I managed to put her down in a clearing in an orchard. I gathered afterwards from some monks who pulled me clear that the wings were torn off and the engine had made an excellent bulldozer. When I was fit to be moved, I was taken to England."

At about 0920 the machines were approaching Grimbergen airfield, clearly visible in the morning sunlight. The plan was to attack in three waves, but as the fifty or so "long noses" came over the target about 650 feet up, the pilots saw that the field was empty. Just four Flying Fortresses, a twin-engine machine and a solitary Mustang stood parked between the hangars. The surprise the Germans had in store for the Allies had rebounded on them. Had German air reconnaissance let the fighters down? The commander, *Oberstleutnant* Priller, was understandably livid at such a strong force of fighters being assigned to an unoccupied airfield.

So the pilots dove on the hangars or the barrack-blocks, set the handful of aircraft on fire and destroyed a good number of trucks and refuellers. Suddenly, there appeared on the middle of the field a Fw 190 on its belly; it was a D-9 from Jagdgeschwader 104, and its pilot was taken prisoner. Unfortunately, the pilot's name is unknown. The Grimbergen perimeter AA had not yet been completely silenced and managed to knock down another of the attackers.

Leutnant Nibel of 10./JG 54 lined up on the parked twin-engine machine, but came under fire from the light AA round the airfield and had to evade. As he was climbing, his engine cut. He dove to gain speed and tried to get clear of the field, but had to make a forced landing at Wemmel, northeast of Brussels, where he was picked up by Belgian police. Perhaps Nibel may not have known that the crash was caused by a partridge, which struck the radiator of his machine.

III./JG 54 had suffered heavy losses the day before, and Operation "Bodenplatte" was a mortal blow for it. Of the seventeen machines which took off only seven returned to base. Five pilots were killed or missing, among them *Hauptmann* Bottländer, *Kapitän* of 11 Staffel; four were captured, and one was severely wounded. *Major* Borris' Gruppe had six killed or missing. One pilot, *Unteroffizier* Wodarczyk, was lost on the return flight; his Fw 190 was shot down near Zwolle. Including *Unteroffizier* Heinz Schulz, who was posted missing, 2 Staffel suffered five casualties.

Unteroffizier Erich Zeidler of 4 Staffel struggled to reach friendly territory in the east after his aircraft "Blue 2", an Fw 190 D-9, was hit by anti-aircraft fire. The overworked Jumo engine continued to function, but the aircraft steadily lost altitude. Ahead, between Fürstenau and Handrup, the pilot could see the Fenster Mountains. His faithful Focke-Wulf could do no more, however. Zeidler was forced to crash-land his machine near Lengerich, practically within sight of his base, and was injured in the process.

As the last machine came in half-an-hour or so before midday, it became clear that the mission against Grimbergen had proved an expensive wild-goose chase.

All the better, then, that the rest of the "*Schlageter*" Jagdgeschwader had a more fruitful day. II and III Gruppen, led by their respective commanders, *Major* Hackl and *Hauptmann* Krupinski, and mustering 100-110 aircraft between them, were airborne at about the same time as I Gruppe. It was still dark when the pilots set off from Nordhorn for their airstrip some six miles away, on the Nordhorn Marshes between the Lingen road and the Ems-Vechte Canal. There the Focke-Wulfs of II Gruppe stood ready, and the snow-covered strip was lit up by the first rays of the sun as they took off to join up with the Messerschmitts of III JG 26, flying from Plantlünne. The formations were led by two Ju 88s, and their outward course was identical to that of I Gruppe, with the same turning points.

As they reached the Zuider Zee the air was suddenly full of brown-black puffs German Flak! Soon afterward a shell burst near "White 11" flown by *Obergefreiter* Hubert Lott of 5 Staffel. His comrades watched in horror as he bailed out successfully but then slipped from his harness as the parachute opened. A Messerschmitt of 11 Staffel was hit by flak over Nijkerk. The pilot, *Oberleutnant* Harald Lenz, failed to get out, and the machine crashed on the ice of the Zuider Zee not far from Harderwijk. *Unteroffizier* Speer of 7 Staffel was shot down and killed in the same area.

After changing course, west of Rotterdam, the German fighters flew low over the islands and causeways of the Maas and Schelde estuaries. Here another aircraft fell to the ships' anti-aircraft guns, this time from 12 Staffel. Pilot *Gefreiter* Sengpiel had insufficient height to bail out, and his aircraft disappeared from sight. Sengpiel remains listed as missing.

The formations now made for St. Nicolas, passing west of Antwerp and its harbour; soon the two Gruppen were over the northern edge of Brussels and a moment later Evere airfield came into view ahead. The pilots made out fighters parked in tight-packed rows and a large number of four-engine bombers. Quite a target! To improve maneuverability, the pilots jettisoned their drop-tanks.

At about 0920, almost the exact time planned, the first formations swept over the airfield. At Evere surprise was complete. Three Spitfires of 403 Squadron RCAF had just lifted off, three more were gathering speed, and still more were waiting to take off. While some of the JG 26 machines set about taking out enemy ground defenses, the rest went for the parked aircraft. At the same time *Unteroffizier* Burkhardt, *Oberleutnant* Glunz, *Major* Hackl and *Leutnant* Sy each bagged one of the scrambling Spitfires.

Very soon fires were sending up thick pillars of black smoke into the clear skies over the airfield. Again and again the Germans went in. Refuellers exploded, hangars blazed, aircraft melted into glowing heaps of scrap-metal. The machines were parked too close, and the ravaging fire quickly spread; 416 Squadron RCAF, for instance, were left with only four serviceable aircraft.

The Allies were fighting back, however. *Unteroffizier* Wilhelm Schmitz of 6 Staffel and *Leutnant* Meier of 9 Staffel were shot down and killed during low-level attacks on Evère and Brussels. The aircraft flown by *Unteroffizier* Risky of 6./JG 26 was hit in the engine during the second attack. Risky was able to nurse his damaged aircraft in the direction of Nordhorn, but when the engine suddenly caught fire he was forced to come down near Zwolle. Fortunately, he escaped uninjured.

Jagdgeschwader 26 made between ten and fifteen low-level runs on Brussels-Evere before it broke off and set course for home just 45 minutes after the attack had begun. Their return route was the same as the outward course, but a few pilots finished up a long way off it. One was *Leutnant*

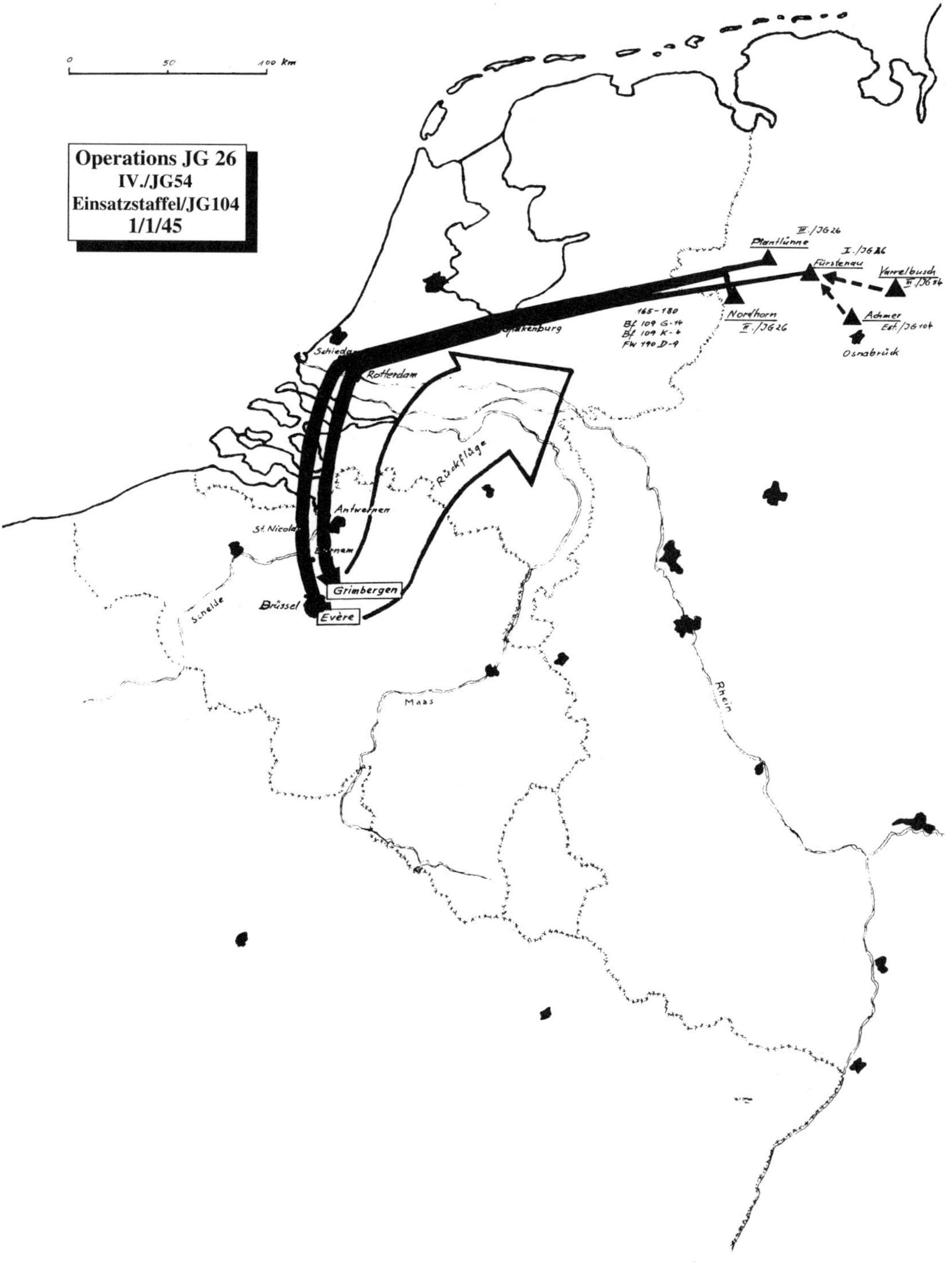
0
50
100 Km
Operations JG 26
IV./JG54
Einsatzstaffel/JG104
1/1/45
III./JG26
Plantlünne
I./JG26
Fürstenau
Varrelbusch
III./JG54
Achmer
Est./JG104
Osnabrück
Nordhorn
II./JG26
165-180
Bf 109 G-14
Bf 109 K-4
FW 190 D-9
Spakenburg
Schiedam
Rotterdam
Rückflüge
Antwerpen
St. Nicolas
Grimbergen
Brüssel
Evère
Schelde
Maas
Rhein

Leinberger, who flew off to the east after being hit by flak, and force-landed his "Black 12" near Kirchhellen, in the northern Ruhr.

The pall of black smoke over Brussels-Evere airfield was visible for miles, a testimony to the major success scored by Jagdgeschwader 26. The Geschwader reported some 120 enemy aircraft destroyed, among them 60-65 fighters of various kinds and 32 heavy bombers – and this for a loss rate of around 19%. But even JG 26's success and its relatively "light" casualties could not conceal the fact that all in all Operation "Bodenplatte" was a failure.

Another Attack on Brussels

On the evening of December 31 a dozen Bf 109 G-14s landed at Rheine airfield. These twelve machines were the total strength of II Gruppe, Jagdgeschwader 27; they were all that was left after the bitter battles of the past week. This meant that each Staffel had scarcely more than three Messerschmitts available for the "Bodenplatte" mission. I./JG 27 was not much better off, as only 16 aircraft from the Gruppe took part. It was due to their meager strengths that II Gruppe had flown in from its base at Hopsten, barely twenty kilometers away. The two Gruppen were to take off together.

The mission was still under a blanket of secrecy, and none of the pilots suspected what the mission would entail. Pilot briefings took place at about 0700 on January 1, 1945. Aerial photos of the Brussels airfield of Melsbroek were provided for the pilots to familiarize themselves with the target. This was followed by the distribution of flight maps, on which the designated flight path had been pencilled in.

"A Ju 88 will lead the Unit approximately as far as Utrecht," continued the briefer. "The Gruppen will assemble over Rheine, then low-level flight to the target!" The units based at Rheine took off as the morning sun lit the snow-covered fields. It was 0830. III./JG 27 from Hesepe, as well as IV./JG 54, which was attached to the Geschwader, from Vöden, joined the formations, while *Hauptmann* Dudeck's IV Gruppe brought up the rear.

The machines roared low over Münster, heading west, and crossed the

Dutch border near Enschede. JG 27 approached the turning point at Utrecht at a speed of 210 mph. As the pilots left the glistening ice-covered Zuider Zee behind them on the right, two squadrons of B-25 Mitchell bombers were taking off on a mission from Brussels-Melsbroek. They had unwittingly escaped the German low-level attack which was soon to strike the airfield.

Before it came to this, however, JG 27 also had to suffer a bitter experience at the hands of their own anti-aircraft guns. Not far from Utrecht the Bf 109 K-4 of *Unteroffizier* Braun of 2 Staffel was shot down in flames. The next victim was *Feldwebel* Mannchen of IV Gruppe. He, too, failed to get out of his doomed machine. Uneasiness spread throughout the units when a third machine, this time from III./JG 27, went down. Whether the pilot, *Unteroffizier* Frickmann, had been hit by anti-aircraft fire or crashed while trying to take evasive action – a dangerous maneuver at low altitude – is uncertain. His "Yellow 4" crashed into a telephone pole at full speed and broke up. Frickmann was killed.

After crossing the Amsterdam-Rhine canal on the west side of Utrecht, the Geschwader made a thirty-degree course change and headed for Breda. Not far away were other formations of German fighters, probably belonging to JG 1 or JG 26. It was an imposing scene, as the German fighter pilots were not used to seeing so many friendly fighters in the air together. As the formations crossed the front they again came under fire from anti-aircraft guns. 2 Staffel lost its *Kapitän*, *Leutnant* Heinrich Wiese, to a direct hit. His Bf 109 K-4 crashed on the bank of the Waals near Werkendam.

Soon afterwards an airfield came into view east of Breda. Several machines attacked, believing it to be Melsbroek. But this was Gilze-Rijen, which was occupied by three Spitfire- and Mustang-equipped reconnaissance units. It had already been attacked by several aircraft of JG 3.

Meanwhile, JG 27 was deep inside Belgian territory and was flying low over the forests of the province of Antwerp, approaching the capital Brussels. The fighters released their drop-tanks after passing Mechelen, and shortly afterward the airfield of melsbroek came into view. The German pilots in their cockpits went over the plan of attack one more time. "Each pilots is to fly four attacks with the objective of destroying an enemy aircraft on the ground each time."

At Melsbroek the British ground crews looked tensely to the north. Were the Mitchells back so soon? But the aircraft approaching at low altitude were not British. By the time the observers on the ground realized their mistake the Germans were upon them. JG 27's attack on Melsbroek began. At the time of the attack the airfield was home to three reconnaissance units, 16 Squadron (Spitfires), 69 Squadron (Wellingtons) and 140 Squadron (Mosquitoes), as well as three medium bomber squadrons, 98, 180 and 320 Squadrons, all equipped with the North American B-25 Mitchell.

Anti-aircraft fire throughout the attack was sporadic. The Messerschmitts of I and II./JG 27 roared down the long, north-south runway, followed by the Focke-Wulfs of IV./JG 54. In many places dark columns of smoke rose into the air, marking aircraft destroyed on the ground. Eleven of the Wellington squadron's aircraft were totally destroyed and a further two damaged.

After his second attack *Unteroffizier* Härtlein of 7 Staffel flew to far south and suddenly found himself over Evère airfield, located only a short distance from Melsbroek, where the "long-noses" of JG 26 were making their attack. Hartlein turned around and set course back to Melsbroek, but was hit by flak and had to bail out. He landed safely and was taken prisoner.

IV./JG 27 was the last unit to attack Melsbroek. *Hauptmann* Dudeck led his aircraft out of the sun and from a distance could already see a number of fires. After about five attacks the Gruppe flew away to the east. The attack on the Brussels airfield had lasted scarcely forty minutes. Eight Mitchells, three Spitfires and two Wellingtons were left damaged. According to British sources, only three Spitfires were destroyed, as well as the eleven Wellingtons already mentioned. None of the Mitchells or Mosquitoes present were destroyed.

The German units suffered further losses on the way home. *Unteroffizier* Maus of 12./JG 27 was wounded in both legs in the Eindhoven area, while further south, near Helden, *Unteroffizier* Fink of 1 Staffel was shot down and killed by a Spitfire.

The *Kommandeur* ofIV./JG 27 also failed to return to Achmer. Near Venray *Hauptmann* Dudeck's Bf 109 G-10 was hit by flak and caught fire. His parachute was torn as he bailed out and Dudeck seemed doomed as he fell at high speed toward the earth. His fall was broken by a tree, however, and the injured officer was taken prisoner and brought to a hospital. Also shot down and captured was *Fähnrich* Otto Theisen. The loss of *Leutnant* von Stechow, who was shot down and killed near Aalten, just short of the German border, brought 2 Staffel's losses to four pilots. *Unteroffizier* Werner Köpp of JG 54 was killed when his aircraft crashed northeast of Nijmegen, probably a victim of anti-aircraft fire. *Unteroffizier* Ohlenschläger of 15./JG 54 was listed as missing, and the Bf 109 K-4 of *Feldwebel* Gäbel was shot down near Kerkwijk, the pilot being killed. At the time of his death

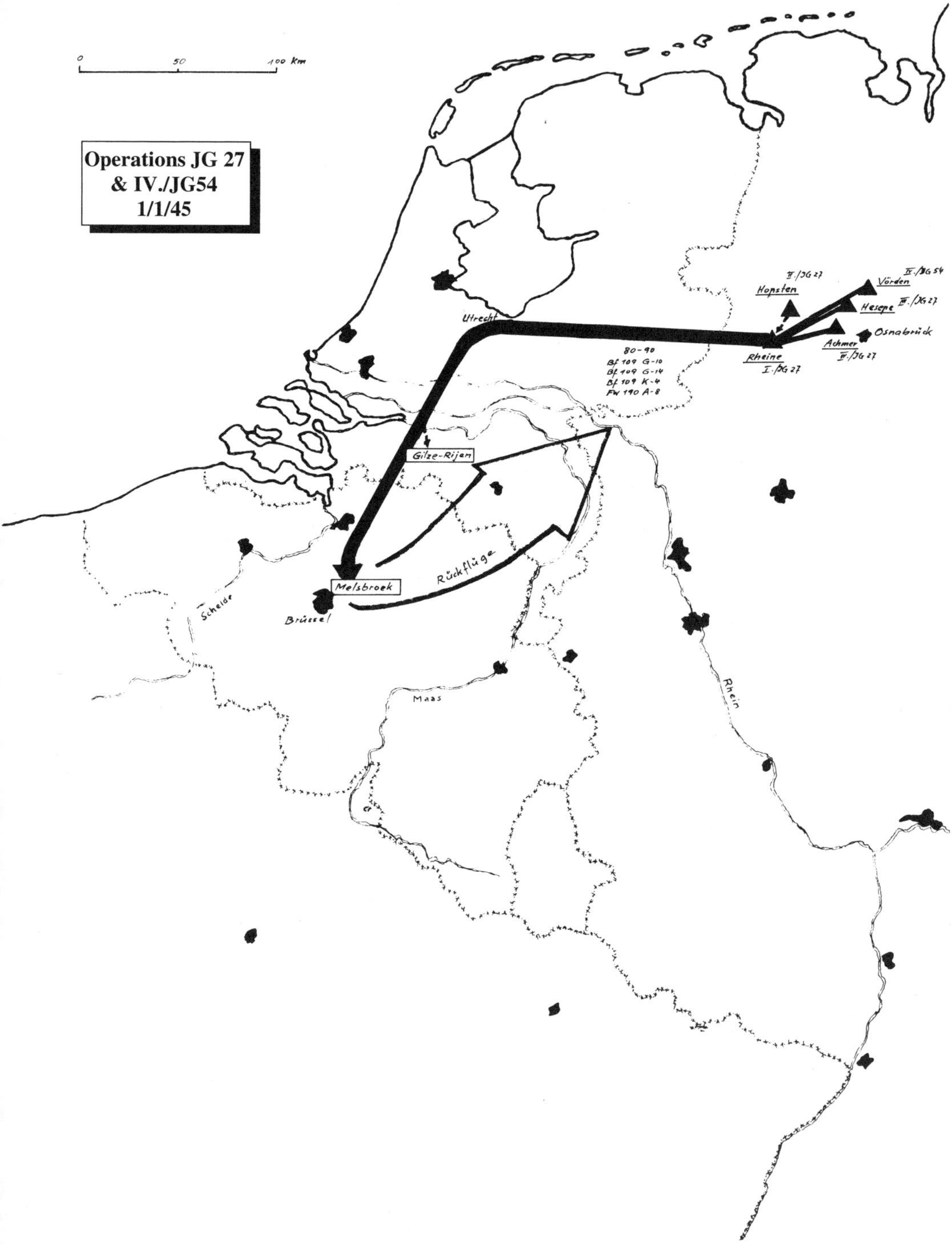

0
50
100 Km
Operations JG 27
& IV./JG54
1/1/45
Utrecht
II./JG 27
Hopsten
IV./JG 54
Vörden
III./JG 27
Hesepe
Osnabrück
Achmer
IV./JG 27
Rheine
I./JG 27
80-90
Bf 109 G-10
Bf 109 G-14
Bf 109 K-4
Fw 190 A-8
Gilze-Rijen
Rückflüge
Melsbroek
Brüssel
Schelde
Maas
Rhein

the young Gert Gäbel had shot down three enemy aircraft, two of which were twin-engine bombers.

When the mission was over JG 27 and the attached IV./JG 54 counted thirteen pilots killed or missing as well as four captured. At this point in the war the loss of two unit leaders, one of them a *Gruppenkommandeur*, weighed especially heavy. Whether the damage inflicted at Melsbroek outweighed these losses is difficult to assess. It is noteworthy that most of the losses – some of them at the hands of German anti-aircraft gunners – occurred during the approach and return flights.

"Pik As" Over Metz

Following a successful transfer flight from Donaueschingen to Stuttgart-Echterdingen Hauptmann Friedrich Müer had only a few minutes to reflect on the events of the past weeks. The assignment of his Gruppe, IV./JG 53, which had been formed the past autumn from elements of III./JG 76, had been to defend the airspace over southern Germany together with the three other Gruppen of the "*Pik As*" Geschwader. The unit had been employed exclusively defending against attacks by Allied fighter-bombers. When the unit leader was informed of the imminent attack against the enemy ground organization, *Hauptmann* Müer believed that the mission in the 5th Jagddivision's area of operations might be for other reasons. After Hitler had been forced to recognize that the Ardennes offensive was not going to achieve the desired success, at the end of December he issued orders for the preparation of a second offensive from northern Alsace: Operation "Nordwind" (North Wind).

As the Allies had already learned of this plan from statements from prisoners and was expecting the attack on December 29 – in fact it began on January 1, 1945 – *Hauptmann* Müer had no difficulty figuring out that the American fighter-bombers must also have completed their preparations. On December 27, the Thunderbolts of the 365th Fighter Group, 9th US Air Force, had transferred from their Belgian airfield to Metz-Frescaty, close to the front. The German troops in the Vosges front at that time were manning a line Hagenau-Bitsch.

On New Year's Morning, the pilots of II, III and IV./JG 53 of were divided into *Schwärme*. The Geschwader was to make a concerted attack against the French airfield southwest of Metz. The Gruppen would assemble in quadrants "05 South Ulrich-Richard" and "04 North Anton-Richard"; the approach route led over Weissenburg, Pirmasens and the St. Avold area. Whether III Gruppe also formed up over the planned assembly point Karlsruhe or proceeded from Kirrlach airfield directly west and joined the other two Gruppen beyond Pirmasens is not known with certainty.

After takeoff *Feldwebel* Friedrich Scheer of 11 Staffel went over his assignment once again: his *Schwarm* was to try and eliminate the airfield's anti-aircraft guns. This was not to be the case, however, because III./JG 53 did not reach Metz. As the Gruppe was flying over the Pfalz Forest it was attacked by a strong force of Thunderbolts. Because of the strict radio silence the attack came as a total surprise. The German pilots had no choice but to give battle. The Messerschmitts jettisoned their drop tanks and pulled up, because evasive maneuvers at such a low altitude were impossible. The Thunderbolts had the advantage of superior numbers, however. They shot down at least nine of the Gruppe's aircraft between Kaiserslautern and Pirmasens. All of the pilots, among them *Feldwebel* Scheer, escaped by parachute. Only two were injured: *Feldwebel* Plettner of 11 Staffel and *Unteroffizier* Göller of 12 Staffel. Plettner had rammed an enemy aircraft before bailing out.

Hauptmann Luckenbach, the *Staffelkapitän* 12./JG53, was flying a brand-new Bf 109 G-14 that day. During the battle he had to bail out, as "the engine could not stand the tempo of the air battle and blew up around my ears," as Luckenbach described it. *Feldwebel* Polak of 11 Staffel was supposed to take part in the operation but failed to receive notification in time. Unaware of the coming mission Polak took advantage of a Sunday evening pass. When he returned to the base his Gruppe was already in the air. Not many fighter pilots had been lucky enough to pass New Year's Eve in this fashion and possibly escape fate once again. Polak's *Staffelkapitän*, *Leutnant* Landt, was also absent, as he had just checked into the Luftwaffe rest and rehabilitation facility at Bad Wiesee.

In the meantime all the Gruppen of JG 53 stationed in the west were on their way to Metz. The airfield was located two to three kilometers west of National Highway 57, south of Metz, and had formerly been used by several German night fighter units, such as Stab/NJG 4.

There is little to report over the attack itself, as information from American records is meager. It is also uncertain how many aircraft were lost

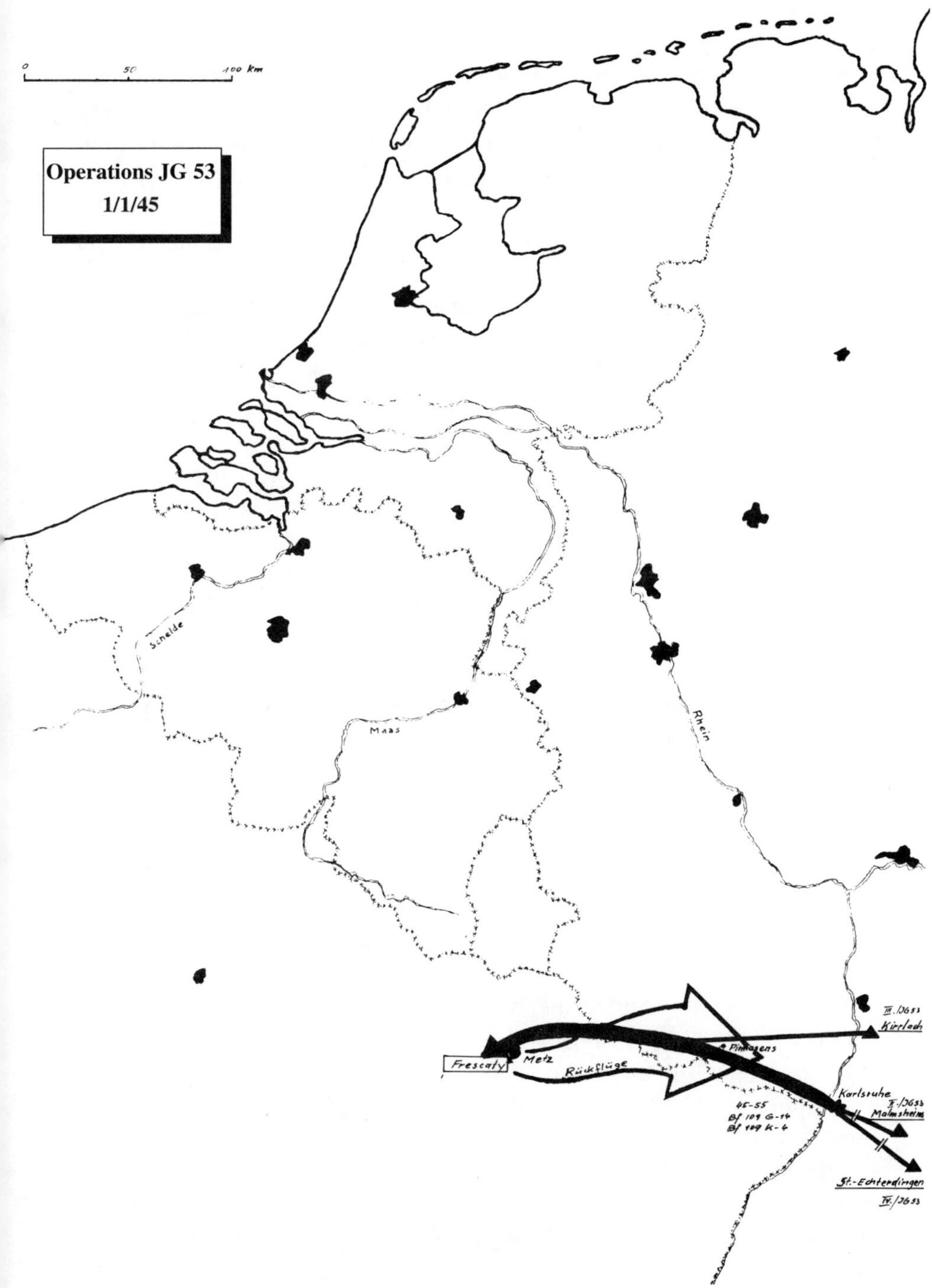

Operations JG 53
1/1/45
0
50
100 km
Schelde
Maas
Rhein
III./JG53
Kirrlach
Pirmasens
Frescaty
Metz
Rückflüge
Karlsruhe
II./JG53
Malmsheim
45-55
Bf 109 G-14
Bf 109 K-4
St.-Echterdingen
IV./JG53

over Metz-Frescaty. When the Messerschmitts attacked, about forty yellow-nosed P-47s were parked on the airfield, possibly the entire 365th Fighter Group. After the first enemy machines went up in flames the airfield defenses opened up, bringing down a number of Messerschmitts. *Gefreiter* Alfred Michel of 16 Staffel was shot down on his first pass in "Blue 2." Michel survived and was taken prisoner – (latest information is that Michel was not over Metz, but apparently made a belly landing after developing engine trouble and was then taken prisoner). *Unteroffizier* Pechardscheck of the same Staffel was also hit by flak, but managed to get his damaged aircraft back. Although wounded, he succeeded in making a forced landing at Echterdingen.

Three pilots of I Gruppe were killed and four more were listed as missing, although at least two of these turned up in American captivity. Among the fallen was *Feldwebel* Johannes Müller, a wearer of the German Cross in Gold. Müller had recently transferred from *Nahaufklärungsgruppe* 13 to the fighter unit. He was probably brought down by anti-aircraft fire; the Americans later reported that *Feldwebel* Müller of 7./JG 53 had died as a result of third-degree burns on January 2, 1945. Also killed were *Feldwebel* Nachotzky of 6 Staffel and *Feldwebel* Ernst Off, who had initially been reported missing near Metz. Müller and Off are both buried in foreign soil: Müller in Luxembourg and Off at Niederbronn in Lorraine (formerly Lothringen).

Hauptmann Müer's IV Gruppe suffered a total of eight pilots lost during "Bodenplatte." Five of these are still listed as missing: *Oberleutnant* Benz and *Unteroffizier* Maxis of 13 Staffel, *Fähnrich* Leese of 14 Staffel, and *Feldwebel* Jascheck and *Fähnrich* Rosenberger of *Hauptmann* Mayer's 15 Staffel. When troops of the US Army Signal Corps advanced to Saarlouis on February 1, a month after "Bodenplatte", they found the fuselage of a partly-cannibalized Bf 109. Still clearly visible was the black fuselage band of JG 53, the insignia of IV Gruppe and the code number, a white 13. It is still unclear whether this was the machine of the missing *Unteroffizier* Herbert Maxis, although Maxis was flying a Bf 109 G-14 coded "White 13" on January 1, 1945.

After "Bodenplatte", JG 53 only disposed of about thirty serviceable aircraft. Not twenty-four hours later American aircraft were later in the air over southwestern Germany. *Hauptmann* Friedrich Müer, commander of IV./JG 53, was killed in battle with fighter-bombers over Echterdingen on January 2, 1945, only one day after the attack on Metz.

Jagdgeschwader 77's Last Major Operation in the West

From the outbreak of war onwards, in every theatre, JG 77 "*Rotherz*" ("Red Hearts") Geschwader had always found itself in the thick of the fighting. It had begun in April 1940 when II./JG 77 was the only fighter unit to take part in Operation "Weserübung", the occupation of Denmark and Norway. Then came France and the Balkans, the southern sector of the Russian Front and later North Africa and Italy. When Müncheberg, who had commanded the Geschwader since October 1942, was killed in the Mediterranean Theater at the end of March 1943, *Major* Steinhoff took over. Under his command the unit took part in the bitter defensive fighting in Tunisia, and was later, together with elements of Jagdgeschwader 53, cut to pieces in the costly air battles over Sicily and the Italian peninsula.

It was when it was transferred to the *Reichsverteidigung* that the lack of aircrew reinforcements first began to show. The losses mounted steadily. In autumn 1944 JG 77 was committed against the Allied airborne operation at Arnhem and had to pay a heavy price for its success. Between September 21-28, 1944 it had seventeen pilots killed or reported missing, among them *Leutnant* Hans-Dieter Student, *Generaloberst* Student's son. A whole series of distinguished fighter pilots and commanders had left their mark on the Wing – men like Bär, Deicke, Freytag, Gollob, Huy, Köhler, Leie, Mader, Müncheberg, Reinert, Setz, Steinhoff, Ubben, and Wiese, to name but a few.

In mid-December 1944, when the launching of the Ardennes offensive brought about a sharp rise in fighter pilot casualties, the Geschwader took its full share. After particularly heavy losses over the Christmas period, little was left of the hard core from the Mediterranean days. *Major* Wiese having been very seriously wounded on Christmas Eve, Erich Leie took over on December 29, and *Hauptmann* Armin Köhler moved from 2 Staffel to take over III Gruppe. Now they faced a new operation. As the following account shows, it was to be a bungled one, not so much because of casualties, which in fact amounted to only 10% of those taking part, but rather because the execution of the attack went completely awry.

Before the German counter-thrust in the West Jagdgeschwader 77 was placed under command of II Jagdkorps and moved to its new bases in the Ruhr. I Gruppe was transferred from Schönwalde to Dortmund and II Gruppe to Bönninghardt, while III Gruppe switched from Seyring to Düsseldorf-Lohausen. On January 1, 1945, the Geschwader was about 100 first-line aircraft strong. The ground staff had gone to the most extraordinary lengths to get 100% serviceability. So this was a healthy unit, the more so when one considers that some fighter Gruppen were practically down to Staffel strength. But on this occasion a muster rarely attained by Home Air Defense wings was to prove of no avail. The punch thrown by JG 77 was to land on thin air.

At Bönninghardt, Dortmund and Düsseldorf the preparations for Operation "Bodenplatte" by and large followed the same pattern as at other airfields. JG 77's target was the Belgian airfield at Antwerp-Deurne; and to get there the pilots had to follow a flight path of almost 200 miles. The direct route was shorter by half, but to ensure surprise the Geschwader was to make a wide sweep to the north, taking account of the configuration of the front line, and to fly into its target from Rotterdam.

Staffel after Staffel took off into the clear morning air. The machines at once turned north across the Lippe and in fifteen minutes they were over Borken. Visibility was excellent, and all was going according to plan. A quarter of an hour later the Messerschmitts turned southwest and headed for their third fix south of Rotterdam. As they approached the front line, the German Naval AA let fly at them with everything it had.

One of the first machines to go down was that of *Leutnant* Abendroth. It was later learned that he had been captured near Rosendaal. *Gefreiter* Kofler and *Gefreiter* Mannweiler were initially listed as missing, but it turned out that Kofler had been killed and Mannweiler captured.

But the fighter formations had more than the German Flak to contend with. A mile or two from the east bank of the Ooster Schelde lay the airfield of Woendsrecht, also known as Bergen op Zoom. When several vics mistakenly went in to strafe it, they could see hardly a single machine on the ground. The German pilots were not to know that all its five Spitfire squadrons were already airborne.

Meanwhile the city and port of Antwerp, gleaming in the sunlight, loomed up to the south. Most conspicuous of all were the port, with the largest docks in Europe, and the towering cathedrals. But the pilots had little time to enjoy the sight, for as they crossed the Schelde up came the Flak. Suddenly, "Yellow 1" of Knight's Cross wearer *Leutnant* Hackler was missing. The *Staffelkapitän* of 11./JG 77 must have been shot down somewhere near Antwerp; his fate remains a mystery.

B-70 (Deurne) was a base for British Hawker Typhoon fighters. Only one of them, a 266 Squadron machine, was lost in the attack, although another dozen or so were more or less severely damaged. Against this, two Jagdgeschwader pilots were shot down in the Antwerp area and taken prisoner: *Unteroffizier* Twietmeyer and *Fähnrich* Braband, both of III Gruppe.

The orders were that the pilots were to make four runs over the field, operating singly or in pairs. But it didn't work out this way, perhaps for two reasons – the unexpected diversion onto Woendsrecht ending in fiasco, and the strength of the British defenses at Antwerp-Deurne. II./JG 77 appears to have been unable to find the target at all; the Messerschmitts made several circuits over the northeast of Antwerp, but they never attacked Deurne airfield.

After the failure of their attack, the Geschwader turned northeast for the return flight. "White 17" was shot down near Tilburg, while the British brought down "Red 7" just short of the German border. Both pilots, *Unteroffizier* Munninger and *Leutnant* Schumacher, belonged to 10 Staffel.

Seen as a whole against an initial strength of some 35 aircraft per squadron, the losses – ten pilots in all – were very light, certainly in comparison to those of other Geschwadern. It seems as though one of the Gruppen, probably I Gruppe, shot its bolt at Woensdrecht and got completely split up. This means that only III Gruppe was over the target, as on their own admission II Gruppe had been unable to find Antwerp-Deurne. Thus it may well be true that only some thirty machines ever appeared over Deurne.

German casualty lists show four pilots as killed; two more were listed missing and four were taken prisoner. The Allies, however, reported the capture of five pilots from Jagdgeschwader 77, including one from 6 Staffel. It may well be – and this applies to the other units also – that the German casualty reports have some small gaps in them, in which case all the casualty figures given would tend to be on the low side. Only one loss is known from II./JG 77: *Feldwebel* Paul Tank from 8 Staffel, who was listed as missing.

Soon after the unfortunate Operation "Bodenplatte" new orders reached the Geschwader: transfer to the Eastern Front. With this began a further chapter in the downfall of the German fighter arm.

Operations JG 77
1/1/45

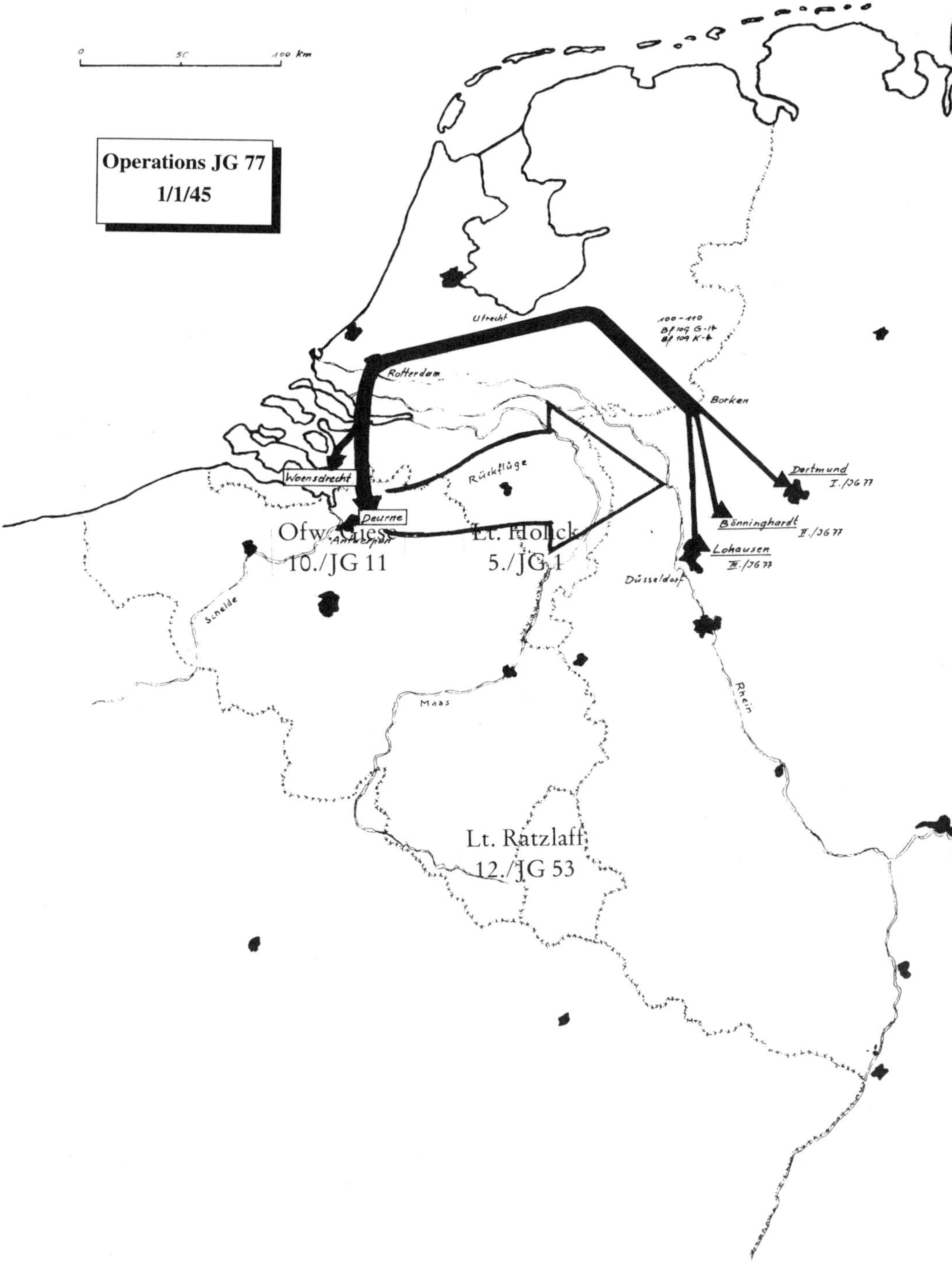

The Losses

> "New Year's Day 45 – The Execution Order from the Bunker – 304 Machines failed to return – 59 Geschwader commanders sacrificed to the murderous defenses of the Allies."

How much truth is there in these headlines from the post-war press and other publications? Almost 28 years have passed since "Bodenplatte" was flown. Many of the pilots then reported missing in fact survived the war; as many again have had to be added to the list of those killed in action. Some four dozen cases are still open at the time of writing; of some of the missing no trace whatever has been found, so that no one knows whether they were killed or came back. But after over four years of intensive research the fighter force casualties on January 1, 1945 are now reasonably firm. The resulting figures are published here for the first time.

In Operation "Bodenplatte" the German day-fighter force alone lost 214 pilots. 151 were killed or reported missing (the cases of 48 of the missing still being under investigation); a further 63 were taken prisoner. In addition there were eighteen wounded, but these cannot be counted as a total loss, since most of them were able to return to flying duties sooner or later.

While the casualties have now been established within a small margin of error, it is more difficult to arrive at figures for materiel; no list of aircraft losses as such is available, if indeed one ever existed. In every unit there must have been machines which crashed as a result of enemy action, German AA fire or technical failures while their pilots escaped unhurt. It is thus safe to assume that, in addition to the 232 incidents which caused casualties, a further 60-70 aircraft were lost, bringing the probable total for the German fighter force on January 1, 1945 to around 300. This corresponds to a loss rate of 30% of all aircraft involved in the operation.

Allied sources quote the discovery of 137 wrecked machines – 98 in the British sector and 39 in the American; of these 57 are said to have been shot down by fighters and 80 by Allied AA defenses. Adding to these the 48 as yet untraced and the eighteen flown by pilots who were wounded, we get a total of some 200 aircraft. The rest must be laid at the door of the German AA gunners. These figures can in fact never be exact, as some of the machines hit by German AA fire crashed in enemy territory and were thus counted in the figure of 137. Nevertheless the final total is probably not all that far out.

On the other hand the figure that is constantly being bandied around of 59 commanders lost in "Bodenplatte" is quite ridiculous. It is a mystery how anyone could ever have arrived at such a figure. The summary below shows clearly the actual number of commanders who became casualties:

3 Geschwaderkommodore (including *Oberst* Druschel of SG 4)
5 Gruppekommandeure
11 Staffelkapitäne (including 1 wounded)

19 unit commanders

+ 236 crew (including 19 wounded)

255 pilots

And while we are talking statistics, it is worth mentioning that the units JG 4 and JG 53 lost none of their commanders. As against this JG 6 had the highest total – six in all. In terms of pilots, Jagdgeschwader 77 had the fewest casualties and Jagdgeschwader 4 the most. At Gruppe level, it was III Gruppe of Jagdgeschwader 54 that suffered the highest casualties; of the seventeen machines that took off only seven returned – a loss rate of almost 60%.

Operation "Bodenplatte" amounted to a total defeat. The home air defense formations equipped with the standard types of fighter never recovered from the blow. Their subsequent operations were insignificant seen against the situation as a whole and offered no further threat to the domination of the Allied air forces.

Controversy continues to rage over the entire operation. The gaining of a dubious advantage at the cost of 151 fighter pilots killed or missing, all within a period of four hours, can only be described as nonsensical. When the up-and coming generation ask their inevitable questions, it will not be easy to make them see how all these things could have come about.

Notes

[1]Feuchter quotes a figure of 800. Allied estimates put the number of machines taking part as 790-870, while the OKW operations log for January 1, 1945 gives a total of 1,035.

[2]This distinction is drawn because in the German Armed Forces structure of the time the AA artillery

formed part of the Air Force (or in certain cases of the Navy).
[3]The Focke-Wulf Fw 190 F-8, like all F-Series marks, was drastically modified for the ground-attack role and was easily recognizable by its under-wing bomb-racks.
[4]Among the Allied aircraft destroyed by the German fighter force on 1 January 1945 there was not a single Tempest. Even the two aircraft logged by *Oberstlt.* Bär as Tempests destroyed on the ground were in fact Typhoons. The Tempest and the Typhoon, both developed by Hawkers, differed in appearance only in the shape of their tail.
[5]RAF/UK name – "Dakota."
[6]Albert Leo Schlageter was a World War I officer who became a national hero when he was executed by the French in 1923 for his part in the resistance to occupation of the Ruhr.

IV

FIGHTING A LOSING BATTLE

The End of the German Air Defense

Monday, January 1, 1945

As we have seen, Operation "Bodenplatte" broke the back of the corps of fighter pilots. But this was not the whole story. While the bulk of the fighter units were pouring out their blood in the Western Theater, operations over Germany itself continued.

To avoid leaving German territory completely defenseless in face of any major daylight incursions by Allied bombers, Jagdgeschwader 300 and 301 were held back at their stations in Central Germany. At that moment these two experienced formations constituted the entire home air defense force; normally their seven fighter Gruppen would have held between them over 300 first-line aircraft, by no means a negligible force. But now, at the turn of 1944/45, the earmarking of just two Geschwader to cover the whole of Germany was totally inadequate, for both were severely under-strength. Only the day before, on December 31, JG 300 and JG 301 had been on operations, hunting the enemy down and worrying him like terriers; but that day too their recent losses had left their mark on operational capability. The Allies on the other hand was growing more powerful day by day. What good were courage and resolve and acts of desperation against such odds?

As the lead formations of American bomber forces some 1,000 strong approached the islands of East Friesland that January morning, JG 300 was scrambled to intercept the stream of bombers, while JG 301 was brought to cockpit readiness. In I Jagdkorps Control Center at Treuenbrietzen they wanted to wait and see how things shaped up before committing their final fighter reserves.

First contact with the US 8th Air Force B-24 Liberators, and B-17 Flying Fortresses was made shortly before midday between Bremerhaven and Bremen. By this time the bulk of the fighters returning from their attack on the Allied infrastructure had already landed, but it was clearly out of the question to send them up again at once to intercept incoming bombers. So the Messerschmitts of II and IV./JG 300 Geschwader were the only Luftwaffe units to take on the Americans as they flew in. IV./JG 300 had been formed from the former I Gruppe of ZG 76.

This time the Mustang escort did not entirely succeed in keeping the Germans away from the bombers, and a large number was shot down. But as the battle went on German losses also grew. One of the first was *Feldwebel* Klenow of 14 Staffel. He was shot down and crashed with his "Black 18" about six miles west of Stade near Oldendorf. Soon afterward *Unteroffizier* Lickert of 12./JG 300 was also shot down and killed. In the meantime I Gruppe had also arrived in the area of operations and had made contact with the enemy near Lüneburg. "Black 1", the Bf 109 G-10/R-6 of *Unteroffizier* Horst Szurde, was hit and went down trailing black smoke. The pilot failed to escape from the plunging aircraft.

South of Hamburg a formation of about 100 Flying Fortresses broke away from the main force and turned south. Its target was the hydrogenation plant at Dollbergen, about twenty miles east of Hanover on the Hanover-Wolfsburg railway line. They must have had a brief contact over the Uelzen-Soltau area with one or more Messerschmitt Me 262s of III Gruppe, Jagdgeschwader 7. This is evidenced by the loss of one of these jet fighters, when *Leutnant* Lönnekker was shot down and killed southwest of Fassberg in a dogfight with the fighter escort. This aircraft must have been on a test flight or some kind of trial; certainly Jagdgeschwader 7 was not operational at this stage.

Meanwhile the main bomber force had reached the Elbe near Wittenberge. Headquarters, I Jagdkorps now assumed a raid on Berlin and scrambled the whole of Jagdgeschwader 301. The capital's air-raid sirens sounded at 1251, but the great city on the Spree was to be spared that day. The Americans changed heading in grid square "Dora-Dora" and made a wide sweep to the south of Berlin, making for central Germany. But first the heavy bombers came into the operational zone of Jagdgeschwader 301 with its three Gruppen of Focke-Wulfs, and bitter fighting developed south of Stendal. *Unteroffizier* Berkler of 4./JG 301 and his *Staffelkapitän*, *Leutnant* Otto Frank, fell over Letzlinger Heath near Lüderitz and Gross-Schwarzlosen.

III Gruppe reported four pilots wounded near Stendal, among them *Leutnant* Reinicke, leader of 5 Staffel. II Gruppe's only loss was *Oberfeldwebel* Schönaich, who was listed as missing.

To the north of Halle the Americans changed course again, this time to the west, and at last their intention became clear. The target was Kassel! But Jagdgeschwader 300 and 301 were now low on fuel. Back at their bases the machines were refuelled and rearmed as quickly as possible and sent straight back into the air. But the German fighters could not catch up with the heavy bomber formations, now on their way home, and had to return to base without intercepting.

On January 1, the Americans also bombed communications targets in the Coblenz-Trier area, and RAF Bomber Command put in an attack on the Dortmund-Ems Canal. Both these raids were unopposed; the two fighter Geschwader available in Germany had been drawn off by the operation against Kassel. They scored sixteen kills for the loss of 27 of their own machines. Nine pilots, six of them from JG 300, were killed, four wounded and one reported missing over Central Germany.

The air operations of the first day of the fateful year of 1945 were over. "Bodenplatte" and the subsequent defensive operation were the beginning of the end.

Tuesday, January 2, 1945

> "2.1.45: Incursion by strong American bomber formations in western and southwestern Germany. Approximately 1,400 Allied fighters! Three Gruppen of JG 4, including the last nine operational aircraft of the former Sturmgruppe, II./JG 4, took off from airfields in the Palatinate to intercept.
>
> Heavy fighting against numerically far-superior enemy forces in the Kaiserslautern-Karlsruhe-Pirmasens triangle. Three killed: *Uffz.* Bojus (10 Staffel), *Uffz.* Hener (7 Staffel) and *Oblt.* Siller (Kapitän 6 Staffel).
>
> Three wounded: *Uffz.* Hässler (1 Staffel) forced landing,
>
> *Ofhr.* Meinke (1 Staffel) and *Uffz.* Henkel (3 Staffel) bailed out.
>
> II and IV./JG 53 engaged Allied fighter-bombers in the Stuttgart area. Four pilots were killed: *Gruppenkommandeur Hptm.* Müer (IV./JG 53) and *Uffz.* Ankelmann (13 Staffel).
>
> *Gefreiter* Engel and *Ofhr.* Rubel, both of II./JG 53, were shot down and killed by Spitfires over Heimsheim as they were preparing to land at their airfield at Malmsheim."

Sunday, January 14, 1945

When the two pilots in the Arado 96 TG+UK spotted the large number of enemy aircraft on their tail, it was already too late. *Feldwebel* Hassinger and *Unteroffizier* Foerster, both from the fighter training Geschwader JG 102, had taken off early on a training flight and headed south. It must have been about 1045 when the Mustangs appeared; they shot down the lone Arado near Eggebek, killing both pilots. This marked the start of Black Sunday for the two home-based Geschwader of I Jagdkorps. Two weeks after the sacrificial action by the German fighter units in the west, JG 300 and JG 301, which had escaped January 1 relatively unscathed, were to suffer their worst defeat.

January 14 was a clear, cold winter's day. For the first time since the New Year, the US 8th Air Force was headed for the German heartland in strength. 600 heavy bombers in all – the Flying Fortresses of 3rd Air Division and some Liberators from 2nd Air Division – were already between the islands of Föhr and Pellworm and about to cross Schleswig-Holstein north of Husum, when the Mustangs of 357th Fighter Group, fanning out ahead of their bombers, chanced upon the German trainer at Eggebek.

Then the leading American formations turned southeast and headed for Schwerin on a broad front between Kiel and Neumünster. When the bombers reached grid square "*Cäsar-Cäsar*" on their usual route in over Ludwigslust, the German air defense expected a daylight raid on the German capital.

But the American strategic air force, based in England, had quite different intentions. Their targets for the day were industrial installations in Central Germany, and in particular the large military fuel depot on the Elbe near Derben-Ferchland, some eight miles west of Genthin. Other bomber elements were directed onto Magdeburg; and a second force about 400 heavy bombers strong was operating the same day in the Cologne area, attempting to take out the Rhine bridges there.

The Mustang formations screening 3rd Air Division had penetrated almost as deep as Perleberg when Col. Dregne and his 357th Fighter Group met Jagdgeschwadern 300 and 301, which had been scrambled for an interception. A major, very costly battle was about to begin. Fighting was heaviest in the area between the Havel and the Elbe, and here the Germans took appalling casualties. The pilots made desperate efforts to break through to the bombers, but most of them simply did not have enough operational experience; their attacks tended to be tentative and were carried out without vehemence.

Visibility was excellent and virtually no maneuver made by either side remained undetected by the other. But the Americans were quicker off the mark and continually got on the tails of the grey-mottled German machines; every attack on a Flying Fortress quickly turned into evasion of the Mustangs. At least five fighters were lost over Havelberg, and another dozen or more shot down in the Kyritz area. 13 Staffel of Jagdgeschwader 300 suffered worst and was virtually wiped out. One of this Staffel's Messerschmitts crashed near Glöwen on Reichstrasse 107. The pilot, *Feldwebel* Kanzek, did not get out. *Obergefreiter* Schlüter was wounded in combat only a few miles to the northeast, while "White 9" crashed in the nearby community of Görike with *Oberfeldwebel* Esche still aboard. A third Bf 109 of 13./JG 300 crashed near Breddin, killing *Gefreiter* Leinbach.

Jagdgeschwader 301 too, notably 2, 4 and 8 Staffeln, suffered heavy casualties in the same area. 2 Staffel reported three pilots having baled out near Kyritz, and 4 Staffel reported *Unteroffizier* Funken, *Feldwebel* Walter Schmidt and *Fähnrich* Strauss shot down and killed and two other pilots wounded in the triangle Barenthin-Kyritz-Gumtow, an area of under ten square miles. But that was not all. The Fw 190 A-9 of the *Staffelkapitän* of 6./JG 301, Knight's Cross wearer *Hauptmann* Hankamer, was shot down over Kyritz. Hankamer was killed. As well, the leader of 11 Staffel, *Oberleutnant* Herzog, was wounded over Kyritz.

The two German units committed 189 aircraft to this operation, and in the face of casualties on this scale it is all the more remarkable that I Jagdkorps pilots succeeded in shooting down a number of bombers. Their most notable success was against a flight of 390th Bomb Group which came down low to make its run over the Derben fuel depot. All eight Flying Fortresses were shot down in a running battle.

The American escort pilots reported an encounter with several Me 262s northwest of Berlin. These jets were from *Hauptmann* Georg Eder's 9./JG 7 based at Parchim. The Americans managed to shoot down one jet fighter near Wittstock on the east edge of the Prignitz; its pilot, *Feldwebel* Wurm, was killed.

Meanwhile the main bomber force was over the area between Stendal/ Tangermünde and Rathenow. Once again the German fighters went in, attacking the Flying Fortresses with their bristling armament head-on, or diving on them singly, in pairs or in formation from behind, in the traditional manner. But only rarely did they succeed. The silvery Mustangs knew just how to protect their bombers and inflicted heavy casualties on the Germans. A Focke-Wulf from Stab/JG 301 crashed near Strodehne at the north end of Gülper Lake. The pilot of "Black 2", *Unteroffizier* Albert Hoffmann, was killed. Not six miles west of this elements of III Gruppe ran into enemy fighters which shot down two machines – "Yellow 9" with *Unteroffizier* Friederich Diestel crashed near Wulken, and *Fähnrich* Wipfli was killed when his Bf 109 G-14 crashed near Jederitz. Another formation was jumped by Mustangs in the Rhinow-Friesack area, losing three pilots killed: *Fähnrich* Spanka of 10./JG 300, as well as *Unteroffiziere* Kilzer and Maximini of JG 301.

The bombers had already been over their targets for some time, while a whole string of engagements was taking place east of the Elbe. At this stage the Americans finally sealed off access to the bombers. III./JG 300 lost four pilots in the area of the lakes round Rathenow: *Oberfähnrich* Grothues, *Leutnant* Klostermann, *Unteroffizier* Reiche and *Oberfeldwebel* Schachtner. Twenty-two-year-old Gerhard Reiche was posted missing. *Gefreiter* Frank and *Oberfähnrich* Weissin of I./JG 300 were shot down and killed a few miles farther south, near Böhne and Premnitz on the Havel.

The 357th Fighter Group claimed 56 kills on January 14; with it in the massacre over Brandenburg were the 20th and 56th Fighter Groups, the latter being Colonel Schilling's Thunderbolt unit which had already made its mark at Christmas time 1944. One of the biggest dogfights of the day took place over the Stendal area, where elements of Jagdgeschwader 300 attempted to attack the heavy bombers. This action cost the lives of five pilots: *Oberfähnrich* Bremer and *Feldwebel* Christoffer of III Gruppe, as well as *Oberfeldwebel* Johannes Deutscher and Josef Pornkopf (missing) of IV./JG 300. The fifth pilot, *Unteroffizier* Kettmann, was a member of 8./JG 301. The Mustangs pursued his "Blue 8" as far as Wittenmoor, where they shot it down.

And thus these two Geschwader's costly operation drew to its end. The following day's Supreme Headquarters communique put the German losses at 78 machines, while the casualty lists show 69 pilots, 39 of them from Jagdgeschwader 300 and 301. Compared with the number of sorties, this amounts to a loss rate of 41%. The Allies on the other hand reported many more kills – 161 in fact. This probably refers to the total of aircraft kills for the day; taking Germany and the Western Theater together, the German fighter force lost at least 150 aircraft. Or perhaps that famous "air gunners' multiplication table" was in operation.[1] If the Americans had really shot down 161 aircraft over Central Germany, Jagdgeschwader 300 and 301 would have had only 28 machines left.

Nonetheless German casualty figures must be regarded as very high, with III and IV Gruppen of Jagdgeschwader 300 (12 and 14 respectively) at the head of the list, 13 Staffel took a punishing blow with six pilots lost, three of them killed. But the hardest hit was 10 Staffel, with five killed. Then came 4, 6 and 8 Staffel of Jagdgeschwader 301, with five pilots killed or wounded each.

The figures for kills on Allied aircraft over Germany are also conflicting. The communique mentioned above quotes 37, but the Americans reported only nine bombers and sixteen fighters (thirteen P-51s and three P-47s) lost.

Luftflotte Headquarters West also had a busy day on January 14th. As mentioned above, 400 US 8th Air Force bombers raided the Cologne area and a heavy bomber formation from RAF Bomber Command attacked the Dortmund-Ems canal. In addition 2nd TAF flew a large number of missions, mainly in west and northwest German airspace.

In the morning three Spitfire squadrons crossed the front in the east of Holland on an offensive patrol in the Hengelo-Twenthe area. 401 and 442 Squadrons RCAF caught a number of I./ JG 1 Focke-Wulfs as they were preparing to scramble. *Unteroffizier* Günter Sill of the *Gruppenstab* managed to get airborne in his "Dora-9" and shoot down one of the British fighters before being shot down himself and killed. The British destroyed seven other Focke-Wulfs on takeoff or over the Twenthe area. *Oberfähnrich* Wilhelm Ade of 2./JG 1 bailed out over Lünthen, only nine miles south of Enschede. Two other pilots, *Leutnant* Honsek and *Feldwebel* Rosemund of 1 Staffel, were shot down and killed shortly after takeoff.

Meanwhile the third Spitfire unit, 411 Squadron RCAF, had despatched three German machines, so that the eleven kills claimed by the RAF tally exactly with the losses reported by Jagdgeschwader 1. The British reported two Spitfires lost.

Over Münsterland another tragedy was enacted when IV./JG 54, already much reduced in strength from the operations of the past few weeks, was set upon and cut to pieces by Allied fighters between the Dümmer See and the Mittelland Canal. Two *Staffelkapitäne* were killed in this battle – *Oberleutnant* Helmut Radke, leader of 14./JG 54, near Hesepe, and *Leutnant* Carl Resch, 15./JG 54, near Broxten. Over the Grossen Moor an Allied aircraft shot down "White 5" flown by *Oberleutnant* Breitfeld, as well as the Focke-Wulf of *Oberfeldwebel* Seifert. Both pilots were killed. 16 Staffel also had two killed, *Unteroffiziere* Krawack and Schwarz. Krawack was shot down east of Bramsche near Engter, and Erhard Schwarz' machine came down near the Osnabrück-Diepholz rail line.

Counting *Feldwebel* Lehmann of 13 Staffel, IV Gruppe finished up with eight pilots killed and two wounded. That made their flight on January 14 the Gruppe's last defensive operation of the War.

Just before noon a group of Tempests from 3 and 486 Squadrons, based at Volkel, intercepted a formation from IV./JG 3. In the dogfight which followed, Flight Officer Payton shot down and killed *Unteroffizier* Helmut Kenne of 14 Staffel near Gütersloh. A second Focke-Wulf, "Blue 2", crashed to the southwest near Rheda, killing *Feldwebel* Landschützer. 10 Staffel lost *Oberfähnrich* Nikolaus, who was shot down near Lippstadt. On the same day IV Gruppe lost six other machines over Holland; four pilots baled out. *Feldwebel* Otto Erhardt of 13 Staffel and *Stabsfeldwebel* Wilhelm Scheschonka of 15 Staffel were killed in the Arnhem area.

The general area of Kaiserslautern was another focus of action. Here a battle group made up of five Staffeln from Jagdgeschwader 4 and 11, as well as IV./JG 53, became involved with Allied fighters whose dual task was to cover the raid on Saarbrücken and to seal off the Lorraine combat zone. Jagdgeschwader 4 lost two *Staffelkapitäne* between the Rhine and the Haardt hills. *Oberleutnant* Stark, who led 3./JG 4, fell north of Ludwigshafen near Oppau, and the former JG 5 "*Eismeer*" pilot, *Leutnant* Josef Kunz was shot down over Neustadt. In spitea of his wounds, Kunz was able to bail out of his "White 1." Nearby at Gimmeldingen, the Allied fighters shot down two Messerschmitts, one from 1./JG 4 and another from 8./JG 11. The pilot of the first machine, *Feldwebel* Willi Becker, bailed out, but the second, *Unteroffizier* Winter, was unable to do so and was still aboard "Blue 13" when it smashed into the ground.

Elements of IV./JG 53, based at Stuttgart-Echterdingen, encountered some American fighter-bombers west of Karlsruhe. In the scrap that ensued *Leutnant* Liebscher was killed. A second pilot, *Feldwebel* Erich Kramp, was wounded and had to abandon his Bf 109 G-14.

Jagdgeschwader 26 was assigned to patrol the Ardennes sector on January 14. About midday it met a strong force of enemy fighters over the Cologne-Bonn area. The outcome – ten pilots killed in action, three missing and two wounded. Among the fallen was the *Kapitän* of 5./JG 26, Knight's Cross wearer Gerhard Vogt, who was shot down near Cologne with 48

Fighter Losses on January 14, 1945

Units Involved	Killed/ Missing	Wounded	Total Casualties	Aircraft	Locale
I/JG1	10	1	11	Fw 190 A-8/A-9	Enschede, Twenthe, Venlo
I/JG2	3		3	Fw 190 D-9	Altenstadt
III/JG2	1	1	2	Fw 190 D-9	Lich, Hagenau
			5		
III/JG3	1		1	Bf 109 K-4	Arnheim, Deelen
IV/JG3	4	4	8	Fw 190 A-8/A-9	Gutersloh, Lippstadt
			9		
I/JG4	1	2	3	Bf 109 G-14/K-4	Gemmeldingen
IV/JG4		1	1	Bf 109 G-10	Neustadt, Oppau
			4		
III/JG7	1		1	Me 262 A-1	Wittstock
II/JG11	2	1	3	Bf 109 G-14	Gemmeldingen, Kaiserslautern
I/JG26	2	1	3	Fw 190 D-9	Cologne-Bonn
II/JG26	8	1	9	Fw 190 D-9	Lengerich
III/JG26	3		3	Bf 109 G-14/K-4	Steinbeck, Overath
			15		
I/JG27	1		1	Bf 109 G-14	Ibbenburen
II/JG27	1		1	Bf 109 G-14	
			2		
IV/JG53	2	1	3	Bf 109 G-14	Bad Durrheim, Kandel
IV/JG54	8	2	10	Fw 190 A-8/A-9	Bramsche, Hesepe, Vorden
I/JG77	2		2	Bf 109 G-10/K-4	Dusseldorf
II/JG77	3	2	5	Bf 109 G-10/G-14	Krefeld, Warendorf, Zutphen
			7		
I/JG300	5	1	6	Bf 109 G-10/G-14	Brandenburg
II/JG300	5	2	7	Fw 190 A-8	Havelberg
III/JG300	11	1	12	Bf 109 G-10/G-14	Perleberg, Nauen
IV/JG300	11	3	14	Bf 109 G-10	Salzwedel, Stendal
			39		
*Stab/JG301	1		1	Fw 190 D-9	Barenthin
I/JG301	7	5	12	Fw 190 A-9/R11	Haverberg
II/JG301	10	1	11	Fw 190 A-9/D-9	Gumtow, Kyritz
III.JG301	4	2	6	Fw 190 A-8	Perleberg, Pritzwalk
			30		
Total Losses (Western Theatre and Germany)	107	32	139 (including 5 Staffel leaders killed, 3 Staffel leaders wounded)		

*Stab = Staff (headquarters)

victories to his credit. *Unteroffizier* Karl Ullerich was shot down by a Spitfire near Lengerich. He managed to abandon his aircraft but was unable to pull the ripcord. *Unteroffizier* Karl Russ was killed after ramming a Spitfire near Steinbeck.

At last Black Sunday was over; and the balance-sheet was a grim one. It bore witness to the German fighter pilots' desperate efforts to achieve something in face of all the odds by barring the Allies way into German airspace. For the picture that the men in their Focke-Wulfs and Messerschmitts saw in their minds' eye was always the same – the daily destruction of German cities, buildings reduced to rubble, conflagrations and civilians dead and injured. January 14, 1945 cost the German fighter force 107 pilots killed or missing and 32 wounded. The fighter pilots had shown themselves full of dash and ready to give their lives. But the air defense of Germany, and indeed German airpower in the West had taken yet another hard blow. The day-fighter force equipped with piston-engine aircraft was no longer in a position to make a significant impact on the course of events.

January 14-17, 1945

Night fighter operations in January 1945 remained far more profitable than the day fighters' actions. For the loss of "only" 47 machines, Jagdkorps I night fighters could still claim 113 kills – admittedly not a very significant figure when seen against the number of Allied sorties. On the British side the trend was to make greater use of the Mosquito bomber. These fast machines flew in almost nightly in an attempt to break civilian morale by harassing attacks on German cities. But they were seldom troubled by German defenses; in the whole of the month only one Mosquito was shot down.

On the night of January 14-15, a large-scale deception plan by RAF Bomber Command succeeded in diverting the defense from the real target, the Leuna hydrogenation plant. Nevertheless some of the 250 night fighters which had been scrambled in pursuit did find the enemy. This nocturnal encounter cost the British twelve bombers against six German machines. Among the German losses was the Bf 110 coded G9+EZ of 12./NJG 1, which crash-landed east of Werl. All members of the crew, which comprised *Leutnant* Schlage, *Feldwebel* Dornebusch and *Obergefreiter* Hildebrandt, sustained injuries.

Of over twenty night operations flown during the month, the largest took place on the night of January 16-17, when the RAF put in some 250 heavy bombers against Magdeburg. The city had been bombed by Americans during the day, and fires were still burning to guide the British onto their target. On this occasion only 128 German night fighters were committed, and again several were lost. One was shot down by a British long-range night fighter just before 2300 about four miles northeast of Paderborn. The aircraft involved was Ju 88 G-1, 3C+HR, of 8./NJG 4. Pilot *Oberfähnrich* Karsten, radio/radar operator *Feldwebel* Bartsch and gunner *Unteroffizier* Pasch died in the crash.

Monday, January 22, 1945

After the failure of Operation "Bodenplatte" and the costly January 14 air defense operation, and in face of the tremendous toll that these had taken of the fighter pilots, Hitler appeared no longer to give priority to countering the bombing raids on Germany. Towards the middle of the month an order went out from Luftwaffe High Command to the division headquarters transferring seven day fighter squadrons to the Eastern Front, to support the Army in the "struggle for freedom in the East." The first to be affected by this order were JGs 1, 3, 4, 11 and 77, but the two Reich Geschwader, JG 300 and JG 301, were also to take part in the final battle.

Conflicting orders, the disciplining of distinguished commanding officers and deprecation of the fighter pilots' personal achievements combined to bring to a head the loss of confidence in the Luftwaffe High Command that was once more making itself increasingly felt towards the end of 1944 and Operation "Bodenplatte." Göring's standing among the first-line aircrew had long since sunk to nothing. The Commander-in-Chief of the Luftwaffe naturally did not remain unaware of this; back in the late autumn of 1944 he had called the Geschwader commanders to discuss what could be done to change the situation for the better. But so many differing views were put forward that nothing really came of this conference; certainly it did nothing to solve the crisis of confidence in the Luftwaffe.

General Galland's sudden dismissal from his appointment in the middle of January was the last straw. Embittered by the recent decisions, experienced, battle-proven Geschwader commanders, the senior fighter officers of regions, Jagddivision commanders and inspectors drew up a memorandum which put the situation as it really was to the *Reichsmarschall* in the plainest and frankest of terms, with complete disregard of possible consequences. Göring quickly made a day available.

So it was that about noon on Monday, January 22, at the "*Haus der Flieger*" in Berlin, there opened the meeting that historians have since often named "The Mutiny of the Aces." But this name is scarcely to the point; there could be no question whatever of a "mutiny", for it was not the interests of individual Luftwaffe officers that were at stake. The moving spirit behind this unique assembly was *General* Galland, seen by the High Command as one of those responsible for the failure of the fighter force and therefore removed from his appointment as *General der Jagdflieger*. Thus the reason which had brought distinguished, experienced fighting men like Graf, Lützow, Rödel, Steinhoff and Trautloft together on that January day was not simply to have a long overdue heart-to-heart talk with the *Reichsmarschall*. Over and above this, they were determined to subject the current Luftwaffe leadership to severe criticism, as set out point by point in the memorandum submitted by this group of senior officers.

A short extract from the draft of this memorandum will serve to indicate to the reader the problems which those taking part intended to have out with Göring. The reasons for the crisis were as follows:

> 1. The dismissal of *General* Galland was incomprehensible to the men of the fighter units. He was recognized by the fighter arm as its outstanding personality and leader and – despite the demands he made on those under him – enjoyed its loyalty and love.
>
> 2. The frequent accusations of cowardice directed at the fighter pilots by the *Reichsmarschall*, and this despite the fact that their losses were probably higher than those of any arm of the Luftwaffe or the Wehrmacht as a whole.
>
> 3. Although he is held in personal and professional respect, *General* Peltz can never gain the confidence of the fighter arm, because:
>
> > (a) At this turning-point in the nation's history he held IX Luftwaffe back from operations by imposing exaggerated training requirements, while at the same time committing the ill-trained day fighter pilots to battle with no thought for the consequences.
> >
> > (b) He is not a fighter pilot.

> (c) He was responsible both for the operation of January 1, 1945 and for the losses that followed the launching of the Ardennes Offensive (i.e. from December 17th 1944), which together cost the Air Force:
>
> 2 Geschwaderkommodore
> 14 Gruppenkommandeure
> 64 Staffelkapitäne
>
> In the view of the fighter arm these losses were basically attributable to command errors.

Göring was accompanied by the Luftwaffe Chief of Staff, *General* Koller, and a number of other officers. He was handed the memorandum, and his face hardened as he read it. Then *Oberst* Lützow, who had been nominated as spokesman, stood up and began to speak. This is roughly the course of the dialogue that ensued:

> "Herr *Reichsmarschall.* In the name of the officers present I must ask you to allow me to speak freely for fifty minutes and to give me your assurance that you will not interrupt. Unless you do this our aim, which is to put you fully in the picture, will be frustrated."
>
> "I've never heard anything like it!" Göring raged, "Are you trying to accuse me of not having built up a strong Luftwaffe?"

The intrepid Lützow was not to be put off like that. He agreed that Göring had created a strong Luftwaffe and had used it with success in Poland and France. But then he told the *Reichsmarschall* straight to his face:

> "But since then, *Reichsmarschall*, from that moment on, you have been asleep."

Göring was beside himself with rage:

> "What's that you're saying?" he roared, "This is a fine council of war! A ring of mutineers! I'll have the lot of you shot!"

With these words, face flushed with anger, he stormed out of the room. Lützow was relieved from his position and "exiled" by the *Reichsmarschall.*

He had to leave Germany forthwith and was posted as Commander of Fighters, Italy – an appointment which had long since lost any importance.

Trautloft, too, had to go and the end of January 1945 saw the final shuffling of personnel in the Luftwaffe. *Oberst* Gollob took over at Kladow as *General der Jagdflieger*. *Oberstleutnant* Dahl replaced him as *Inspekteur der Tagjagd*, handing over Jagdgeschwader 300 to *Major* Hackl, then commanding II./JG 26, who was widely recognized as an outstanding fighter man.

But the slaughter of fighter pilots went on.

January's End

After the transfer of a large number of fighter units to the Eastern Front in mid-January, only four day fighter Geschwader remained available to the Home Defense Forces and Luftflotte Headquarters West. And all four were well below strength. The Allied bombers in their hordes droned their way across Germany every day. The raids continued with unabated weight. Augsburg, Hamburg, Magdeburg, Paderborn, Bielefeld, Mannheim, Heilbronn, Duisburg, Düsseldorf, Cologne, Kassel, Hamm, Münster – these were just the main bomber targets for the second half of the month.

The German air defense in the I Jagdkorps' area had by now become virtually meaningless. Losses amounted to almost 30% of sorties flown, while kills did not even amount to 0.2% of the Allied aircraft committed.

In the last fifteen days of January 1945 the fighter force lost at least a further 125 pilots, 80% of them flying close support missions on the Eastern Front. Seven Staffel leaders failed to return. Jagdgeschwader 6, operating in the Oder-Vistula sector, was the hardest hit. It lost eighteen killed or missing, among them two Staffel leaders.

On January 26, the day that *Oberstleutnant* Dahl was appointed Inspector of Day Fighters, I Jagdkorps was redesignated IX Fliegerkorps (Fighters). The weak forces at its disposal from that point on left little scope for effective action. Only the formations which had converted to the new Me 262 jet fighter were still to achieve successes which, though noteworthy, were in no way decisive.

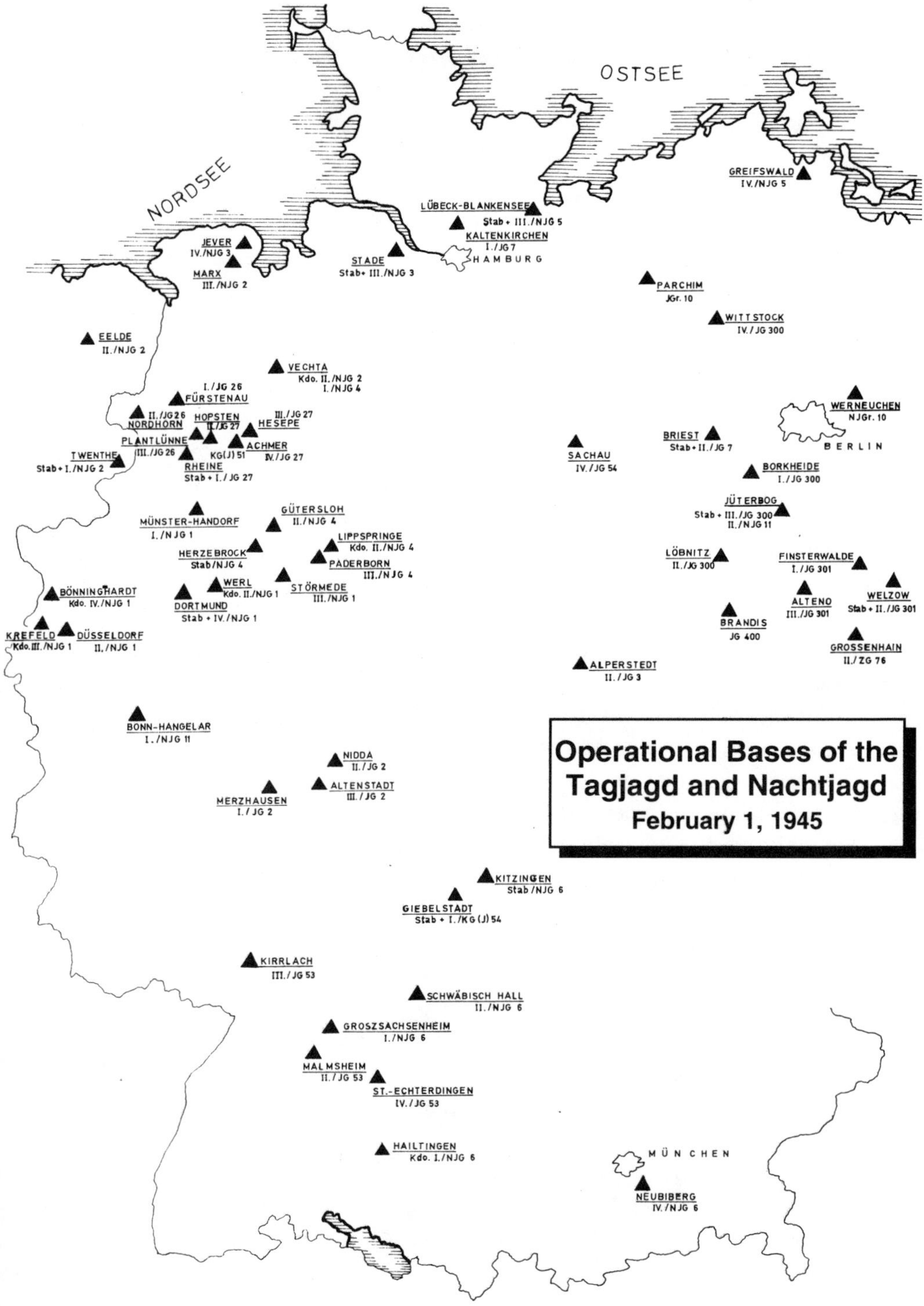

Operational Bases of the Tagjagd and Nachtjagd
February 1, 1945

Friday, February 9, 1945

The War had entered its final phase. In East and West alike Allied forces already stood on German soil and was pressing forward relentlessly to deliver the final back-breaking blows. By now the Soviet armies had closed up to the Oder and were concentrating for their final major thrust on Berlin, while in the West the Allies were preparing their leap across the Rhine. Because of this, the Allied air effort continued to be mainly directed against communications targets and the fuel industry. But the Luftwaffe had little left to put up against the bombers' incursions.

Right at the beginning of February a number of German towns, among them Mannheim, Ludwigshafen and Bochum, had suffered massive terror raids. On February 3, Berlin was subjected to a raid that proved to be the most damaging and the costliest in civilian casualties so far. Two days later Regensburg was the target for US 15th Air Force's heavy bombers. AA apart, German air defense activity was slight; for the Luftwaffe High Command had issued orders to the wings that fighters should no longer be scrambled if the operation stood little chance of success. But the question was whether a promising opportunity of this kind would ever again present itself.

In the forenoon of February 9, almost 1,300 heavy bombers from US 8th Air Force, in several large formations, flew in over West Germany to take on communications targets in the German heartland. At the same time one of these groups was ordered to take out the hydrogenation plant at Lützkendorf, ten miles west of Merseburg.

It was over the Rhine-Main area that the first encounter took place between the Americans and I Gruppe of the new KG(J) 54, which was ordered to intercept. Kampfgeschwader 54 had turned in its Ju 88s and, like Kampfgeschwader 51, had converted onto the Me 262. The weather was bad when *Oberstleutnant* Freiherr zu Eisenbach, the unit's commander, led fifteen machines off from Giebelstadt; as far as is known, this was the Gruppe's first operational mission. Near midday the Me 262 jets sighted the bomber formations to the north of a line between Frankfurt on Main and Wiesbaden. But in breaking through the cloud the German formation had got so split up as to make a coherent attack impossible. The Americans' heavy defensive fire knocked down three German jet fighters one after the other. At noon the Geschwader commander was killed in action: *Oberstleutnant* Volprecht Riedesel Freiherr zu Eisenbach was killed in the crash of his

Messerschmitt a mile east of Camberg. Soon afterward another Me 262, B3+GL, crashed near Neuhof with *Oberleutnant* Günter Kahler aboard. *Major* Otfried Sehrt, commander of I Gruppe, was wounded near Frankfurt. West of Gelnhausen Mustangs of the 55th Fighter Group shot down a further Me 262. The pilot, *Oberleutnant* Walter Draht, was also killed.

Some seventy fighters from JG 300 and JG 301 were scrambled against the bomber formations heading for Thuringia and Saxony, but the chances of success appeared remote. Yet again, as on every occasion in the past, the Mustangs were able to screen their bombers effectively. For only two bomber kills the German units lost eleven machines, with four pilots killed and two wounded. There was no chance of warding off the raid on Magdeburg, for the American fighters had pushed forward in strength thirty miles or more to the east of the city and forced I and III Gruppe of Jagdgeschwader 300 to give battle. *Unteroffizier* Lohrey and *Oberfähnrich* Josef Miller of III Gruppe were shot down and killed near Belzig. "Red 9", flown by *Gefreiter* Meinhard of 2 Staffel was also shot down in this area, but Meinhard was able to escape by parachute. Elements of I Gruppe would appear to have got closer to Magdeburg, as two Messerschmitts were lost near Zerbst and Burg. They were the aircraft of *Feldwebel* Zeder and *Feldwebel* Gärtner, both of whom were shot down and killed.

JG 301 reported another pilot, *Oberfeldwebel* Salzgruber of 6 Staffel, as wounded, after his Fw 190 D-9 was shot up by American fighters over Grieben, near Stendal. Far to the north in the Wittenberge area the leader of 4./JG 300, *Oberleutnant* Burghoff, was shot down. This brought the number of unit leaders lost in the defensive battle against the US 8th AF on February 9 to three.

Wednesday, February 14, 1945

The heaviest and cruellest air raid to which any German city was subjected in the whole of World War II was only a few hours past. Dresden, the splendid Baroque city on the Elbe, had been obliterated. The folly of war reached its peak on the night of February 13-14, when the RAF, with a total of 770 Lancasters and a force of Mosquitos, carried out a two-phase attack on the capital of Saxony, dropping some 2,700 tons of bombs of all sizes. First estimates gave a figure of 20,000 killed. Home Air Defense could put up only 27 night fighters against this operation; their score was nil.

To complete the catastrophe, another heavy bomber force appeared over the Dresden area on the morning of February 14th. This time it was the Americans, who penetrated to Saxony via Kassel and the Harz Mountains – 311 Flying Fortresses, with an escort of twice that number of Mustangs! Their bombs ravaged the already devastated city anew and sent another 10,000 to their death in the flames; for at this time Dresden was giving shelter to a host of refugees from the Eastern regions. At the same time two other terror raids were made – one on Chemnitz, and one, the seventh since the New Year, on Magdeburg.

On February 14, the Americans put 945 heavy bombers into the overcast skies of Central Germany. To counter the three enemy incursions, Home Air Defense could muster only 145 machines from IX Fliegerkorps (Fighters); and once again it was JG 300 and JG 301 who bore the brunt. On their own figures twenty of their aircraft went down. The Americans, on the other hand, lost only two bombers, a further testimony to the impotence of the German fighter force.

To the west of Riesa, in grid square "Ludwig-Gustav 4", two Gruppen of Jagdgeschwader 300 were in action against American escort fighters, who brought down a Messerschmitt from 4 Staffel and an Fw 190 from 6 Staffel in the Oschatz area: the Messerschmitt pilot, *Leutnant* Gerhard Achard, fell over Dahlen, while *Obergefreiter* Rösch was killed when his "Yellow 14" crashed near Lönnewitz. II Gruppe suffered two further losses in the attack on the American force attacking Chemnitz. All three pilots were killed, including *Unteroffizier* Walter Beuchel of 5./JG 300, who was initially posted missing.

Meanwhile the Messerschmitts of III Gruppe had scrambled from Jüterbog and reached the operational zone. They intercepted just after crossing the Elbe, and this encounter cost the lives of two pilots, *Oberfähnriche* Heyer and Howe failed to return.

Unhampered and in parade formation the American bombers flew on toward their targets. Fighter-bomber formations went over to low-level attacks, turning their guns on anything left over from the bombing. And the home air defense fighter units were impotent; they could do nothing more to put up an effective defense against the resulting inferno.

Jagdgeschwader 301, in particular the elements of II Gruppe from Welzow, had its losses too. The Fw 190 D-9s flown by *Oberfeldwebel* Frank and *Leutnant* Stuck were shot down east of Leipzig. Stuck was wounded, but survived. A third pilot of 7 Staffel, *Feldwebel* Helmut Stöber, fell somewhere over Saxony in the unequal battle against the superior numbers of escort fighters.

Jagddivision 1 ended the day with ten pilots killed and one wounded.

And after the Americans had reduced three cities of Central Germany to rubble and twisted metal overhung with the stench of death, the late afternoon of February 14 brought action for Luftflotte Headquarters West in the shape of an encounter between British Spitfire formations and the Focke-Wulfs of III./JG 54,[2] which was flying takeoff and landing cover over the Rheine fields for the Me 262 jets of KG(J) 51.

In 2 TAF's favorite hunting-ground, the Rheine-Osnabrück area, *Unteroffizier* Seidenfuss and *Obergefreiter* Zogbaum fell to the guns of Flight-Sergeant Moyle and Flight Lieutenant Woolley of 41 Squadron (Spitfires). Shortly after 1700 Flight Lieutenant Gaze of 610 Squadron shot down an Me 262 with *Feldwebel* Hofmann at the controls; the machine crashed near Emmerich, killing the pilot.

February 21/22, 1945

German night fighters were to score one more major success before the war ended. A massive terror raid on Dortmund on the night of February 20-21 had cost the British 25 heavy bombers. The following night, in a two-wave attack on Duisburg and a raid on Worms, 62 more British bombers were shot down. On the evening of Wednesday February 21, over 800 Allied four-engine machines flew in over Germany, 450 of them headed for Duisburg. 129 night fighters from NJGs 1, 2, 3, 4 and 6 were scrambled against this RAF Bomber Command operation.

In the moonlit skies bitter fighting developed and spread out over wide areas. Of the 62 kills, 28, or 45%, were added to the tallies of just four night fighter pilots, *Oberfeldwebel* Bahr of NJG 6 shot down seven bombers; and *Hauptmann* Hager of II./NJG 1 knocked eight out of the sky within the space of seventeen minutes. *Hauptmann* Rökker, leader of 2./NJG 2, sent six heavy bombers down, and *Major* Schnaufer, commander NJG 4 and undoubtedly the greatest night fighter ace of the war, accounted for seven.

Over the whole of the Ruhr, the Bf 110s, Ju 88s and He 219s clung to the enemy bomber stream. The ground control centers directed their pilots on to the bomber formations passing to and fro, and pilots then sought out their targets. Tracer criss-crossed the night sky, and gaudy torches of flame, plunging like comets, marked the end of the bombers. Traffic was brisk on all the night fighter nets.

It was the Mosquito long-range night fighters, whose task was to escort and protect the bombers, that posed the greatest threat and brought about most of the German losses. South of Duisburg, *Hauptmann* Schirmacher and *Feldwebel* Waldmann, the crew of Heinkel 219 "G9+TH" from 1./NJG 1, had to make a forced landing in which Waldmann, the radar operator, was injured. A Bf 110 from 9 Staffel of the same wing was shot down by a Mosquito night-fighter twelve miles east of Störmede.

On the night of February 21-22, the British lost about 8% of the bombers committed against Duisburg and Worms. But what made the measure of success even more remarkable was the very light German losses of only four aircraft. Six aircrew were killed and two wounded.

While the major air battle was in progress over the West and Southwest, the RAF also flew about 100 Mosquito bomber sorties in two groups for a harassing raid on Berlin. For the first time the Me 262 B-la/Ul, a night-fighter version with the "Lichtenstein" SN-2 airborne radar, went up to meet them. These machines, from 10./NJG 11, under *Oberleutnant* Welter ("*Kommando Welter*") were based at Jüterbog; they had specialized in Mosquito interception, as the Me 262 had the performance necessary to catch these fast, highly maneuverable British bombers. That night they shot down three Mosquitos over Berlin.

But in proportion to the RAF Bomber Command effort, the British casualties in those February nights were light, only exceeding those of the previous month by rather under 2%.

Thursday, February 22, 1945

> 22.2.45: "The Allies carried out Operation "Clarion." A demonstration of enemy air power over the entire Reich with focal points in southern Germany, the Ludwigslust-Lüneburg-Salzwedel triangle and the Halberstadt-Hildesheim area.
>
> In 1st Jagddivision area more than thirty Me 262s of JG 7 in action. The jet unit lost five machines with one pilot, *Ofw*. Helmut Baudach (10./JG 7), killed in action.
>
> In the area of LwKdo West heavy fighting involving I and III./JG 26, III./JG 54 as well as elements of all four Gruppen of

JG 27. JG 26 reported one killed (*Fw.* Girstenbreu near Altenrheine) and two wounded (*Uffz.* Gehrke over Hopsten and *Uffz.* Weiss over Greven) after combat with Spitfires and Tempests. In addition, III./JG 54 lost two Fw 190 D-9s near Varrelbusch, shot down by Mustangs and Tempets respectively.

Fw. Gasser (10 Staffel) and *Fw.* Westedt (11 Staffel) killed.

JG 27 also suffered six killed. *Uffz.* Steinke crashed on approach to Rheine due to battle damage and was killed. *Ofw.* Kühl (5./JG 27) was shot down by our own flak north of Hopsten. *Lt.* Eugen Bau, flying "White 3" of 9./JG 27, bailed out over Alverskirchen, but his parachute failed to open.

1450 hours. Combat involving IV./JG 27 and seven Tempests of 486 Squadron over the Münster area. *Staffelkapitän Hptm.* Grapp (15./JG 27), *Fhr.* Balluf and *Ofw.* Wittke killed, *Lt.* Schindler and *Fw.* Tschertner wounded.

In 5th Jagddivision area combat in the Stuttgart area between Mustangs and three Staffeln of JG 53. Two pilots lost their lives in tragic fashion after bailing out: *Lt.* Hans Fischer bailed out too low, and *Ogfr.* Fred Hellig came down in the Neckar River and drowned.

Uffz. Reichenberger (5 Staffel) was shot down by a Mustang south of Heimsheim. Only *Lt.* Moser of 14./Jg 53 survived this action – albeit wounded – after bailing out over Reutlingen.

It is noteworthy that during this last massed incursion the enemy also carried out numerous secondary attacks, mostly by fighter-bombers against less important targets."

Sunday, February 25, 1945

The closing days of February were marked by another period of unusually intensive Allied air activity over Germany. On February 24, strong US 8th Air Force heavy bomber formations attacked hydrogenation plants in the Hamburg and Hanover areas. These raids met no opposition and only two bombers failed to return.

On the following day the Americans launched a major operation against the German communications system, at the same time attacking a number of airfields, mainly those used by Me 262 units. The towns of Aschaffenburg, Friedrichshafen, Munich and Ulm also suffered raids of varying weight. The

Fighter Losses on February 25, 1945

Units Involved	Killed/ Missing	Wounded	Total Casualties	Aircraft	Locale
I/JG2	1		1	Fw 190 D-9	Groß Umstadt
III/JG2	1		1	Fw 190 D-9	Odenwald
			2		
I/JG26	6		6	Fw 190 D-9	Greven, Nord-
II/JG26	1	1	2	Fw 190 D-9	horn, Köln-Wahn
			8		
I/JG27	3	2	5	Bf 109 K-4	Ahaus, Coesfeld
II/JG27	2	4	6	Bf 109 G-14	Hesepe, Münster,
III/JG27		1	1	Bf 109 K-4	Osnabrück
IV/JG27	4		4	Bf 109 G-10/K-4	
			16		
I/JG301	4		4	Fw 190 A-9/R11	Salzwedel,
II/JG301	1		1	Fw 190 A-9/D-9	Stendal
			5		
Total Losses (Germany)	23	8	31		

American fighter escort, over 600 strong, once again succeeded in holding off the German fighter defense and allowing the 1,177 heavy bombers used to reach their targets unimpeded. The RAF also flew another daylight operation, this time against Dortmund.

IX Fliegerkorps (Fighters) scrambled a large number of fighter units against this massive incursion, but all were immediately contained by the escort fighters or the Allied fighter-bombers, which were out in strength. Elements of I./JG 2 "*Richthofen*" took off from the strip at Merzhausen in the Taunus Hills to intercept a Liberator formation returning from a raid on Aschaffenburg. A spectacular dogfight between this unit's Focke-Wulfs and the American escort fighters developed over Gross Umstadt. A group of twelve Mustangs and six Lightnings dove on the handful of German machines and shot two down. *Unteroffizier* Ewald Kamman of 3 Staffel and *Oberleutnant* Rossbach of 9 Staffel were killed. Kamman was listed as missing until 1963 when the crash site was discovered by chance.

Jagdgeschwader 27 once again took substantial casualties when its four Gruppen became involved with British fighters over the Münster-Osnabrück

Dawn takeoff — the start of Operation Bodenplatte. On the early morning of January 1, 1945, 33 fighter Gruppen were ordered into attacks against the Allied infrastructure in Holland, Belgium and France. The German fighter force's most costly operation was under way. The photographs show to Fw 190 A-8s and a D-9 taking off.

Formation takeoff by Messerschmitt Bf 109G's on a snow covered field.

A fighter Staffel flying on an air defense operation — and (below) in the ground-attack role.

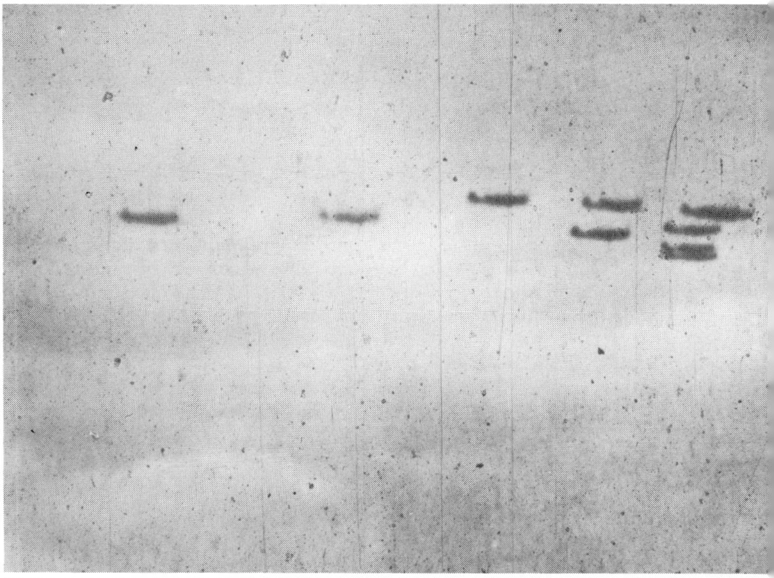

At low level over an enemy airfield. Two Bf 109s of II./JG 11 in the surprise attack on Asch airfield in Belgium. But the operation cost JG 11 dearly; among the pilots killed or missing was its commander Oberstlt. Günther Specht.

Shot down! A Focke-Wulf is hit and the pilot bales out.

This photograph, taken somewhere in Belgium or Holland, shows the spot at which a German fighter crashed on January 1, 1945.

Destroyed on the ground — a burning Lancaster, Hawker Typhoon and a Spitfire. Operation Bodenplatte cost the Allied air forces some 400 aircraft, however, they were able to make these losses good very rapidly. The German fighters' greatest success was at Eindhoven airfield, where the Typhoons of a complete Canadian fighter squadron were destroyed.

His aircraft riddled with bullets, Gefreiter Wagner of 5. Staffel/JG 4, landed on the enemy airfield at St. Trond and was taken prisoner by the Americans. His "White 11", repainted of course, was put to good use by US 404th Fighter Group as a liaison aircraft.

One of the many crashes in enemy territory on January 1, 1945. In their forward sectors, the Allies counted in all 137 crashed German fighters.

After a hit in the radiator, Lt. Nibel of 10. Staffel/JG 54, had to make a forced landing at Wennel, northwest of Brussels, and was taken prisoner. Some British soldiers showed great interest in his "Dora 9", especially in its two MG 131 machine guns.

On a roadside somewhere in Belgium, January 1, 1945. The end of an Fw 190 D-9.

BERLINER
MORGENPOST

Wöchentlich 50 Pf. Einzeln 10 Pf.

10 PFENNIG

Vereinigt während des Krieges mit Berliner Lokal-Anzeiger

Mittwoch, 3. Januar 1945
47. Jahr / Nr. 2 / Deutscher Verlag

Angriff gegen die Flugplätze im belgisch-holländischen Raum

Großer Erfolg unserer Jagdflieger

Die Heftigkeit der Kämpfe im Raum von Bastogne nahm weiter zu — Geländegewinn an der Saar und in Lothringen — Stärkere sowjetische Angriffe im ungarischen Kampfraum abgewiesen

Aus dem Führerhauptquartier, 2. Januar

Das Oberkommando der Wehrmacht gibt bekannt: Im Raum südwestlich und südlich Bastogne nahm die Heftigkeit der Kämpfe noch zu. Die mit starken Kräften angreifende 3. amerikanische Armee erlitt schwere Ausfälle und Verluste, ohne zu dem angestrebten Durchbruch in Richtung auf Houffalize zu gelangen, und büßte erneut 48 Panzer ein. Die Gesamtzahl der seit dem 16. 12. in der Schlacht zwischen Maas und Mosel abgeschossenen oder erbeuteten feindlichen Panzerkampfwagen ist damit auf über tausend gestiegen.

An der Saarfront und der lothringischen Nordostgrenze wurde der Geländegewinn aus der Neujahrsnacht vertieft, unser Brückenkopf nordwestlich Forbach erweitert und der Eisenbahnschnitt nordöstlich Saargemünd überschritten. Im Gebiet nördlich Rohrbach und in den unteren Vogesen wurde der Feind in verschiedenen Frontabschnitten aus seinen Stellungen geworfen. Im Nachstoß eroberten unsere Divisionen zahlreiche Ortschaften südlich der Maginotlinie.

Starke Geschwader deutscher Kampf-, Schlacht- und Jagdflieger führten am Neujahrsmorgen einen überraschenden Schlag gegen die feindlichen Flugplätze im belgisch-holländischen Raum. Nach den bisher vorliegenden Meldungen wurden durch diesen Großangriff mindestens 400 feindliche Flugzeuge am Boden zerstört, 100 weitere schwer beschädigt. Darüber hinaus wurden die Flugplätze selbst und ihre Einrichtungen stark getroffen. Bei diesen Angriffen kam es zu heftigen Luftkämpfen, in denen weitere 79 Flugzeuge abgeschossen wurden. Damit verlor der Feind im Westen gestern mindestens 579 Flugzeuge, wahrscheinlich mehr.

Das Fernfeuer auf Lüttich und Antwerpen wurde fortgesetzt.

In den meisten Frontabschnitten in Mittelitalien hält die Kampfpause an. Nur im Raum nördlich Faenza lebte die Gefechtstätigkeit gestern wieder auf.

Im ungarischen Kampfgebiet wiesen unsere Truppen stärkere sowjetische Angriffe im Abschnitt südwestlich Felsögalla zurück. Im übrigen kam es zwischen der Drau und der slowakischen Grenze zu keinen größeren Kampfhandlungen. Die Besatzung von Budapest schlug an der Ost- und Westfront heftige von Schlachtfliegern unterstützte Angriffe der Bolschewisten ab und beseitigte einzelne Einbrüche im Gegenstoß.

Im Grenzgebiet der Slowakei sind nördlich der Eipel Kämpfe mit den nach Norden drängenden Sowjets im Gange. Bei einem überraschenden Vorstoß im Quellgebiet des Sajo machten Gebirgsjäger über 350 Gefangene und erbeuteten eine große Anzahl Waffen.

An der gesamten übrigen Ostfront kam es zu keinen größeren Kämpfen.

Deutsche Schlachtflieger bekämpften im Raum von Budapest bei Tag und Nacht den feindlichen Nachschubverkehr. Im Monat Dezember verloren die Sowjets durch unsere Jäger und Flakartillerie der Luftwaffe 588 Flugzeuge.

Anglo-amerikanische Terrorbomber flogen am Neujahrstag in das westliche und nordwestliche Reichsgebiet ein. Durch Abwurf zahlreicher Spreng- und Brandbomben entstanden vor allem in Wohnvierteln von Kassel erhebliche Gebäudeschäden. Das Gebiet westlich des Rheines war verstärkten Angriffen feindlicher Tiefflieger und schneller Kampfflugzeuge ausgesetzt, die wahllos Bomben auf kleine Ortschaften warfen und die Zivilbevölkerung mit Bordwaffen angriffen. Nachtangriffe der Briten richteten sich besonders gegen den rheinisch-westfälischen Raum. Luftverteidigungskräfte schossen über dem Reichsgebiet gestern 25 feindliche Flugzeuge, fast ausschließlich viermotorige Bomber, ab.

Groß-London wird weiterhin beschossen.

*

Ergänzend zum Wehrmachtbericht wird gemeldet:

An dem Gelingen des Durchbruches eines unserer Armeekorps aus dem Raum von Podgorica nach Nord-Montenegro hatte eine Kampfgruppe unter Führung von Oberst Neumann hervorragenden Anteil. In schwierigsten Gebirgskämpfen gegen einen mit dem Gelände vertrauten Feind durchbrach die Kampfgruppe zahlreiche feindliche Bergstellungen und zerschlug die gegnerischen Kräfte, die ihr den Weg verlegen wollten. Nach wochenlangen Gefechten gelang es ihr schließlich, den von Norden zu ihrem Entsatz herunterstoßenden deutschen Kräften unter Führung von Generalleutnant Friebe die Hand zu reichen.

Schicksalswende

BMP **Berlin,** 2. Januar

Goldenes Eichenlaub mit Schwertern und Brillanten

Cutting from the "Berliner Morgenpost" of January 3, 1945. The headlines still show no change in tune, and there is of course no mention of the loss of over 200 pilots.

The Headline reads:

"Attack on Dutch and Belgian airfields
A MAJOR SUCCESS FOR OUR FIGHTERS
Fighting in the Bastogne area becomes more intense — Our forces gain ground on the Saar and in Lorraine — Heavy Russian attacks repulsed on the Hungarian sector."(TR)

Fw. Bachhuber
15/JG 54

Oblt. Bartels
3./JG 77

Ogfr. Büttner
3./JG 2

Lt. Doppler
I/JG 11

Ogfr. Dwora
3./JG 2

Uffz. Gattner
10./JG 11

Ofw. Giese
10./JG 11

Lt. Holick
5./JG 1

Fw. Jaschek
15./JG 53

Ofw. Jung
5./JG 6

Uffz. Katzer
4./JG 2

Fhr. Leese
14./JG 53

Lt. Ratzlaff
12./JG 53

Fhr. Rosenberger
15./JG 53

Uffz. Richte
II./JG 4

Oberstlt. Specht
Kdre JG11

Fw. Tanck
II./JG 77

Oblt. Graf. v.
Treuberg
12./JG 3

Fhr. Wiethoff
3./JG 11

Major Vowinc
III./JG 11

Missing on January 1, 1945. These are only 20 fighter pilots of the Luftwaffe who were killed or reported missing, presumed dead, in Operation Bodenplatte. They represent a far greater number of casualties of this ill-fated "New Year" mission.

Focke-Wulf Fw 190 A-8s — and their opponents — in the skies over Germany. (Center) Thunderbolts of US 9th Air Force on operations. (Below) Mustangs of US 8th Air Force pull out after a low-level attack.

Above left: General-Lt. Josef Schmid, commander Jagdkorps I, was in charge of the home air defense units. From December 1, 1944 to the end of the war he commanded Luftwaffe Headquarters West.

Above right: Oberst Hajo Hermann champion of many new ideas, some of them controversial, commanded Jagdivision 30 which he had himself set up with single-engine night fighters, and Jagdivision I in the Berlin area. It was on his initiative that "Sonderkommando Elbe" was set up; this formation flew its first and last operation on April 7, 1945, losing a high number of pilots.

Below: Oberst Walter Dahl became the last Inspector of Day fighters, taking over when Oberst Gollob was appointed Director of Fighters. With III./JG 3 the "Special Purpose" Jagdgeschwader and JG 300, Dahl was outstandingly successful in home air defense, and he was probably the fighter pilot with the highest individual tally of Mustangs.

The North American P-51D Mustang, one of the deadliest, most maneuverable and most stubborn opponents German fighters had to face. Thanks to their numerical superiority, the Allied fighter forces succeeded again and again in screening their bomber formations from the German air defense, inflicting heavy losses into the bargain. But not even a Mustang was invincible, as the lower photograph shows.

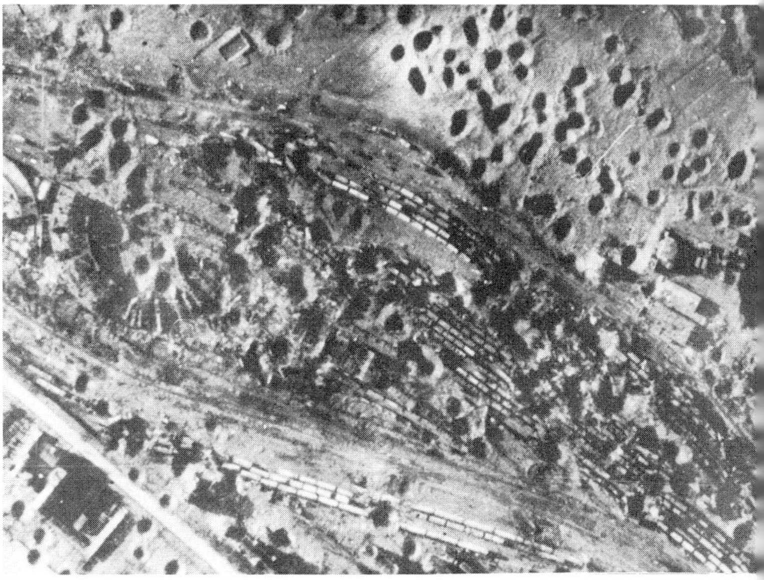

In the last resort three factors decided the outcome of the war: the offensive against the fuel industry — raid on the hydrogenation plant at Hanover-Misburg (top), the smashing of the German communications network —Giessen marshalling yards, December 24, 1944 (center), and the destruction of German aircraft on the ground (below) throughout Germany itself and the Western theatre as a whole.

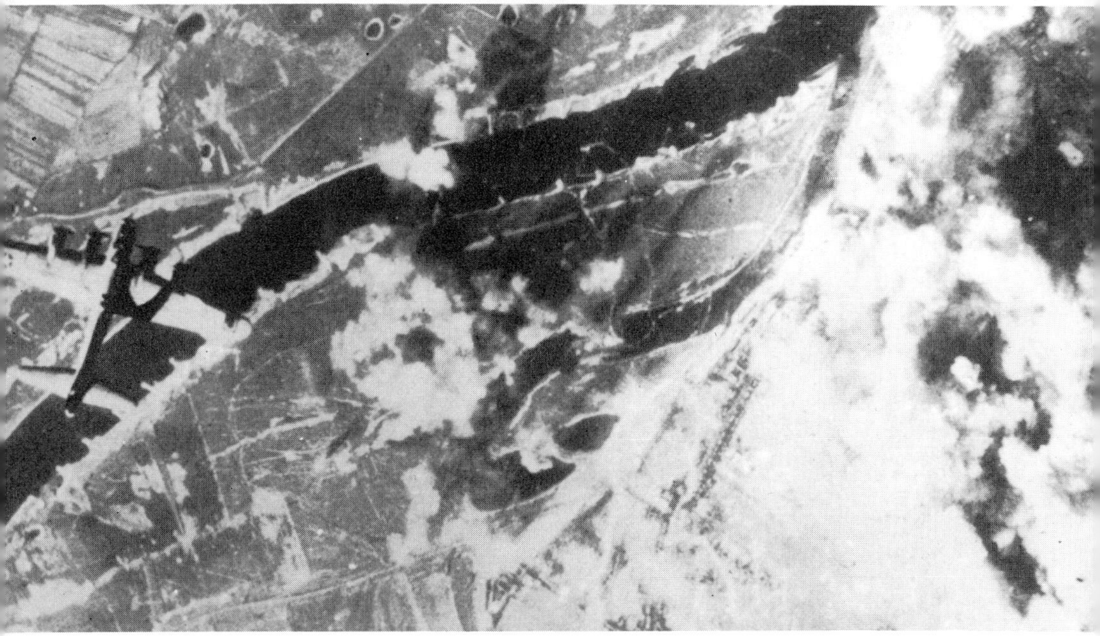

Above: The raid by 390th Bomber Group on the Wehrmacht Fuel Depot at Derben-Ferchland, January 14, 1945. On this day the fighters of JG's 300 and 301 once more succeeded in shooting down a fair number of enemy aircraft, but themselves lost 55 pilots in the process.

Below: After take-off, a Bf 109 G-10/R6 skims the airfield only a few feet up.

Lt. Broeckelschen, one of the few survivors of "Sonderkommando Elbe." All available machines were assembled to form this force. This G-14 still wears the 3-digit tactical sign of a flying school and, as the "Ace of Spades" ("Pik As") indicates, has also had a spell with JG 53.

A German aircraft crashed here. Long after the war was over wreckage like this continued to bear witness to the sacrifice of German fighter pilots.

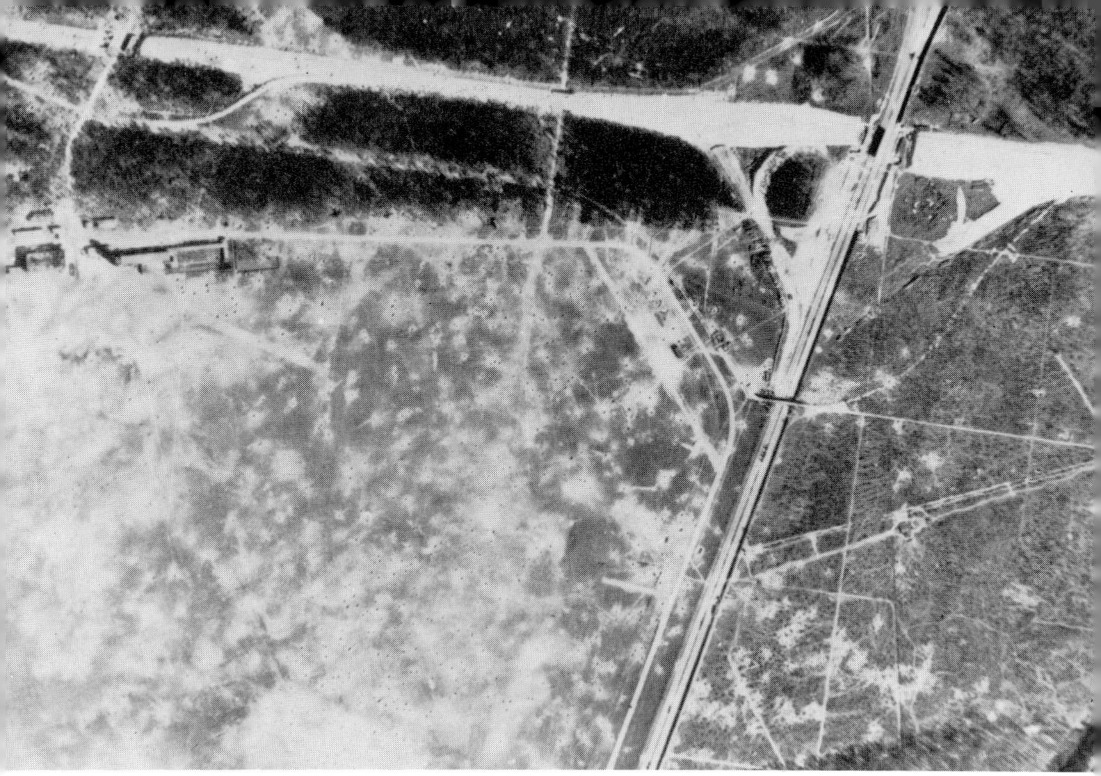

March 12, 1945 and the Rhine-Main Airfield is ploughed up by American bombs. Who then would have guessed that it would become Europe's third largest airport? The "Frankfurter Kreuz" (top right) motorway intersection, under construction at the time.

The remains of the Luftwaffe, as they were to be found at the end of the war in airfields and airstrips all over Germany.

The end comes. In the middle of April, American fighters attacked South German airfields and destroyed hundreds of German machines on the ground (top). A last cigarette before facing the rigors of the prison camp. A German fighter pilot with his Bf 109 G-14 on an American held airfield (center). The night fighter force as well lies shattered, and the unequal struggle is over (below). But the German fighter pilots had fought with every ounce of their strength, and their efforts had taken its appalling toll in blood. Their splendid achievements should never be forgotten.

area. 1, 2 and 3 Staffeln lost one pilot each. The whole Münster Basin was suddenly alive with Allied aircraft, and one German machine after another went down in face of these crushing odds.

In the same area I and II Gruppen, JG 26 reported contact. Both units were flying Fw 190 D-9s, and Flight Lieutenant Reid of 41 Squadron shot one of these machines down between Gronau and Rheine – very probably that of *Oberleutnant* Kittelmann, who failed to return from this operation. Born in 1914, Kittelmann was one of the older fighter pilots; he flew with 2 Staffel, which had two other pilots killed that day.

5 Staffel was just taking off from Nordhorn when some Tempests bounced the airfield and shot up the "long noses", wounding *Leutnant* Bott. Other elements of the two Gruppen of JG 26 were directed onto the Cologne area, where they encountered a Thunderbolt formation and lost two aircraft.

A Mustang pilot from US 364th Fighter Group had a rare bit of luck when he caught a twin-jet Arado 234 B from KG(J) 76 over Bohmte, about ten miles south of the Dümmer See, and shot it down, killing the pilot, *Unteroffizier* Przetak. And in an attack on Giebelstadt airfield the US 55th Fighter Group destroyed a total of six Me 262s of II./KG(J) 54 which were on a training flight. Three of these pilots were killed. In the Nuremberg area the Mustangs spotted two Messerschmitt G-14s belonging to JG 104 at Roth, and shot them down in quick succession.

Apart from three Staffeln of Jagdgeschwader 301, the units of IX Fliegerkorps (Fighters) which scrambled to intercept the US 8th Air Force had no contact. The American force attacking communications centers in Jagddivision 1 sector had railway junctions in the triangle Salzwedel-Stendal-Wittenberge on their target list. Over map square "*Emil-Cäsar 4*" 1./JG 301, led by *Leutnant* Benning, an old hand from the single-seat night fighter days with over twenty kills to his name, became involved with the Allied fighter escort over Salzwedel. This encounter cost the Staffel three Focke-Wulfs and the lives of their pilots.

Notes

[1]The American four-engine bombers had an average of six machine-gun positions. If three or four of the gunners in the crew shot at an attacking fighter and saw him go down, each of them would claim a kill (which would probably be confirmed). Imagination boggles at the number of kills which had to be sorted out at the debriefing of a large bomber formation.

[2]III Gruppe, Jagdgeschwader 54, had been withdrawn from the Russian Front in the summer of 1943, and placed under the command of Jagdgeschwader 26 in the West. With effect from February 25, 1945 the Gruppe was absorbed by Jagdgeschwader 26 and redesignated IV Gruppe.

V

THE HUNT IS OVER

Friday March 2, 1945

Not the least of the indications that the Allies now sought to put a speedy end to the War was the further intensification of their air activity. On no single day or night of the month of March did German airspace remain free of their intrusions; and only a few weeks before the end of the murderous worldwide conflagration many more cities had to suffer further heavy air-raids with appalling results; among them were Berlin, Dortmund, Chemnitz, Dessau, Essen, Hanau, Hildesheim, Mannheim, Paderborn, Ulm, Unna and Würzburg.

The German air defense had been shattered. The Geschwader, most of them by now reduced almost to Gruppe strength, went down in a series of last desperate encounters. March 2, was to spell the end for the Gruppen of Jagdgeschwader 301, but first a number of skirmishes in the familiar battleground of Rheine-Osnabrück provided a curtain-raiser for the major air battles.

It was still early morning when two squadrons each of Tempests and Spitfires from 2nd TAF took off on one of their surveillance patrols over the Me 262 airfields. These had become almost a daily routine, for the Allies never gave the German jet fighter units a moment's peace. Almost every day led to encounters with German fighters trying to keep the British away from these fields or at least to prevent the jets being attacked during takeoff and landing, when they were at their most vulnerable. That Friday it was the turn of some Focke-Wulfs from II./JG 26 and a stronger force of Messerschmitts of II, III and IV Gruppen, JG 27.

The German machines had been airborne only a few minutes when a dogfight started between the Tempests and Bf 109 K-4s of JG 27 in the Osnabrück area. Eventually, when Spitfires joined in, the German pilots had their work cut out to avoid being completely wiped out. JG 27 lost four pilots over the western spurs of the Teutoburger Wald.

Fighter Losses on March 2, 1945

Units Involved	Killed/ Missing	Wounded	Total Casualties	Aircraft	Locale
I/JG2	3	2	5	Fw 190 D-9	Mainz area
III/JG26	1		1	Fw 190 D-9	Osnabruck, Rheine
II/JG27	1		1	Bf 109 G-14	Achmer, Saerbeck
II/JG27	3		3	Bf 109 K-4	Steinbeck
IV/JG27	2	2	4	Bf 109 K-4	Tecklenburg
			8		
II/JG300	4		4	Fw 190 A-8	Belzig, Grosstreben,
III/JG300	2	1	3	Bf 109 G-10	Torgau, Saxony area
			7		
I/JG301	3		3	Fw 190 A-8/A-9	Aussig, Burg
II/JG301	6	1	7	Fw 190 A-9/D-9	Dresden, Stresow
IV/JG301	8	5	13	Bf 109 G-10	Wurschwitz
			23		
Total Losses (Against incursions from West and South)	33	11	44 (including 1 Gruppe commander and 2 Staffel leaders killed)		

After this encounter the British claimed a total of eight Messerschmitts shot down, one of them by Wing Commander Keefer, and two Focke-Wulfs. The German fighters accounted for two Spitfires.

As the morning wore on strong American bomber formations, with an overwhelming fighter escort, penetrated as far as the Elbe and flew on into Saxony. Some 200 German home air defense fighters were scrambled against them, and intense fighting developed at various places, stretching in some cases as far south as Sudetenland.

One of the centers of this fighting was over the south edge of Annaburg Heath between the Elbe and the Black Elster. In this encounter with the Americans II.(Sturm)/JG 300 lost four pilots. III Gruppe intercepted about seventeen miles from its base at Jüterbog, in grid square "Heinrich-Friedrich", and lost two pilots in the Belzig area.

Another focus formed north of Magdeburg. JG 301 had once again put every serviceable machine into the air against the US 8th Air Force's heavy bomber formations. Its newly-formed IV Gruppe took off on its first and last operation. The unit succeeded in shooting down a few bombers, but the Mustangs quickly gained the upper hand and the battle ended in defeat for Jagdgeschwader 301. By the time they landed back at their bases – Finsterwalde, Gahro, Gardelegen, Stendal and Welzow – seventeen pilots had been killed or reported missing.

IV./JG 301 met its fate some 25 miles southeast of its base at Gardelegen, when its three Staffeln tried to head off the American bomber force directed onto Magdeburg. The Allied fighter escort was too strong for the Germans; between Magdeburg and Burg a veritable massacre ensued, some twenty Messerschmitts being shot out of the sky in quick succession. The fighting over map squares "*Gustav-Dora*" and "*Heinrich-Dora*" became one vast dogfight. The brave young German pilots made desperate efforts to limit the scale of the disaster; and a few of them did succeed in bringing fire to bear on the silver Mustangs, so that they should at least go down fighting.

With four pilots killed and two wounded, 13 Staffel also suffered severely, the more so as the Staffel leader, *Oberleutnant* Johann Patek, was amongst the dead.

Away to the south, over southern Saxony and the Moravian marshes, the Americans took on the bulk of II./JG 301. Here it was 8 Staffel that took the worst punishment; their encounter with the Mustangs cost them three pilots killed and one wounded. The flight had just received its first Focke-Wulf 190 D-9s, replacing the A-9 version.

For the IX Fliegerkorps (Fighters) units the day of March 2 ended with a loss of 43 aircraft against fifteen kills. JG 300 and JG 301 together had 23 pilots killed and one reported missing.

But that was not the end of the story. In the afternoon a fairly strong formation of Martin B-26 Marauder twin-engine bombers from 9th US TAF was targeted onto a military depot near Giessen. As the Americans approached the Rhine-Main sector I./JG 2, which was to lose its commander, *Hauptmann* Hrdlicka over the Vogelsberg on March 25, was scrambled. The Germans intercepted near Mainz, and the usual dogfights with the fighter escort quickly developed. By then it was around 1730. The Focke-Wulf pilots tried approaching the B-26s from every imaginable angle, but could not get into firing position. Only one Marauder went down, and three German pilots were killed.

Wednesday, March 14, 1945

"14.3.45: The Americans are now outside Bad Kreuznach. Fighter sweeps between Rhine and Odenwald in the Oppenheim-Darmstadt-Bensheim triangle. II./JG 53 in combat with P-47s:

Lt. Harms bailed out over Dieburg, breaking his ankle in the process. *Uffz.* Schwarz killed over Worfelden.

III./JG 53 likewise engaged by Thunderbolts immediately after takeoff in Darmstadt-Griesheim area at about 1600.

Four pilots failed to return: *Lt.* Henkell of the Gruppenstab shot down and killed east of Oppenheim, *Fw.* Wagener (9 Staffel) in Cochem area, *Uffz.* Tesarik (11 Staffel) and Dröge (11 Staffel) over Bickenbach and Biebesheim. *Lt.* Bernhard of the Gruppenstab was shot down by a Thunderbolt near Oppenheim and bailed out."

Sunday, March 18, 1945
Monday, March 19, 1945

Fighter sweeps against Allied fighter-bombers and other ground-attack aircraft continued, but defense against the heavy bomber formations made little further impact. The jet fighter units, on the other hand, were rather more successful, even though Allied domination of German airspace and the effects of raids on fuel installations meant that they could only be used intermittently. Mention must be made at this point of *General* Galland's JV (*Jagdverband*) 44 with its Me 262s; Galland himself has given a full account of its setting up and operation.[1] This force was made up of experienced and highly decorated fighter pilots; operating in conjunction with *Oberstleutnant* Bär's EJG 2, it was to have further successes against the American bomber forces. But to pose a real threat to the Allies, a far stronger jet fighter force would have been needed. Plans along these lines did indeed exist, but the tumultuous course of events prevented their ever reaching fruition.

On March 18, a force of over 1,200 heavy bombers, bombing through heavy cloud cover, delivered another shattering blow on Berlin. Some forty Me 262s, including *Major* Sinner's III./JG 7 from Parchim, dove onto the Americans as they headed for home and shot down eight Flying Fortresses and five escort fighters. With a further sixteen four-engine machines going down to AA, this amounted to another local success for Home Air Defense. But for the Allies it meant a loss rate of barely 2%, and at this stage of the war the Americans would not lose much sleep over the loss of 24 bombers out of 1,200.

On the German side, two Me 262s were lost, JG 26 lost two pilots that day and I./JG 2 reported three killed.

On the following day US 8th Air Force was joined by RAF Bomber Command over West Germany, and their escort fighters were able to pin down the German defense so thoroughly that they never came close to getting through to the bombers.

Both British 2nd TAF's Spitfires and American fighters in strength put in low-level attacks on German fighter airfields. Jagdgeschwader 27, which at the time was just in the process of redeploying to the new airfields south of the Teutoburger Wald, suffered severely at their hands. For IV Gruppe, which had taken off from Achmer, March 19 proved to be the end of their existence as an operational unit. The Americans shot down virtually a whole Staffel over the Osnabrück area, killing six pilots and wounding five.

The 78th Fighter Group's Mustangs were on a ground-attack mission against the airfields between Rheine and Osnabrück. As they approached, they met between 40-50 machines from JG 26 and JG 27. The Americans went straight into the attack, catching some of the German formations while they were still climbing.

Their first victims were four of Jagdgeschwader 26's "long noses", which had already reached their tactical altitude. Three pilots were killed.

To the north of Osnabrück, IV./JG 27 never really had a chance against the Mustangs. The Americans took on 14 Staffel over Wallenhorst and Hollage, and pursued them as far as the Wiehen Hills. The Americans claimed 32 kills but themselves lost five Mustangs.

Elements of I Gruppe took off about 1000 on their transfer flight to Störmede, but a group of Spitfires from No. 130 Squadron were on them in a flash. Flying low over the field, they caught some machines before they were even airborne. Two pilots were shot down in flames, and one crash-landed in a wooded area.

Over the Brandenburg area the Mustangs accounted for two Me 262s bringing the German fighter force's losses for March 19 to eight pilots killed and seven wounded in air defense operations.

Saturday, March 24, 1945

With the cutting to pieces of JG 301 at the beginning of the month, 1st Jagddivision had already lost a substantial part of the force under its command, and on March 24 JG 300 also suffered a decisive defeat. On this day US 8th Air Force put up a total of 1,400 bomber sorties in a major operation against a dozen or more Luftwaffe bases east of the Rhine, some in Holland and some in West Germany. These raids were carried out in support of the Allied airborne operations at Wesel, where Montgomery's British troops were about to cross the Rhine.

It was about noon when the Americans, flying low, swept across the countryside between the Teutoburger Wald and the Lippe to take on the airfields in that area. There can be no doubt that the destruction wrought on the German bases and the loss of hundreds of machines on the ground very severely impaired the German day and night fighter effort.

Over Störmede, where I./JG 27 were based at this time, a major battle developed between a strong force of Mustangs and the Messerschmitts of I and III Gruppen. The unit had already been stretched to the limit, and now it lost another twelve pilots, four from I Gruppe and eight from III Gruppe. Over and above this, three pilots were wounded by machine-gun fire on the Störmede field.

A little later Jagdgeschwader 300's turn came, just east of Göttingen. II Gruppe under the 24-year-old *Oberleutnant* Radener and small elements from I and IV Gruppen had flown west from Thuringia to be directed by ground control on to the reported American incursion. In a bitter action II Gruppe, the Sturmgruppe, was completely wiped out, losing twenty of its Focke-Wulfs. 5 Staffel lost five pilots, and 6 Staffel simply ceased to exist, six of its pilots were killed in action. With 7 Staffel also losing two pilots, II Gruppe casualties amounted to fourteen killed and one wounded – a blow from which it was never to recover. American losses on the other hand were negligible.

Now the German fighter force was well down the slope of its decline. Another six costly weeks of attrition were to go by before Germany finally collapsed, and a further 200 pilots were to lose their lives.

Saturday, April 7, 1945

As long as fuel and aircraft were available, the remnants of the fighter units battled on day by day. But then came that mad enterprise known as "*Sonderkommando Elbe*", which delivered the knockout punch to the fighter force. The originator of the "Elbe" operation was *Oberst* Hajo Herrmann, who had already made a name for himself with other proposals, all of them controversial but not always to be dismissed out of hand. When for instance he was commanding 1st and 30th Jagddivisions at the time of the Battle of Berlin, it was his idea to lift the blackout so that the RAF bombers with their dark camouflage would stand out against the bright background and offer the night fighters a better target. There was no reason to suppose that a lit-up city would be bombed any less haphazardly than a blacked-out one.

But the formation of a "ram unit", which from the very beginning took on the character of a suicide squad, produced a flood of objections; both *Oberst* Gollob, *General der Jagdflieger*, and the *Inspekteur der Tagjagd*, *Oberst* Dahl, turned it down. Despite this, and for reasons which can perhaps only be understood against the background of the situation at the time, "*Sonderkommando Elbe*" was set up at Stendal. Few members of it survived the day of April 7, 1945, and their lips still remain sealed. This account must therefore confine itself to the facts.

Two days earlier, on April 5, over 1,000 heavy bombers had flown in over Central and South Germany for heavy raids on Nuremberg and Plauen. Nineteen were shot down, but at the cost of 42 German machines. On the morning of April 7, 1,200 bombers and 800 fighters from US 8th Air Force were again headed for North Germany. From their bases near Stendal and Gardelegen 183[2] Focke-Wulfs and Messerschmitts of the *Kommando* scrambled, covered by a strong force of Me 262 jet fighters from JG 7 and KG(J) 54.

The pilots were briefed to close to point-blank range before opening fire, to come back with at least one kill on a heavy-bomber to their name and – if necessary – to destroy the enemy bomber by ramming it. No details are available of the units from which this *Kommando* was formed or how the pilots came to be selected for it. Certainly men from JG 300 and JG 301 were among them.

It was a very cold morning on April 7th. Visibility was almost ten miles and the sky was about three quarters overcast. Up at 36,000 feet, the height from which the German fighters were to dive onto the Americans, it was about 20 degrees below. The "Elbe" fighters made a sighting over the south of Lüneburg Heath, Nienburg and the Steinhuder Meer. They drove their attack home hard; the Mustangs reacted vigorously but simply could not stop the German machines breaking through to the leading bomber formation. About fifty piston-engine fighters and a few Me 262s reached the bomber spearhead. The Americans appeared to be taken by surprise at the strength of the fighter attack; they were on the receiving end of an operation that bore a certain resemblance to the Japanese Kamikaze tactics. A handful of Focke-Wulfs would come roaring in, pressing their attack home with complete disregard of danger; the 452nd Bomb Group lost two Flying Fortresses and the 385th and 388th Bomb Groups one each. And a Messerschmitt accounted for a fifth B-17 from 490th Bomb Group.

The battle raged on for at least three quarters of an hour; the Me 262s managed to account for one Flying Fortress each from the 100th and 390th Bomb Groups and an Bf 109 rammed a Liberator head on. It was a day of sacrifice for the Americans too.

But in the last analysis the outcome was horrifying and, predictably enough, fell far short of expectations. Only fifteen German machines of those that took off returned to base. Seventy-seven pilots were reported

Fighter Losses on March 24, 1945

Units Involved	Killed/ Missing	Wounded	Total Casualties	Aircraft	Locale
III/JG7	3	3	6	Me 262A	Grossen, Harz, Wittenberg
I/JG27	4	3	7	Bf 109 K-4	Osnabruck,
III./JG27	8	1	9		Teutoburger Wald, Stormede
			16		
I/JG300	2		2	Bf 109 G-10	Gottingen, Lobnitz
II/JG300	14	1	15	Fw 190 A-8/A-9	Kothen
IV/JG300	1	1	1	Bf 109 G-14	
			18		
Total Losses	31	9	40		

(Against incursions from the West and South)

killed or missing; the rest had successfully taken to their parachutes. A pointless sacrifice. The German side admitted 133 machines lost and claimed a total of fifty enemy aircraft shot down. Even if these figures were correct, they could have had no influence whatever on the course of the War. The Americans by contrast reported the destruction of 100 German aircraft, 59 of them by fighters, for a loss of only eight bombers. One figure is probably too high, the other definitely too low. But what of it – what matters is that this desperate throw sent to their death over 75[3] young Germans, many of them fresh from the flying schools.

April 10-17, 1945

The proof that home air defense was now effectively at an end came on Thursday, April 10, when a massive American raid went in on the jet fighter fields in North Germany. Briest, Burg, Oranienburg, Lärz and Parchim suffered extensive damage to installations and machines. This resulted in the move of the Me 262 units to Czechoslovakia, where US 8th Air Force could no longer get at them. Meanwhile Hitler raged away at the Luftwaffe; he simply could not understand why the runways could not be restored overnight. On Friday, April 13, the Americans really began to take the Luftwaffe out on the ground. Thunderbolts from the 56th Fighter Group destroyed 95 machines on North German airfields, including Eggebek in the northwest of Schleswig-Holstein. Three days later, on the following Monday, it was the turn of the South German fields, the 353rd Fighter Group destroying some 110 aircraft on the ground. And 125 machines went up in smoke on airfields in the Sudetenland. The next day the Mustangs were back again to send another 200 aircraft up in flames. This sealed the fate of the Luftwaffe, and of the fighter force in particular. The achievements of the German fighter pilots, their fearlessness and their resolve, must never be forgotten, least of all when the conditions under which they fought are borne in mind. It was perhaps best summed up in the words of an unknown fighter pilot, though even these hardly began to reflect the true measure of the tragedy:

> "We were losing pilots all the time, and had to get used to seeing new faces and hearing new names. So now I can hardly recall a single name – things were all mixed up. Almost every day new

> pilots came up from the reinforcement units or the schools, full of hope and optimism. The quartermasters were reluctant to find billets for any more pilots; they hated to see these young men take the air when the grim routine of bringing back their remains had to be so often repeated."

Now, or so we hope, those grim days are over. The enemies of yesterday are now friends. And long may it remain so, for a new Operation "Bodenplatte" must never happen and another *Sonderkommando Elbe* must never come into being.

One Fighter Staffel's Losses in Home Air Defense

5 Staffel, Jagdgeschwader 300, October 1944-March 1945

In conclusion it would be well to review the casualties in a home-based assault Staffel over a period of only six months. 5 Staffel, Jagdgeschwader 300, with its Fw 190 A-8s lost nineteen pilots killed or missing and six wounded in this time, so that its aircrew virtually had to be replaced twice over. At the turn of the year, three Staffel leaders were killed within four weeks.

And this example does not stand alone.

Other Staffeln had a similar story to tell – some of them an even sadder one.

Pilot	Casualty	Date	Cause	Tactical Number
Uffz. Alois Auth	MIA	10/7/44	Air Combat	Red 17
Uffz. Werner Conradt	KIA	10/18/44	Factory Test Flight	Black 1
Ofhr. Herbert Schneider	KIA	11/27/44	Air Combat	Red 6
Ofhr. Gerhard Piel	KIA	11/27/44	Air Combat	Red 5
Fw. Claus Richter	Wounded	11/27/44	Air Combat	Red 17
Gefr. Karl-Heinz Hachmann	Wounded	11/27/44	Air Combat	Red 10

Uffz. Leo Kühnert	KIA	11/30/44	Air Combat	Red 18
Uffz. Karl Rief	Wounded	12/17/44	Air Combat	Red 7
Uffz. Walter Grund	KIA	12/17/44	Air Combat	Red 15
Lt. Klaus Bretschneider (*Staffelkapitän*)	KIA	12/24/44	Air Combat	Red 1
Ofw. Heinz Deil	KIA	12/24/44	Air Combat	Red 17
Fw. Kurt Schoepp	KIA	12/31/44	Air Combat	Red 15
Lt. Norbert Graziadei (*Staffelkapitän*)	Wounded	12/31/44	Air Combat	Red 14
Fw. Heinrich Schlüter	Wounded	1/7/45	Training Flight	Red 19
Uffz. Mathäus Erhardt	Wounded	1/14/45	Air Combat	Red 6
Oblt. Heinz-Dieter Gramberg (*Staffelkapitän*)	KIA	1/24/45	Air Combat	Red 2
Lt. Wolfgang Karsosky	KIA	2/14/45	Air Combat	Red 7
Uffz. Walter Beuchel	KIA	2/14/45	Air Combat	Red 6
Fhr. Richard Löfgen	KIA	3/2/45	Air Combat	Green 2
Fhr. Siegfried Felske	KIA	3/2/45	Air Combat	Red 8
Uffz. Karl Lerner	KIA	3/2/45	Air Combat	Red 6
Uffz. Hans Basteck	KIA	3/24/45	Air Combat	Red 11
Ofw. Claus Richter	KIA	3/24/45	Air Combat	Red 9
Uffz. Fritz Dürrling	KIA	3/24/45	Air Combat	Red 5
Gefr. Karl-Heinz Hachmann	KIA	3/24/45	Air Combat	Red 16
Lt. Gerald Schaller	Wounded	3/24/45	Air Combat	Red 20
Fw. Günther Kublank	KIA	3/24/45	Air Combat	Red 6

Notes

[1]In his book *The First and the Last.*

[2]Other sources quote only 120.

[3]This number is much too high, and relates to reports made just after the mission. In fact, many pilots had made off field landings.

Bibliography

Bartz, Karl, *Als der Himmel brannte*, Hannover, 1955

Bundesarchiv, Koblenz

Craven, Wesley Frank & Kate, Lea, *The Army Air Force in World War II*, Vol. III, USA, 1951

Dahl, Walter, *Rammjäger,* Heusenstamm, 1961

Department of the Air Force, Washington, D.C., USA and USAFE, Wiesbaden

Deutsche Dienststelle für die Benachrichtigung der nächsten Angehörigen von Gefallenen der ehemaligen Wehrmacht (WASt), Berlin, Ref. II and VII

DRK-Suchdienst, München

Freeman, Roger A., *The Mighty Eighth*, London, 1970

Freeman, Roger A., *Mighty Eighth War Diary*, London, 1981

Flugbuch Oberstlt. Bär

Galland, Adolf, *Die Ersten und die Letzten*, Damstadt, 1953

Girbig, Werner, *Die nicht zurückkehrten*, Stuttgart, 1976

Girbig, Werner, *Abgeschossen, gefallen, verschollen*, Stuttgart, 1976

Headquarters US 8th Air Force, Westover AFB, Massachusetts, USA

Hoffmann, Karl Otto, *Die Geschichte der Luftnachrichtentruppe*, Neckargmünd, 1968

Jacobsen, H.A., 1939-1945, *Der Zweite Weltkrieg in Chronik und Dokumentation*, Damstadt, 1961

Koch, Adalbert, *Flak*, Bad Nauheim, 1954

Koller, Karl, *Doe letzen Tage*, Mannheim, 1949

Militärgeschichtliches Forschungsamt, Freiburg

OKL, Ic (27.1.1945), *Einsatz der Jagdverbände 1. Januar 1945*

Ploetz, Karl, *Auszug aus der Geschichte*, Würzburg, 1956

Priller, Josef, *Geschichte eines Jagdgeschwaders (JG 26)*, Stuttgart, 1956

Ring, Hans & Girbig, Werner, *Jagdgeschwader 27*, Stuttgart 1971

Rust, Kenn, *The 9th Air Force in World War II,* USA, 1967

Shores, Christopher, *2nd Tactical Air Force*, Reading, 1970

Schramm, Percy Ernst, *KTB des Oberkommandos der Wehrmacht*, Band IV, 1944-1945, Frankfurt/Main, 1961

Sims, Edward H., *Jagdflieger*, Stuttgart, 1967

Sims, Edward H., *Amerikanische Asse im Luftkampf*, München, 1958

Studiengruppe der Luftwaffe, Hamburg (Führungsakademeie der Bindeswehr)

Toland, John, *Das Finale*, München/Zürich, 1968

The United States Strategic Bombing Survey, Washington

Unterlagen des Reichswetterdienstes

USAF Historical Division, Air University, Alabama, USA, Monographs: No.164: German Air Force Air Defense Operations, No.166: German Air Force Counter Air Operations

USAF Historical Studies, (Galland, Adolf-1945/46) *Die Reichsluftverteidigung 1943* (C/IV/2bb, Karlsruher Dokumente, jetzt z.T. auch MGFA, Freiburg)

Warlimont, Walter, *Im Hauptquartier der deutschen Wehrmacht*, Frankfurt/Main, 1962

APPENDIX

Appendix A

Luftwaffe Casualties in Operation "Bodenplatte"

Jagdgeschwader 1

Uffz. Ardner, Edgar	5.Staffel	Captured
Gefr. Bauch, Karl-Heinz	2.Staffel	MIA
Uffz. Behrens, Gerhard	8.Staffel	KIA
Uffz. Böhmer, Heinz	3.Staffel	KIA
Uffz. Comptesse, Egon	1.Staffel	KIA
Uffz. Fritzsche, Alfred	4.Staffel	Captured
Lt. Guha, Anton	10.Staffel	Captured
Hptm. Hackbarth, Georg (Gruppenkommandeur)	Stab/I.Gruppe	KIA
Fw. Hahn, Karl	5.Staffel	MIA
Fw. Hofmann, Fritz	3.Staffel	Captured
Lt. Holick, Walter	5.Staffel	MIA
Lt. v.Johannides, Ernst	5.Staffel	KIA
Fw. Kilian, Heinz Jürgen	3.Staffel	KIA
Fw. Klints, Harrys	2.Staffel	KIA
Fw. Kräuter, Wilhelm	10.Staffel	KIA
Ofhr. Kreb, Hilmar	7.Staffel	MIA
Uffz. Kuntzsch, Otto	5.Staffel	KIA
Fw. Mayr, Paul	8.Staffel	KIA
Oblt. Meinhof, Hans Gottfried (Staffelkapitän)	4.Staffel	KIA
Ofw. Niedereichholz, Kurt	7.Staffel	MIA
Uffz. Schober, Reinhold	8.Staffel	MIA
Uffz. Vetter, Oskar	7.Staffel	Wounded
Uffz. Wenniges, Erich	5.Staffel	KIA
FjFw. Wichardt, Willi	9.Staffel	Captured
Uffz. Wunderlich, Paul	2.Staffel	Captured

Jagdgeschwader 2

Ofhr. Aickelin, Rudolf	7.Staffel	KIA
Uffz. Altpeter, Fritz	11.Staffel	KIA
Uffz. Binger, Siegfried	10.Staffel	Captured
Uffz. Bollwerk, Helmut	5.Staffel	MIA
Uffz. Breitweg, Helmut	1.Staffel	Captured
Gefr. Büscher, Fritz	3.Staffel	KIA
Ogfr. Büttner, Albert	3.Staffel	MIA
Lt. Clemens, Christfried	10.Staffel	KIA
Uffz. Dost, Otto	1.Staffel	KIA
Ogfr. Dworak, Franz	3.Staffel	MIA
Lt. Edelhoff, Werner	Stab	Captured
Uffz. Eggert, Wilhelm	4.Staffel	MIA
Lt. Enge, Martin	10.Staffel	KIA
Uffz. Hilbert, Werner	9.Staffel	Wounded
Fw. Hohenberg, Werner	4.Staffel	Captured
Uffz. Jäger, Johann	12.Staffel	KIA
Uffz. Katzer, Erwin	4.Staffel	MIA
Fw. Keppler, Fritz	8.Staffel	KIA
Uffz. Klein, Ernst	10.Staffel	KIA
Uffz. Körber, Herbert	3.Staffel	Wounded
Uffz. Optenhostert, Freidrich	4.Staffel	KIA
Fw. Peschak, Josef	10.Staffel	Captured
Gefr. Piesker, Werner	4.Staffel	KIA
Uffz. Redlich, Adolf	12.Staffel	MIA
Uffz. Ruppel, Richard	11.Staffel	KIA
Uffz. Scherwadt, Wilhelm	11.Staffel	Captured
Hptm. Schröder, Georg (Gruppenkommandeur)	Stab/II Gruppe	Captured
Ofw. Schuler, Fritz	12.Staffel	KIA
Ogfr. Schyma, Hubert	2.Staffel	Captured
Uffz. Spiess, Michael	12.Staffel	MIA
Fhr. Storkan, Richard	1.Staffel	Missing
Lt. Swoboda, Fritz	11.Staffel	KIA
Fw. Tschelesnig, Karl	2.Staffel	Captured
Lt. Wagner, Helmut	5.Staffel	Wounded
Uffz. Wilkens, Georg	4.Staffel	Captured
Ofw. Wylezick, Otto	10.Staffel	Wounded
Uffz. Wyssola, Hans	2.Staffel	Captured

Jagdgeschwader 3

Uffz. Busch, Erich	14.Staffel	KIA
Uffz. Dors, Alfred	10.Staffel	Wounded
Fw. Fischer, Paul	2.Staffel	Captured
Uffz. Grell, Hansjoachim	15.Staffel	KIA
Ofw. Hameister, Friedrich	4.Staffel	Captured
Lt. Jung, Hans (Staffelkapitän)	10.Staffel	KIA
Fw. Leipholz, Gerhard	14.Staffel	KIA
Ofhr. Naumann, Uwe	11.Staffel	KIA
Uffz. Reinecke, Helmut	1.Staffel	Captured
Ofw. Reiser, Robert	10.Staffel	Wounded
Fw. Rutkowski, Walter	4.Staffel	Captured
Uffz. Schmidt, Alois	16.Staffel	MIA
Uffz. Schmidt, Gerhard	15.Staffel	Captured
Fw. Schmitt, Theodor	3.Staffel	KIA
Uffz. Schöne, Horst	3.Staffel	MIA
Fhr. Tazreiter, Friedrich	1.Staffel	Captured
Oblt. v.Treuberg, Eberhard, Graf (Staffelkapitän)	12.Staffel	MIA
Gefr. Wieschhoff, Rudolf	4.Staffel	KIA

Jagdgeschwader 4

Uffz. Anetzhuber, Walter	13.Staffel	KIA
Uffz. Bartels, Georg	9.Staffel	KIA
Fw. Berg, Karl	15.Staffel	MIA
Uffz. Breves, Willi	7.Staffel	MIA
Uffz. Dierks, Hans Gustav	5.Staffel	KIA
Lt. Ecker, Elmar	16.Staffel	KIA
Ofhr. Grüner, Horst	15.Staffel	KIA
Uffz. Güldenpfennig, Erich	7.Staffel	KIA
Uffz. Holtkötter, Hermann	13.Staffel	KIA
Uffz. Hübner, Walter	7.Staffel	Crash landed
Uffz. Keller, Erich	5.Staffel	MIA
Gefr. lack, Kurt	3.Staffel	KIA
Lt. Morio, Gottfried	7.Staffel	Wounded
Gefr. Noppener, Karl	13.Staffel	KIA

Ogfr. Peschel, Hans	5.Staffel	MIA
Uffz. Richter, Heinz	II.Gruppe	MIA
Ofhr. Russow, Arnulf	15.Staffel	Captured
Ofhr. Schaar, Franz	5.Staffel	MIA
Uffz. Schmidt, Lothar	15.Staffel	Captured
Fw. Schneider, Franz	4.Staffel	MIA
Uffz. Schwarzenau, Günther	8.Staffel	Captured
Uffz. Tharann, Horst	8.Staffel	Captured
Gefr. Wagner, Walter	5.Staffel	Captured
Uffz. Zetzschke, Werner	4.Staffel	KIA

Jagdgeschwader 6

Uffz. Betz, Karl	10.Staffel	KIA
Uffz. Fries, karl	4.Staffel	KIA
Oblt. Gerlach, Lothar (Staffelkapitän)	9.Staffel	MIA
Lt. Grabmair, Karl	5.Staffel	KIA
Fw. Grislawski, Helmut	5.Staffel	Captured
Ofw. Jung, Walter	2.Staffel	MIA
Hptm. Katz, Norbert (Staffelkapitän)	5.Staffel	Captured
Hptm. Kindler, Wilhelm (Staffelkapitän)	11.Staffel	Captured
Oberstlt. Kogler, Johann	Stab	KIA
Ofhr. Krumm, Johann	12.Staffel	KIA
Major Kühle, Helmut (Gruppenkommandeur)	Stab III.Gruppe	KIA
Oblt. Pfleiderer, Eberhard	3.Staffel	Crash landed
Uffz. Riedel, Karlheinz	7.Staffel	MIA
Uffz. Rose, Hans Joachim	9.Staffel	Captured
Uffz. Schaupp, Hans	10.Staffel	KIA
Uffz. Schlossborn, Rudolf	9.Staffel	Captured
Uffz. Schneider, Paul	7.Staffel	MIA
Uffz. Schröttle, Franz	8.Staffel	KIA
Ofw. Schwerdtfeger, Paul	11.Staffel	KIA
Hptm. Trost, Ewald (Staffelkapitän)	2.Staffel	Captured
Uffz. Voss, Willi	1.Staffel	KIA
Lt. Wulff, Hans	8.Staffel	Captured
Uffz. Zangerle, Josef	1.Staffel	MIA

Jagdgeschwader 11

Uffz. Barion, Hermann	12.Staffel	KIA
Gefr. Böhm, Gerhard	9.Staffel	KIA
Lt. Doppler, Alwin	2.Staffel	MIA
Oblt. Engel, August	8.Staffel	KIA
Hptm. v.Fassong, Horst Günther (Gruppenkommandeur)	Stab/III.Gruppe	MIA
Oblt. Fiedler, Hans	Stab/III.Gruppe	Captured
Uffz. Gattner, Walter	10.Staffel	MIA
Ofw. Giese, Xaver	10.Staffel	MIA
Ofw. Hiller, Karl	12.Staffel	Captured
Fhr. Hoffmann, Günther	Stab/II.Gruppe	MIA
Fhr. Huss, Herbert	6.Staffel	Captured
Fw. Kraschinski, Herbert	7.Staffel	KIA
Ofw. Meindl, Franz	8.Staffel	MIA
Uffz. Milkreiter, Max	12.Staffel	MIA
Lt. Neumann, Gerhard	2.Staffel	MIA
Uffz. Noreisch, Ernst	10.Staffel	KIA
Uffz. Nüssle, Kurt	9.Staffel	MIA
Fw. Reschke, Peter	6.Staffel	KIA
Uffz. Schmidt, Sophus	Stab	MIA
Fw. Schwartz, Harald	7.Staffel	KIA
Ogfr. Sistenich, Karlheinz	1.Staffel	KIA
Major Specht, Günther (Kommodore)	Stab	MIA
Fw. Tempel, Alfred	8.Staffel	Captured
Major Vowinkel, Günter	Stab/III.Gruppe	MIA
Ofhr. Wiethoff, Heinrich	3.Staffel	MIA

Jagdgeschwader 26

Frh. Ahrens, Erich	7.Staffel	Captured
Uffz. Berndt, Karlheinz	12.Staffel	Captured
Ogfr. Braunert, Karlheinz	4.Staffel	KIA
Gefr. Götz, Hans Karl	7.Staffel	MIA
Fw. Hartmann, Karlheinz	4.Staffel	MIA
Ogfr. Heuser, Helmut	6.Staffel	MIA
Fw. Hött, Karl	6.Staffel	Wounded

Ogfr. Krägeloh, Dieter	3.Staffel	Captured
Oblt. Kunz, Franz (Staffelkapitän)	2.Staffel	Wounded
Gefr. Kunz, Willy	7.Staffel	KIA
Uffz. Lampferhoff, Ernst	5.Staffel	Captured
Lt. Leinberger, Rudolf	11.Staffel	Wounded
Oblt. Lenz, Harald	11.Staffel	KIA
Ogfr. Lott, Hubert	5.Staffel	KIA
Lt. Meier, Gottfried	9.Staffel	KIA
Uffz. Schmitz, Wilhelm	6.Staffel	KIA
Uffz. Schulz, Heinz	2.Staffel	MIA
Gefr. Sengpiel, Horst	12.Staffel	MIA
Uffz. Speer, Leo	7.Staffel	KIA
Uffz. Sydow, Willy	2.Staffel	KIA
Ogfr. Vogel, Bodo	2.Staffel	KIA
Fhr. Werner, Hans-Joachim	3.Staffel	Captured
Uffz. Wodarcyk, Heinz	2.Staffel	KIA
Uffz. Zeidler, Karl Erich	4.Staffel	Wounded

Jagdgeschwader 27

Uffz. Braun, Heinrich	2.Staffel	KIA
Gefr. Diesing, Arno	4.Staffel	KIA
Hptm. Dudeck, Hanns-Heinz (Gruppenkommandeur)	Stab/IV.Gruppe	Captured
Uffz. Fink, Ferdinand	1.Staffel	KIA
Uffz. Frickmann, Heinrich	11.Staffel	KIA
Fw. Gäbel, Gert	3.Staffel	KIA
Uffz. Gisevius, Petermichel	7.Staffel	KIA
Uffz. Härtlein, Johannes	7.Staffel	Captured
Ogfr. Heymann, Erich	10.Staffel	MIA
Fw. Mannchen, Alfred	16.Staffel	KIA
Uffz. Maus, Heinrich	12.Staffel	Wounded
Uffz. Rehak, Karl	13.Staffel	KIA
Lt. von Stechow, Joachim	2.Staffel	KIA
Fhr. Theisen, Otto	2.Staffel	Captured
Lt. Wiese, Heinrich (Staffelkapitän)	2.Staffel	KIA

Jagdgeschwader 53

Oblt. Benz, Otto	13.Staffel	MIA
Fw. Bermpohl, August	8.Staffel	Wounded
Uffz. Göller, Karl	12.Staffel	Wounded
FjFw. Jascheck, Werner	15.Staffel	MIA
Uffz. Juszczak, Florian	7.Staffel	MIA
Uffz. Koenitzer, Rudolf	5.Staffel	Captured?
Ofw. Kohl, Stefan	13.Staffel	Captured?
Fhr. Leese, Siegfried	14.Staffel	MIA
Uffz. Maxis, Herbert	13.Staffel	MIA
Gefr. Michel, Alfred	16.Staffel	Captured
Fw. Müller, Johannes	7.Staffel	KIA
Fw. Nachotzky, Ernst	6.Staffel	KIA
Fw. Off, Ernst	8.Staffel	KIA
Ofw. Opitz, Kurt	5.Staffel	Captured?
Uffz. Pechardscheck, Horst	16.Staffel	Wounded
Fw. Plettner, Heinz	11.Staffel	Wounded
Gefr. Reichert, Wolfgang	7.Staffel	MIA
Fhr. Rosenberger, Wolfgang	15.Staffel	MIA

Jagdgeschwader 54

Fw. Bachhuber, Fridolin	15.Staffel	MIA
Hptm. Bottländer, Willi (Staffelkapitän)	11.Staffel	MIA
Fw. Drutschmann, Paul	9.Staffel	Captured
Ofw. Eckert, Walter	11.Staffel	KIA
Fw. Egli, Günther	11.Staffel	Captured
Uffz. van Hooven, Aloysius	12.Staffel	KIA
Uffz. Köpp, Werner	13.Staffel	KIA
Uffz. Kroll, Gerhard	9.Staffel	Wounded
Lt. Nibel, Theo	10.Staffel	Captured
Uffz. Ohlenschläger, Gerhard	15.Staffel	Captured
Lt. Ratzlaff, Jürgen	12.Staffel	MIA
Fw. Steinkamp, Hans-Joachim	12.Staffel	Captured
Uffz. Thoss, Gerhard	11.Staffel	MIA

Jagdgeschwader 77

Lt. Abendroth, Herbert	9.Staffel	Captured

Oblt. Bartels, Karlheinz	3.Staffel	MIA
Fhr. Braband, Rolf	11.Staffel	Captured
Lt. Hackler, Heinrich (Staffelkapitän)	11.Staffel	KIA
Gefr. Hoffschmidt, Alfred	6.Staffel	Captured
Gefr. Kofler, Helmut	3.Staffel	KIA
Gefr. Mannweiler, Edwin	4.Staffel	Captured
Uffz. Munninger, Heinrich	10.Staffel	KIA
Lt. Schumacher, Hans-Jürgen	10.Staffel	KIA
Fw. Tanck, Paul	8.Staffel	MIA
Uffz. Twietmeyer, Johann	10.Staffel	Captured

Jagdgeschwader 104 (Einsatzstaffel)

Ofhr. Schmoll, Heinz	1.Staffel	Captured

Schlachtgeschwader 4

Oberst Druschel, Alfred (Kommodore)	Stab	MIA
Fw. Fye, Rudolf	9.Staffel	KIA
Fw. Heinz, Richard	7.Staffel	MIA
Ofw. Schmieder, Hans	7.Staffel	Captured

Flugzeugüberführungsgeschwader 1

Uffz. Altendorf, Rudolf	4.Staffel	MIA

Nachtjagdgeschwader 1

Uffz. Böhle, Heinz	5.Staffel	KIA
Ogfr. Dagn, Simon	5.Staffel	KIA
Uffz. Ehret, Wilhelm	9.Staffel	KIA
Uffz. Fischer, Wilhelm	5.Staffel	KIA
Lt. Hettlich, Josef	9.Staffel	KIA
Fw. Gutzeit, Arthur	7.Staffel	KIA
Uffz. Mayr, Ingomar	9.Staffel	KIA
Uffz. Meinert, Karl	9.Staffel	Captured?

Gefr. Steinhauer, Georg	9.Staffel	Captured?
Ogfr. Stocklöw, Alois	5.Staffel	KIA
Uffz. Woll, Hartmut	9.Staffel	KIA

Nachtjagdgeschwader 3

Uffz. Hoppe, Gerhard	10.Staffel	KIA
Uffz. Maus, Gerhard	4.Staffel	KIA
Uffz. Ofenschiessl, Franz	10.Staffel	KIA
Fw. Werthner, Johann	10.Staffel	Captured?

Nachtjagdgeschwader 101

Ogfr. Zechner, Karl	6.Staffel	MIA

Kampfgeschwader (J) 51

Lt. Hettlich, Josef		KIA
Ofw. Kaiser, Erich	2.Staffel	KIA

The above named losses of NJG units can in part have resulted as part of night bombing missions on the night of 12/31/44-1/1/45.

Unit	Killed/Missing	Captured	Wounded	Including Commanders	Total Casualties	Average Number of Aircraft Committed	Casualties %
I/JG1	7	3		2	10		
II/JG1	10	1	1		12		
III/JG1	1	2			3		
	18	6	1	2	25	80	31
Stab/JG2					1		
I/JG2	10	5	1		16		
II/JG2	3	1	1	1	5		
III/JG2	10	3	2		15		
	23	10	4	1	37	90	31
I/JG3	3	5			8		
III/JG3	3		2	2	5		
IV/JG3	4	1			5		
	10	6	2	2	18	70	26
I/JG4	3				3		
II/JG4	8	3	1		12		
IV/JG4	5	3			8		
	16	6	1		23	55	42
Stab/JG6		1		1	1		
I/JG6	5	1		1	6		
II/JG6	6	1		1	7		
III/JG6	6	3		3	9		
	17	6		6	23	70	33

Stab/JG11	2			1	2		
I/JG11	3				3		
II/JG11		6	2			8	
III/JG11	10	2		1	12		
	21	4		2	25	65	38
I/JG26	5	3	2	1	10		
II/JG26	4	4	1		9		
III/JG26	3	1	1		5		
	12	8	4	1	24	160	15
I/JG27	6	1		1	7		
II/JG27	1	1			2		
III/JG27	2		1		3		
IV/JG27	2	1		1	3		
	11	3	1	2	15	85	18
II/JG53	5	2	1		8		
III/JG53			2		2		
IV/JG53	5	2	1		8		
	10	4	4		18	50	36
III/JG54	5	4	1	1	10	17	60
IV/JG54	2	1			3	25	12
I/JG77	2	1			3		
II/JG77	1				1		
III/JG77	3	3		1	6		
	6	4		1	10	105	10
Day Fighter Force Totals	151	63	18	18	232	875	

Unit	Killed/Missing	Captured	Wounded	Including Commanders	Total Casualties	Average Number of Aircraft Committed	Casualties %
Est/JG104		1			1		
Stab/SG4	1			1	1		
III/SG4	2	1			3		
	3	1		1	4		
FlüG 1	1				1		
NJG1	9	2			11		
NJG3	3	1			4		
NJG101	1				1		
	14	3			16		
KG(J)51	2				2		
	19	4		1	23		
Day Fighter Force	151	63	18	18	232		
Other Forces	19	4		1	23		
Total Losses	170	67	18	19	255		

Appendix B

The Last Commanders of the German Jagdwaffe May 1945

Tagjagd

Jagdgeschwader 1		*Oberstlt.* Ihlefeld
I.Gruppe	He 162A	*Oblt.* Demuth
II.Gruppe	He 162A	*Major* Zorner
III.Gruppe	Bf 109 G-14	*Hptm.* Moldenhauer
Jagdgeschwader 2		*Oberstlt.* Bühlingen
I.Gruppe	Fw 190 D-9	*Oblt.* Eickhoff
II.Gruppe	Fw 190 D-9	*Hptm.* Karch
III.Gruppe	Fw 190 D-9	*Hptm.* Lemke
Jagdgeschwader 3		*Major* Schroer
II.Gruppe	Bf 109 G-10	*Hptm.* Bäker
III.Gruppe	Bf 109 K-4	*Hptm.* Langer
IV.Gruppe	Fw 190 A-8/A-9	*Hptm.* Schack
Jagdgeschwader 4	Fw 190 D-9 (Stab)	*Oberstlt.* Michalski
II.Gruppe	Fw 190 A-8/A-9	*Major* Moritz
III.Gruppe	Bf 109 G-14/K-4	*Hptm.* Strasen
IV.Gruppe	Bf 109 G-14	*Hptm.* Laube
Jagdgeschwader 5		*Oberstlt.* Scholz
II.Gruppe	Bf 109 G-14	*Hptm.* Treppe
III.Gruppe	Bf 109 G-14/Fw 190 A-8	*Hptm.* Dörr
IV.Gruppe	Bf 109 G-14	*Hptm.* Stendel
Jagdgeschwader 6		*Major* Leppla
II.Gruppe	Fw 190 A-8/D-9	*Hptm.* Weyl
III.Gruppe	Bf 109 G-14	*Hptm.* Müller

Unit	Aircraft	Commander
Jagdgeschwader 7		*Major* Weissenberger
I.Gruppe	Me 262A	*Major* Späte
II.Gruppe	Me 262A	*Major* Klemm
III.Gruppe	Me 262A	*Hptm.* Naumann
Jagdgeschwader 11		*Major* Hackl
II.Gruppe	Bf 109 G-10/G-14	*Hptm.* Leonhardt
III.Gruppe	Fw 190 A-8	*Hptm.* Kutscha
Jagdgeschwader 26		*Major* Götz
I.Gruppe	Fw 190 D-9	*Major* Borris
II.Gruppe	Fw 190 D-9	*Hptm.* Schauder
Jagdgeschwader 27		*Major* Franzisket
I.Gruppe	Bf 109 G-10/K-4	*Hptm.* Clade
II.Gruppe	Bf 109 G-14	*Hptm.* Keller
III.Gruppe	Bf 109 K-4	*Major* Dr. Werfft
Jagdverband 44	Me 262A	*Generalmjr.* Galland
Jagdgeschwader 51	Fw 190 A-8 (Stab)	*Major* Dr. Lange
III.Gruppe	Bf 109 G-14	*Hptm.* Brendel
IV.Gruppe	Bf 109 G-14/K-4	*Hptm.* Josten
Jagdgeschwader 52		*Oberst* Graf
I.Gruppe	Bf 109 G-14/K-4	*Major* Hartmann
II.Gruppe	Bf 109 G-10/G-14	*Major* Batz
III.Gruppe	Bf 109 G-14	*Major* Borchers
Jagdgeschwader 53		*Oberstlt.* Bennemann
I.Gruppe	Bf 109 G-10/G-14	*Hptm.* Lipfert
II.Gruppe	Bf 109 G-14	*Major* Meimberg
III.Gruppe	Bf 109 K-4	*Hptm.* Luckenbach
IV.Gruppe	Bf 109 G-14	*Hptm.* Hammer
Jagdgeschwader 54		*Oberst* Hrabak

I.Gruppe	Fw 190 A-8/A-9	*Hptm.* Eisenbach
II.Gruppe	Fw 190 A-8	*Hptm.* Findeisen
Jagdgeschwader 77		*Major* Losigkeit
I.Gruppe	Bf 109 K-4	*Hptm.* Grosser
Jagdgeschwader 300		*Major* Rall
I.Gruppe	Bf 109 G-10/G-14	*Major* Baier
II.Gruppe	Fw 190 A-8/A-9	*Oblt.* Radener
III.Gruppe	Bf 109 G-10/G-14	?
IV.Gruppe	Bf 109 G-14	*Hptm.* Offterdinger
Jagdgeschwader 301	Ta 152 (Stab)	*Oberstlt.* Aufhammer
I.Gruppe	Fw 190 A-8/A-9/D-9	*Hptm.* Posselmann
II.Gruppe	Fw 190 D-9	*Major* Cescotti
III.Gruppe	Fw 190 A-8/A-9	Major Bascilla
Jagdgeschwader 400	Me 163B	*Hptm.* Opitz

Nachtjagd

Nachtjagdgeschwader 1		*Oberstlt.* Jabs
I.Gruppe	He 219	*Hptm.* Baake
II.Gruppe	Bf 110G	*Hptm.* Breves
III.Gruppe	Bf 110G	*Major* Drewes
IV.Gruppe	Bf 110G	*Hptm.* Greiner
Nachtjagdgeschwader 2		*Oberstlt.* Thimmig
I.Gruppe	Ju 88G	*Hptm.* Rath
II.Gruppe	Ju 88G	*Hptm.* Brinkhaus
III.Gruppe	Ju 88G	*Hptm.* Merker
Nachtjagdgeschwader 3		*Oberst* Radusch
I.Gruppe	Ju 88G	*Hptm.* Husemann
II.Gruppe	Ju 88G	*Hptm.* Hüschens
III.Gruppe	Ju 88G	*Hptm.* Barthe

IV. Gruppe	Ju 88G	*Hptm.* Tober
Nachtjagdgeschwader 4		*Major* Schnaufer
I.Gruppe	Bf 110G/Ju 88G	*Hptm.* Krause
II.Gruppe	Bf 110G/Ju 88G	*Hptm.* Rauh
III.Gruppe	Bf 110G/Ju 88G	*Hptm.* Meister
Nachtjagdgeschwader 5		*Major* Schönert
I.Gruppe	Ju 88G	*Hptm.* Lang
II.Gruppe	Bf 110G/Ju 88G	*Hptm.* Tham
III.Gruppe	He 219/Ju 88G	*Hptm.* Pink
IV.Gruppe	Ju 88G	*Hptm.* Bussmann
Nachtjagdgeschwader 6		*Major* Lütje
I.Gruppe	Bf 110G/Ju 88G	*Hptm.* Spoden
II.Gruppe	Bf 110G/Ju 88G	*Hptm.* Schulte
III.Gruppe	Bf 110G	*Hptm.* Johnen
IV.Gruppe	Ju 88G	*Hptm.* Becker
Nachtjagdgeschwader 11		
I.Gruppe	Bf 109 G-14	*Hptm.* Müller
II.Gruppe	Bf 109 G-14	*Hptm.* Schwab?
III.Gruppe	Bf 109 G-14	*Hptm.* Krause
10.Staffel	Me 262B	*Oblt.* Welter
Nachtjagdgeschwader 100		
I.Gruppe	Ju 88G	*Hptm.* Fischer
II.Gruppe	Ju 88G	*Major* Zorner

Disbanded Units:

I./JG 3	March 1945
I./JG 4	April 1945
I./JG 5	April 1945
I./JG 6	March 1945
I./JG 11	March 1945
III./JG 26	March 1945
IV./JG 26	March 1945
IV./JG 27	March 1945
I./JG 51	April 1945
II./JG 51	April 1945
IV./JG 54	April 1945
II./JG 77	April 1945
III./JG 77	April 1945
NJG 10	Spring 1945
NJG 101	Spring 1945
NJG 102	Spring 1945

Appendix C

Ranks of the Luftwaffe, RAF and USAAF

Luftwaffe	Royal Air Force	US Army Air Force
Generalfeldmarschall	Marshall of the Royal Air Force	General (Five Star)
Generaloberst	Air Chief Marshall	General (Four Star)
General der Flieger	Air Marshall	Lieutenant General
Generalleutnant	Air Vice Marshall	Major General
Generalmajor	Air Commodore	Brigadier General
Oberst	Group Captain	Colonel
Oberstleutnant	Wing Commander	Lieutenant Colonel
Major	Squadron Leader	Major
Hauptmann	Flight Lieutenant	Captain
Oberleutnant	Flying Officer	First Lieutenant
Leutnant	Pilot Officer	Lieutenant
Stabsfeldwebel	Warrant Officer	Warrant Officer
Oberfeldwebel	Flight Sergeant	Master Sergeant
Feldwebel	Sergeant	Technical Sergeant
Unterfeldwebel	- No Equivalent -	- No Equivalent -
Unteroffizier	Corporal	Staff Sergeant
Hauptgefreiter	- No Equivalent -	Sergeant
Obergefreiter	Leading Aircraftsman	Corporal
Gefreiter	Aircraftsman First Class	Private First Class
Flieger	Aircraftsman Second Class	Private Second Class

Additional Hard Cover
Luftwaffe Titles